A Concise History of Russian Literature

About the Author

THAÏS LINDSTROM was born in St. Petersburg, Russia. Her father, a well-known criminal lawyer, was a descendant of a Swedish family which had emigrated from Stockholm in 1719. Her mother's family were landowners who came from Central Russia to settle near Moscow in the fifteenth century. Both parents were members of the Russian intelligentsia. Her mother and she left their country on the last refugee boat out of Sebastopol in 1923. They settled in Paris and later came to the United States.

Miss Lindstrom received her B.A. from Hunter College, her M.A. from the University of California, and her doctorate in Franco-Russian relations from the University of Paris. During the past twelve years she has taught in several American universities and has pursued her chosen career of propagating and interpreting Russian literature as translator, radio and television commentator, and literary critic. She is now Professor of Russian and Comparative Literature at Sarah Lawrence College.

RUSSIA BEFORE THE REVOLUTION

A Concise History

of Russian Literature

Volume I
From the Beginnings to Chekho

by Thaïs S. Lindstrom

New York · NEW YORK UNIVERSITY PRESS
London · UNIVERSITY OF LONDON PRESS LIMITED
1966

RUSSIAN LETTERS vibrate to the echoes of Russian history. No other modern literature of international stature has resounded to the impact of social and political events so strongly; no major Russian writer has failed to record in his work something of the national circumstances of his time and to reflect the great ethnic consciousness of Russia's place as bridge between East and West. Added to this is the recognition of centuries of isolation and estrangement from the mainstreams of Western civilization and the bitterness of its feudally fettered, culturally sterile past. Philosopher Chaadayev wrote in 1827: "At first brutal barbarism, then crude superstition, then fierce and humiliating foreign bondage whose spirit was passed on to our own sovereigns—such is the history of our youth."

Russia's situation on Europe's unprotected southeastern flank invited attack, invasion, conquest, and occupation for centuries at a time, yet, within a thousand years, the Russians managed to build a continental empire that occupies a seventh part of the globe. But the price in terms of violence and alienation was high.

Conversion to Byzantine Orthodoxy augmented Russia's separation from the West and when in defiance and distrust of Rome the Muscovite state proclaimed itself guardian of the true Christian faith, a vacuum was formed between Russia and Western Europe. A gigantic turnabout to break it was effected by Peter the Great. The violence and haste of his bulldozing action, designed to uproot patriarchal tradition within a single generation, produced a deep rift between the reactionary elements in Russian society—which included the semiliterate masses, who clung obstinately to their primitive folk culture—and the nascent Westernizers. Thus, an internal vacuum occurred between the peasants and a minority educated elite, which was not to be dissipated until the nineteenth century, when social agitation and reforms articulated and defined Western and Slavophil positions.

It is a rare work among the novels and plays of the second half of the nineteenth century that escapes some discussion of these problems, their political implication, and a sense of impending national crisis. The unresolved tensions and passionate solutions that abound in this fiction may appear strange, equivocal, even paradoxical to a reader little acquainted with Russia's historical situation and her confrontation with the West. This literature, steeped in high intellectual excitement, dynamic with an exuberant traffic in ideas, cannot be judged by aesthetic standards alone; it must be viewed against its own social and political background to be rightly appreciated and understood.

A major purpose of this work has been to establish an accurate perspective between Russian literature and historical environment. To this end each major section is preceded by a brief historical sketch so that the reader who is less familiar with the course of Russian national development may better appreciate the deep and organic involvement of Russian writers in the continuum of Russia's historical process.

The author has maintained the traditional transliteration of Russian names as a courtesy to the American reader, even though not all philologists are in agreement with this method. For the same reason, some Russian first names have been Anglicized. No attempt has been made to mention all the minor Russian writers, but readers who want brief notes on writers not discussed in this book will find Robert Magidoff's A Guide to Russian Literature helpful (New York University Press, 1964).

The metamorphosis of Russian literature from borrower into lender within less than a century is the most interesting literary phenomenon of our time. Before the mid-1700's Russian secular writing hardly existed, and during the next half-century was distinguished only by its imitation of French classical models. Then, just as its writers of the immediate pre- and post-Napoleonic era were absorbing the new trends of West European romanticism, Russian literature leaped forward and suddenly came of age in the work of Alexander Pushkin. Pushkin transmuted the preceding foreign influences and Russian oral lore into poetry and prose of such originality that his own genius became synonymous with a new Russian literary tradition. This later developed under the panoply of realism. In its fundamental purpose it differs from English and French nineteenth-century novels whose writers concentrated on the changing spirit and morals of their age, in turn fascinated or repelled by the rise of the middle class and the immediate effects of scientific materialism.

In Russia urban capitalism was just beginning to encroach upon an agricultural society. The side effects of the industrial revolution were scarcely felt and the prevailing tyranny was not that of the machine but of the capricious rule of a very few men over countless millions. Remoteness from the practical and increasingly mechanized realities of modern living in Western Europe engendered in the Russian mind a fear, a reaction against ruthless technological advance, and a prophetic awareness of its ultimate consequences on man's individual freedom. This apprehension haunts the works of nineteenth-century Russian writers. With crushing directness, with clarity and lucidity, they were the first to raise questions that our own literary spokesmen are still trying to answer, penetrating beyond the façade of institutions into the bereft situation of modern man.

What these Russian writers, from Pushkin to Chekhov, have done for us is to prognosticate the nature of our twentieth-century experience. They pioneered a new kind of writing, so far removed from escapist art that enjoyment of it seems almost irrelevant since, in the largest sense, its appeal to men lies in its purposeful, serious, and reflective examination of universal human issues that brings into focus all of man's world beyond immediate reality. The themes that now grip the imagination of French, English, Italian, German, and American writers were the substance of serious Russian fiction a century ago.

The dehumanized bureaucrat who became fixed in Gogol's

satire reaches his nadir in Kafka's faceless and Frederic Wake-
man's organization man. Dostoyevsky's underground hero has
become for today's avant-garde critics a precursive symbol of
existentialist postulates and his sense of alienation within his
society has been echoed time and again in the estranged characters in the novels of Albert Camus. The agony of noncom-
munication that works its tragedy of attrition in the Chekhovian
personality is inherent in the works of Albert Moravia, Graham
Greene, and a score of young French and American novelists.

Caught between the illiterate indifferent masses and a
regime hostile to literary activity, the Russian writer found himself isolated from active participation in his society, and his
convictions, based on theory alone, bred their own kind of
intransigence and mania for totality. A parallel situation con-
fronts the serious writer in the free world today. Member of a
mass society which under the inexorable pressures of science
and technology is increasingly conformist, he apprehends a
hostile and dehumanized reality in which he has little part.

CONTENTS

PREFACE   v

1. The Beginnings   1

Origins of Rus   1
Orthodoxy—Unifying Force   2
Earliest Literary Monuments   3
Kiev—The Mother of Russian Culture   9
Slovo o Polku Igoreve—Russia's Greatest
    Heroic Epic   11

2. Russia's Estrangement from the West   15

Under the Mongolian Yoke   15
Creeping Rise of Moscow and Autocracy   17
Consolidation of Muscovite Mentality   23
Literary Novelties—Native and Borrowed   28

3. Russia Goes to School in Europe   33

Period of Apprenticeship   33
Oral Literature   37
Fairy Tales   37
Religious Ballads   37
Peasant Songs   38
Epic Poems   39
Age of Classical Imitation   44
Kantemir (1708–1744)   46
Trediakovsky (1703–1769)   47

3. Russia Goes to School in Europe (Continued)

Sumarokov (1718–1777)	48
Origins of the Russian Theater	49
Lomonosov (1711–1765)	52

4. The Age of Catherine   55

The Age of Catherine (1762–1796)	55
Derzhavin (1743–1816)—Poet Laureate	59
Novikov (1744–1818)	61
Fonvizin (1744–1792)	63
Krylov (1769–1844)	64
Radishchev (1749–1802)	66
Karamzin (1766–1826)	68
Summary of the Eighteenth Century	72

5. The Golden Age of Russian Letters   76

Paul I (1796–1801)	76
Alexander I (1801–1825)	77
The Decembrists	80
Nicholas I (1826–1855)	82
Literary Climate of the Nineteenth Century	83
Zhukovsky (1783–1852)	85
Batyushkov (1787–1855)	87
Ozerov (1770–1816)	88
Griboyedov (1795–1829)	88
Pushkin (1799–1837)	90
Heritage: 1799–1820	91
"The Russian Byron": 1820–1824	94
A Meeting with the People: 1824–1826	96
New Fetters: 1826–1831	98
At Boldino	99
Last Years	103
After Pushkin	105

6. New Ideologies: Trail Blazers to the
   Revolution   111

Between Russian Reality and German Idealism	111
Literary Evangelism	114

6. New Ideologies: Trail Blazers to the
Revolution (Continued)

Herzen (1812–1870): The Aristocratic Rebel 117
Radicalism on the March 123
The Literature of Radical Reform 124

7. Nikolay Gogol (1809–1852): Genius of the
Comic-Grotesque 129

8. The Realists 143

Realism in Earnest 143
Goncharov (1812–1891) 144
Turgenev (1818–1883) 146
Ostrovsky (1823–1886) 154
Nekrasov (1821–1878) 157
Fet (1820–1892) and Tyutchev
(1803–1873): Art for Art's Sake 159
Alexey Tolstoy (1817–1875) 160
S. Aksakov (1791–1859) and Saltykov-Shchedrin
(1826–1889) 160

9. The Great Truth-Tellers 164

Leo Tolstoy (1828–1910) 166
Dostoyevsky (1821–1881) 180

10. The Twilight Age 200

Leskov (1831–1895) 200
Chekhov (1860–1904)—the End of an Era 202

BIBLIOGRAPHY 216

Historical Background 216
Criticism 216
Anthologies 217
Recommended Translations of Individual Works 218

INDEX 225

A Concise History of Russian Literature

1 · The Beginnings

ORIGINS OF RUS

Drumming hoofbeats of horde upon horde of nomadic Asiatic invaders resound throughout the protohistory of the Slavic peoples. Sparsely settled on the steppe between the rivers Vistula and the Don, they were caught in the cross-current of trans-Caucasian migration westward. Historically we hear of them first as the conquered subjects of Attila the Hun during the fifth century A.D. A peaceful, agricultural tribal society, the East Slavs, ancestors of the Russian people, gradually moved northward in search of land that could be cultivated without constant threat of pillage and slaughter. By the ninth century we find them occupying the inland plateau traversed by the 1300-mile-long Dnieper river, the main artery of the navigable water system linking northern Europe with Constantinople and the Mediterranean basin.

A new aggression menaced them there. Down the rivers out of Scandinavia came marauding merchants known as Varangians. Originally traders, they were pirates as well and hired themselves out as mercenaries for the defense of Slavic ships along the river route. The result was inevitable. In the process of protecting the unwarlike Slavs the privateering *knyaz* (leader of a Varangian band) would take over a town with his *druzhina* (military bodyguard) and set himself up as prince.

Most important of these Varangian-dominated centers was Kiev. Strategically situated at the crossroads of the Byzantine-northern European route, it became the capital of a loose federation of petty principalities known as the Land of Rus— the name given, probably, by Finnish tribes to invading Scandinavians. The ruling dynasty of Rus was founded in 882 by Oleg, Norwegian successor to the Norse pirate Rurik, who had seized the northern city of Novgorod. Although the princes of the various territories were related and were bound to the Grand Prince of Kiev by kinship and oaths of fealty, there was more dissent than accord among them. In the absence of right primogeniture, land and its attendant powers were widely dispersed, and under a dynastic principle which prohibited the senior prince from governing the country in his person, political coercion was impossible. Even in the defense of their domains against hostile peoples surrounding Rus, joint action among the princes was sporadic and unsure.

ORTHODOXY—UNIFYING FORCE

It was the Grand Prince Vladimir I (later known as St. Vladimir) who was inspired to consolidate his country through the unifying element of a new and powerful religion. Pagan king of a pagan people, he had three major choices. Catholicism from the West would weld him to the struggles of Europe; Mohammedanism would draw Russia into the Islamic world; Greek Orthodoxy would strengthen his trade relations with Byzantium and incidentally permit Vladimir, a man of many wives, to obtain in marriage, as a Christian prince, the beautiful young sister of the Emperor of Constantinople, whom he coveted. It is difficult to assess the importance of this private consideration. Be it as it may, in a portentous move more willful and arbitrary than political Vladimir chose the Byzantine faith, and the year 988 witnessed the wholesale baptism of the Russian people. By this single act, one man alone fixed the nation's course for the next seven hundred years. Russia was set upon her path of isolation from the West.

The ancillary benefits of the new religion were immediate and titanic. Byzantine theologians, scholars, and master craftsmen now pouring into the converted land brought with them the apparatus needed to transform Kievan Rus into a homogeneous Christian state. Their works were the foundation of an indigenous Russian art and architecture, literature and written language.

Training Russian priests presented no linguistic problems. The Bible and liturgical texts had been translated a century earlier into a Bulgarian dialect which came to be known as Church Slavonic. It was written in a phonetic alphabet based on Greek characters with several new signs added to represent purely Slavonic sounds. This Cyrillic alphabet (so named after its presumed inventor, St. Cyril, a Greek missionary to Bulgaria in the ninth century) is still used today in a modified form among peoples of Slavic ancestry.

Although Church Slavonic was an artificial ecclesiastical language, it was close enough to the spoken idiom to be understood by the congregation. This was its first great advantage. In addition, it made a new and highly developed religious and moral ethic readily available, through historical and liturgical literature. Finally, the evolution of a distinctly Russian literary style was accelerated by early familiarity with Byzantine Greek forms. One cannot evaluate Church Slavonic as a literary vehicle, however, without recognizing its blighting effect on Russian intellectual life. With no pragmatic incentive to learn Greek and Latin, the Russian clergy, as churchmen and teachers, had little contact with pre-Christian thought and so remained in ignorance of the humanism of antiquity and Western medieval learning.

EARLIEST LITERARY MONUMENTS

The Byzantine prose which poured into Russia through the funnel of the Church was either purely liturgical—service books, church prayers, chants, selections from the Old and New Testaments—or religio-historical, that is, lives of saints, excerpts from church history, homilies and discourses of the church fathers.

Lives of saints were most widely read. They were biographies that emphasized the miraculous and the ascetic in the subject's life and highlighted his successful struggles against the devil. They were often copied out into collections called Chetyi-Minei (readings for each day), with the story of each saint written out under, and intended to be read on, the date

of his feast day. Teachings of the early Christian Fathers were
also in great favor and those of St. John Chrysostom were
copied and recopied in the monasteries for several centuries.

A variety of historical chronicles formed no small part of
Byzantine literary production, but only those of a particularly
religious bent were translated and available in Rus. In isolated
contrast stands the widely disseminated and near classical *The
Jewish War* by Flavius Josephus. It is worth noting that the
Russian translator of this work featured the war episodes in
Galilee and the siege and destruction of Jerusalem in especially picturesque vocabulary, departing at times from the
Greek text in his use of poetic similes which he either created
himself or remembered from native oral sources. In describing
battle action he writes: " . . . and you saw the breaking of the
lances, and the clanging of the swords on the helmets, and
the shields bursting apart, and the warriors carried away and
the earth given their blood to drink . . . and as the arrows
flew they made a darkness around the sun. . . ."

After the official church texts, apocryphal writings made
their appearance from about 1050 onward, brought from abroad
by monks and travellers. Though banned by the Church because of its heretical nature, this type of literature was extremely popular, and with reason. Orthodox Christianity and
Catholicism placed emphasis on the soul's destination after
death and the credulous medieval mind liked to dwell on
eschatological facts that made up such stories as *The Visit of
the Virgin to Hell, Adam's Address to Lazarus in Hell, The
Revelation of Paul the Apostle, The Colloquy of the Three
Prelates,* and other books that were concerned with divina-
tion, exorcism, and astrology. The most lasting and best-loved
of these was *The Visit of the Virgin to Hell.* Accompanied
by the Angel Gabriel, Mary descends to the underworld
and there, shaken by the tortures of the damned, she intercedes
with God to ease their suffering. In answer to her plea, a
yearly fifty-day respite is granted them. Somewhat in the manner of Dante's *Inferno,* the roster of sins and appropriate
punishments allotted to sinners of every rank and condition
discloses in capsule form some of the major social and moral
abuses of the times. The Holy Mother's deep compassion and

pity for the unfortunates made this tale a special favorite with the Russian people.

By the end of the eleventh century heroic romances were beginning to compete for the interest of the populace. Most of the stories reached Rus in Bulgarian translations which drew upon a literary legacy, non-Christian and non-Eastern, of ancient Hellenistic and Latin fiction. The romances dealt in the main with military exploits of warriors of antiquity, embellished by Greek writers with the fabulous, the monstrous, the calamitous; and the narrative bulged with descriptions of great armies, splendid armor, breathtaking combats, magnificent accoutrements. They must have appealed hugely to the militant members of the princes' *druzhina*. Best known were *The Adventures of Alexander the Great*, the *Deeds of Troy*, and the *Exploits of Digenes Akritas*.

The popularity of these new heroes in mythical guise was not confined to Kievan Rus. Their biographies were as eagerly read and reported at the French courts of the eleventh and twelfth centuries, but with a difference. Western writers portrayed Alexander as a chivalrous knight, and the amorous complexities of his adventures provided relief from the fierce onrush of military action. In Russian versions of the heroic romances, this kind of pause does not exist; the concept of gallant behavior and courtly love was alien to Digenes, who is otherwise portrayed as the prototype of a feudal knight. In other stories of the same genre, romantic elements are consistently missing.

The oldest dated Russian work is a series of dry, laconic admonitions concerning church dogma, written in 1036 by Luka Zhidyata, the bishop of Novgorod, titled *Instruction*. The work epitomizes Russian writing of that period: strict education was its object, and the clergy its mentor. In such writing there were three sharply defined areas of content: *sermons* intended as vehicles for the propagation of the faith; *saints' lives* which invited emulation; *chronicles* of events where migratory tales and legend blended companionably with fact.

The sermons were couched in rather simple language in order to be comprehensible to congregations all over Kievan

Rus. Of another caliber and composed for a different audience, the "Discourse on Law and Grace" was written by the Metropolitan Hilarion in 1051 and delivered before St. Vladimir's grandson, the Grand Prince Yaroslav. Hilarion was the first Russian to become head of the Russian Orthodox Church. The superb rhetoric and sophisticated allegory of the "Discourse" show that Hilarion had studied and assimilated the ornate, intricate style of his Byzantine masters. The content of the sermon proves that he had outgrown them. Hinting at emancipation from Byzantium, he draws a parallel between replacing the Old Testament with the New and the superiority of the young Russian faith to that of Constantinople. The future destiny of Holy Russia as the torchbearer of Orthodoxy is adumbrated here for the first time, just sixty-three years after the pagan Slavs adopted Christianity.

As the Kiev Crypt monastery, founded in the middle of the eleventh century, became the religious and cultural center for the country, a Russian hagiography made its first appearance. Not boldly original, the composition of saints' lives was patterned on Byzantine models. They followed a stereotyped formula for virtue, piety, miracles, and martyrdom and offered a modicum of personal data. True to pattern are the accounts of Saints Boris and Gleb, the first Russians to be canonized by the Orthodox Church. All we learn from the official *Life* is that they were brothers of Prince Svyatopolk who had them murdered in his attempt to inherit the coveted Kievan throne. The two young princes are warned of their brother's treacherous intent, but, faithful to their Christian upbringing, they prefer death to the sin of fratricide. Other chronicles of this political assassination upon which the *Life* is based are contrastingly vivid—Svyatopolk is fully and colorfully drawn as an unmitigated villain. Here, however, the author, conforming to the idealized concept, has minimized the drama, fearing probably that it might detract from the pious purpose of the tale.

Subsidiary to the production of hagiography was the compilation of the *Paterikon*, episodes from the lives of the monks themselves, dating from the early thirteenth century. The entries are sporadic, often in the vernacular, and include apocryphal inserts, homilies, and stories of monks who had yielded to the temptations of the flesh. The latter are described with verve and horror, the writer giving free rein to his imagination. This more pungent and exciting form of biography was copied and recopied, elaborated and exaggerated throughout the centuries, until the episodes finally became disassociated and achieved the status of novellas and short stories.

But it is the chronicles (*letopisi*) that constitute the most massive and important part of early Russian literature. Much of the primal record is only approximate as to dates and facts, but without it we should have no guide at all to the chronology of Kievan Rus. All the principal cities maintained annals, most of them continuously from the eleventh to the eighteenth centuries. Their beginnings were humble, set up in the form of charts upon which the monks noted Easter and other festivals. Gradually the blank spaces were filled in with accounts of current events, such as diplomatic missions, trade agreements, the weather, death and accession of princes, and even statements that nothing at all had happened at such and such a time. If space was lacking on the chart, commentary would overflow into the margins. Naturally, the entries reflected the interests of individual towns. The Novgorod chronicle is matter-of-fact and especially concerned with its economic activities as a mercantile center; while the South Russian chronicles are wider in scope and more imaginative. As years passed the heterogeneous material from the charts was copied, amplified, and compiled in chronological sequence. Brief comments were elaborated, lengthened, and the chronicler did not hesitate to enliven factual details with anecdote and legend.

The *Primary Chronicle* (also known as *The Tales of Bygone Years*) is the most interesting and cohesive of the annalistic writings. It is the work of six monks of the Kiev Crypt monastery and was compiled from 1040 to 1118. The first part traces the antecedents of the Kievan state; beginning with the Flood, it tells of the building of the Tower of Babel (one of the tongues is identified as the language of the Slavs), locates the Slavs in Russia on the Danube and Dnieper rivers,

and in highly dramatic, loosely linked episodes relates the
coming of the Varangians and the establishment of the great
Kievan dynasty. This colorful part of the chronicle, founded
on various migratory Eastern tales, legends from Byzantium,
and native oral tradition, recalls, in its terse, compressed style,
the Scandinavian sagas. The following passage, *Oleg's Occupation of Kiev*, concerns the second conquest of the city by
the Varangians under the leadership of Oleg, who succeeds
through a stratagem used by merchant pirates in "colonizing"
Slavic ports.

> Oleg set forth, taking with him many warriors from among the
> Varangians, the Chuds, the Slavs, the Merians, and the
> Krivichians. He came to the Hills of Kiev and saw how Oskold
> and Dir reigned there. He hid his warriors in the boats, left
> some others behind, and went forward himself bearing the
> child Igor. He thus came to the foot of the Hunnish hills, and
> after concealing his troops, he sent messengers to Oskold and
> Dir, saying: "I am a stranger on my way to Greece on an
> errand for Oleg and for Igor, the prince's son, and I request
> that you come forth as members of their race." Oskold and Dir
> straightway came forth. Then all the soldiery jumped out of
> the boats, and Oleg said to Oskold and Dir: "You are not
> princes, nor even of princely stock, but I am of princely birth."
> Igor was then brought forward and shown as the son of Rurik.
> They killed Oskold and Dir and took them to the hill and
> buried them there. And Oleg went into Kiev and took it and
> said: "This city is to be the mother of all the Russian cities."

As the record proceeds to the Christian era it becomes
more specific, more garrulous, and the account of the conversion of the Russians is treated in considerable detail; the
scribe dwells on the change in Prince Vladimir who as a
pagan had been ruthless, impatient, and haughty, but who
after his baptism became a gentle, considerate ruler, and such
a lover of learning that he had the children of his *druzhina*
sent away to school despite the lamentations of their mothers
who "mourned them as dead."

Although the Russian chroniclers, like Western medieval
historians, were unselective and naive with their material, they
became inflexible in underlining its moral implications, in this
case, the folly of fratricidal strife, and its crippling effect upon
Rus. Throughout the *Primary Chronicle* the concern for a

united royal family and a cohesive nation appears as a constant admonition and a recurrent plea.

Of all European countries Russia is richest in her fund of medieval annalistic writings. From the literary point of view they are of the greatest interest to us, for they help to determine what literary matter was current at the time of their composition. They are precious depositories which have preserved the legends, oral lore, and history of early Russia, frequently in highly artistic form. Later, they were to serve as a source of inspiration to nineteenth-century writers, such as Pushkin, Gogol, Turgenev, Leskov, and Tolstoy.

KIEV—THE MOTHER OF RUSSIAN CULTURE

For the literary historian, the beginnings of intellectual life in Russia are landmarked by the importation of a written language and Byzantine literary forms. But in the memory of the Russian people, the dawn of culture is a less specific concept.

It is rather the image of a twelfth-century city: holy Kiev of the glittering golden domes where spires rose heavenward in monolithic assertion of the power and serenity of the Orthodox faith and the prosperity of its citizens. Monasteries, libraries, schools, hospitals, palaces, workshops of skilled artists and craftsmen crowded the great cosmopolitan river city, larger than London, more brilliant than Paris, and the cultural center of the Land of Rus.

The presence of a small, educated elite—laymen as well as clergy—insured the patronage of intellectual activities. The Grand Prince Yaroslav (1036-1054), for example, established a large manuscript library at the cathedral of Saint Sophia and built schools for the children of the nobility and wealthy merchants; among them was a school for girls which his three daughters attended. (With chauvinistic care, Russian historians do not fail to remark that Yaroslav's daughter, the Princess Anna, who was versed in five languages and became the wife of Henry I of France, read official documents for her husband and opposed her signature in Latin and French to his straggling X.) Yaroslav's grandson, Vladimir Monomakh (1100-1125), employed a workshop of scribes to copy all available church manuscripts for his private archives and himself wrote original prose. In his *Testament* he not only details his many campaigns but lists sets of precepts to be followed by his children, exhorting them to retain the knowledge they had already acquired and to learn that with which they were not yet familiar. He instructs them to adhere to Christian principles, indispensable to a monarch, and to encourage the growth of scholarship.

That this last injunction was being obeyed is made clear from a manuscript of the next century, extant in only slightly differing copies. It indicates that education was becoming a less exclusive commodity, for it was composed by a boyar's (noble's) dependent who was neither nobleman nor cleric.

The Lament of Daniel the Exile is a petition to a prince, a sophisticated and lengthy piece of prose, showily erudite, sprinkled with aphorisms and scriptural references. Daniel begs the prince to take him into his service, not as a warrior, for he is neither brave nor skilled in arms, but because he is an intelligent and educated man and therefore entitled to an honorable place in the prince's entourage. It has been suggested that the whole content of the petition is fictitious. But if so, this could only add to the significance of the *Lament* as the first Russian literary work concerned with a private human situation wherein no moralizing overtones prevail, but where rather the author solicits the reader's compassion for the predicament of the lettered and underprivileged supplicant.

The Lament is a curious document and a rare one. Its intensely personal tone sets it apart from other literature of the epoch which, reflecting the official outlook of the governing bodies of the Church and State, was stylized and impersonal in approach. Essentially a two-dimensional prose —stranger to both psychological depth and personal perspective—this didactic matter served to propagate the rigid prescriptions of religious and secular rulers and to shape the national image of the emerging Russian state. In this process formal patterns of Old Church Slavonic were gradually penetrated by and admixed with the vernacular; but such "popularization" did not free literary genres from their Byzantine prototypes. Early Russian literature continued to be overburdened by the ponderous rhetoric and circumlocutions of its ecclesiastical antecedents.

SLOVO O POLKU IGOREVE—
RUSSIA'S GREATEST HEROIC EPIC

To the modern reader Kievan literary output would barely merit its classification as literature were it not for the towering monument of the *Lay of the Host of Igor* (*Slovo o Polku Igoreve*) which culminates this first period of Russian writing.

The *Slovo* is written in rhythmic prose and its title (*slovo* meaning "word," "discourse") tells us that it was intended to be declaimed rather than read. It is almost certain that the minstrels, as they recited it, emphasized the rolling alliteration of its phrases with accompanying chords on the *gusli*, an ancient Russian harp.

It is based on Prince Igor's abortive expedition in 1185 against the traditional foes of the Kievan state, the infidel Polovtsi (or Kumans), Turkish-Mongolian tribesmen who were constantly harassing the fertile lands of Kievan Rus. Igor, overlord of Novgorod-Seversk, a small town situated 100 miles northeast of Kiev, sets out with his brother Vsevolod, their nephew, Svyatoslav, Igor's young son, Vladimir, and their knights. Without the knowledge of the sovereign prince of Kiev they do battle with the Polovtsi beside the Don. In the first encounter, Igor wins; in the second, the Russians are disastrously defeated and all four princes taken prisoner, though Igor finally manages to escape. As the actual raid took place in 1185, and lines closing the *Lay* identify the living Volodimir of Pereyaslavl, one of Igor's companions who died in April, 1187, we may place the composition of the epic between these two dates.

It is a tale exemplary of the precipitous history of that time. After the death of Saint Vladimir, Kiev was torn from within by continuous strife among her princes. There was hardly a moment when one petty ruler was not feuding with another. This disunity emboldened barbarian tribes, and such expeditions as Igor's foolhardy one, undertaken vaingloriously and on impulse, were instrumental in weakening still further the dwindling Kievan resources.

Fearful premonition concerning the future of the Land of Rus is the major theme of the *Lay*. As in the political weather warnings sounded by the old Russian chroniclers, the author calls for unity among military leaders and their obedience to the Grand Prince. But no didactic note enters here and Christian motifs are singularly missing. The theme is handled less directly, with an artist's perception and intuition. Probably himself one of the prince's companions, the writer is carried away by the panache of knighthood and he cannot but exalt the valor of Igor and his men:

> . . . swaddled to the sounds of trumpets, nursed under helms, fed from a spear's end; the roads they know and ravines; their bows are taut, their quivers full, their swords sharpened; they race like grey wolves across a field, pursuing honor for themselves and glory for their prince.

But interspersed with the panegyrics are sobering passages in bitter criticism of Igor's foolhardy enterprise:

> Early you began to harass the Kuman lands with your swords and seek glory for yourselves. But you found glory without honor, for dishonorably you shed the blood of the infidel.

There are laments that mourn and view in retrospect acts of disobedience and fratricidal combat which needlessly shed Russian blood:

> O, how the Russian land moans, remembering her early years and princes! Vladimir of yore could not be nailed within the hills of Kiev, and now his banners are dispersed some to Rurik and others to David and in discord their pennons flutter apart.

The prose, as in the first and third of these extracts, abounds in metaphor. Some of it, unlike the examples just cited, is complex and difficult; nevertheless it is invariably rich and powerful, threading the lines with light and dark colors, attuning the splendid words to the height of the tragedy. The Polovtsian host assembles for battle: "The black clouds come from the sea, they want to eclipse the four suns, and in them shiver blue lightnings." The black clouds are, of course, the Polovtsian soldiers; the four suns are the four Russian princes;

and the blue lightning is the flickering of the light on the Polovtsian lances.

Nature is dramatically invoked in the *Slovo*, the very steppe and its denizens, the sun, the wind, the rivers are stirred by Igor's ill-starred venture and react to his passage. As Igor galloped across the fields, "the sun stood in his way with darkness"; the night "howled with the voice of a storm, awakening the birds, and warned the steppe and the river ahead of his knights to hearken to their coming."

By its incorporation of natural elements, pagan references, recurring laments, dreams, blazoned simile and metaphor, the *Slovo* is a literary aggregate of the devices common to that early medieval period. It qualifies as literature, and great, creative literature, by the psychological insight that permeates the epic and by the organization of its content. In structure it is amazingly modern, impressionistic; passages flower into lyric comment, panegyric jostles lament. Everything is unexpected, full of poetry, and passionately persuasive. For the first time in Russian literature the voices of women are heard: Glebovna mourns her son's premature end and in extraordinarily poignant lines which many Russians know by heart, Yaroslavna laments her separation from Igor, her husband:

Wind, O Wind! Why, lord, do you blow so strong? Why do you speed the Khan's arrows against my love's warriors? Were you not content to blow high beneath the clouds, rocking the ships on the blue sea? Why, lord, have you scattered my happiness across the grass of the steppe?

The *Slovo* is comparatively short (some fifteen modern printed pages); yet within this brief compass the author succeeds in satisfactorily developing the motives of the heroes and projecting their emotional reactions to the drama in which they are caught up.

The very fact of the author's strikingly original approach to his subject and the lack of any other epic like it have caused the authenticity of the *Slovo* to be called into question. As is the case with the majority of the writings of this period, the original draft was not preserved; the work survived only in a single, mutilated sixteenth-century manuscript unearthed in a monastery by an amateur collector in 1795. This copy was destroyed during Napoleon's invasion of Russia, but since a duplicate of it had been previously made for Catherine II and an edition of the manuscript had appeared in print in 1800, the work survived. Had the sixteenth-century manuscript not been lost, modern scientific methods of dating would have long ago put an end to the debate as to whether or not it was an eighteenth-century forgery. Pushkin, with a poet's insight, declared that there was not enough poetry in the entire eighteenth century for any part of the *Slovo* to have been written then! In attempts to settle this controversy, modern scholars have examined the text with infinite care, and it is now generally considered that the manuscript extant is a genuine copy of a work composed by a man inspired by the tragedy of events which occurred during his lifetime. Indeed, he had been inspired to see *beyond* these events, for the *Lay's* foreboding refrain lamented a Russian land irretrievably lost, and within fifty years the literary prophecy was fact. In 1240 Mongolian hordes swept once more across the steppe, ravaging most of Kievan Rus, capturing and sacking the city of Kiev itself, and with land and power firmly in grip, settled to complete control of the country for over two hundred years.

2 · Russia's Estrangement from the West

UNDER THE MONGOLIAN YOKE

In the depths of central Asia, the Mongolian chieftain Genghis Khan shaped his vast empire, and, aiming at world conquest, forged a mammoth army of archers, trained in cavalry techniques, rigorously disciplined, and savage. In the spring of 1240, the Khan commanded his grandson, Batu, to lead the assault upon Rus, and with 150,000 armed horsemen Batu thundered over the Siberian steppe, crossing the Volga to devastate the principality of Ryazan and raze the city of Vladimir. Novgorod lay next in his path, but the approach was deterred by marsh and forest, and Batu withdrew to the lower Volga to establish his headquarters at Sarai. Three years later, he moved again against the Russian princes, ravaging the towns of the northeastern principalities, pressing down into areas bordering the steppe, prostrating the towns of Pereyaslavl and Chernigov, and, despite their heroic resistance, slaughtering most of the citizens of Kiev and sacking the city itself. A Western traveller visiting the site in 1246 reported that the hundred-odd houses left standing there were lost in the miles of steppe littered with bones and human skulls. With the remainder of his forces, Batu then drove through Hungary, crushing its army and reaching the suburbs of Vienna before he learned that the Great Khan had died. He turned back to be present at the election of a new chieftain in Mongolia.

Fear dominates the only memory Western Europe re-

tains of the Tartars, the Russian name for Batu's Golden
Horde. But Russia remembers 240 years of relentless oppression, 100 of them unsurpassed for cruelty and ruthlessness,
extraordinary even by Tartar standards and comparable in
modern times only to Nazi brutality. The pattern of Mongolian occupation in Rus was swiftly and inexorably established. Following the second tidal wave of invaders, the prince
of Vladimir had set about restoring order, rebuilding his towns,
clearing the roads of corpses, and providing for refugees from
the devastated south. Now he was summoned to Sarai, there
recognized as sovereign prince, and ordered to journey to Mongolia to pay homage to the Khan. Sarai monopolized the great
trade routes of the south and southwest. The strength of Batu's
army was insured: heavy tributes were levied and collected
with punctual militancy, and a small Mongolian troop saw
to the registration of all male Russians, of whom one in ten
was recruited to fatten the ranks of the Golden Horde. If
the burdensome payments in taxes and men roused the people, punitive expeditions rode out of Sarai and restored order
with a brutality matched only by its dispatch. To underscore
his power, Batu periodically marched his men across the country, allowing them to commit atrocities at will.

While Russia bled beneath Tartar rule, avaricious neighbors to the west made other encroachments on her territory.
The Poles overran Galicia and Volhynia, attacking Russian
Orthodoxy and enslaving the population. Lithuania, last of
the European pagan powers, expanded her dominions to the
southeast, settling in Polotsk, Kiev, and along the Dnieper to
the Black Sea, conquering most of the rich black soil belt of
the steppe. By the middle of the fourteenth century, the
population of the vast stretch of land which is today the
European section of the Soviet Union was subject to either
Lithuanian or Mongolian domination. In 1386, when Lithuania effected a "personal union" with Poland through the
marriage of their respective sovereigns, all of their Russian
acquisitions came under Polish rule. The last link to independence gave way when the Teutonic Knights founded Riga
on the Baltic Sea, gaining control of the Drina River, one
of the two great Russian waterways from northern Europe to

the Black and Caspian seas. Russia was now effectively land-locked.

In Novgorod, German merchants had become, via the Hanseatic League, a powerful party in city affairs. They supported the constitution, which guaranteed equality to all freemen before the law; and they raised the standards of merchant and artisan guilds. Based on the export of fur, Novgorod trade flourished in a prosperity unequalled anywhere else in Russia. Contributing to the success of the mercantile center was Novgorod's swampy, forested terrain, a natural and effective barrier against the Tartar cavalry. But the astuteness of a Novgorod prince also played a leading role in the city's development. Alexander Nevsky, struggling to rout the Swedes from the Neva in 1240, hit upon a plan of cooperation with the Tartars, paying them generous voluntary tribute. For his lavish gifts and studious homage to the Khan—he made the long journey to Mongolia four times—his own men were allowed to levy the yearly tax within his own territories.

No ambitious princeling followed Nevsky's example more assiduously, nor exploited to greater advantage the policy of total subservience to the Khan, than did Nevsky's youngest son, Daniel, Prince of Moscow. Moscow (or *Moskva*, from the Finnish *mos*, meaning "way," and *kva*, or "water") emerges into history for the first time as a summer villa on a quiet river bank. When Yury Dolgoruky, youngest son of Vladimir Monomakh, discovered it in 1147, he liked it well enough to evict and drown the owner, marry his daughter to one of the Dolgoruky sons, and establish the villa as his summer retreat, enclosing the adjacent settlement with a fortified palisade, or *kremlin*. Later, it served as a seat for minor princes of the Vladimir line. By the middle of the fourteenth century, this obscure provincial town had become the capital of Russia, its princes in a position to command the entire Russian state.

CREEPING RISE OF MOSCOW AND AUTOCRACY

Moscow's growth as a commercial center in medieval Russia was probably due to its relatively sheltered location geographically, and its easy access to the Volga and Oka rivers for trade to the east, now that the provinces of the south and west had been lost. But the character of its governing house is primarily responsible for the rise of Moscow as a political force, which gradually gathered unto itself all the Russian lands, conquering even the vast republic of Novgorod, and forming the substance of the modern Russian nation. A succession of eight cunning, tenacious, and long-lived princes pursued with a singleness of purpose rare in history a policy which can best be called "acquisition through stealth." Only such a policy could have succeeded during the period of Mongolian subjugation. Any Russian ruler privately pressing for personal advantage risked immediate reprisal from Sarai. The princes of Moscow, however, were careful to shun the very appearance of ambition, all the while increasing and strengthening their domains with Machiavellian care. To uprooted peasants on scorched lands they rented tools and sold seed. By diplomacy, marriage, and, less frequently, by arms, they appropriated the appanages of junior princes and seized the entailed estates of tax-burdened boyars. They lured able military leaders and discontented nobles into their service. Ransoming Slav prisoners from the Mongols, they subsidized settlements on virgin lands in return for taxes and service. Through taxation and police pressure, they gained control of portages and rivers which led eventually to the open sea.

Effected through unremitting but unobtrusive rapacity, this accumulation of lands, moneys, and political power succeeded because the Tartars, interested only in exacting tribute from conquered territory, exercised general and long-range, not immediate or specific, control from Sarai. Besides, Alexander Nevsky's lesson had been well learned: no prince was more punctilious in his payments, more subservient to the Khan or generous in gifts to him and his concubines, more ready to assault a neighbor at the Khan's bidding, or use Tartar troops to collect taxes from recalcitrant villages, than was the prince of Moscow. It is not surprising, therefore, that to Ivan I of Moscow, better known as Ivan Kalita ("Moneybags"), was granted the position of chief tax collector for all Russia outside his own domains. This extension of temporal authority was further enhanced by spiritual prestige when, in 1326, the Church, tax exempt and itself holder of extremely large land properties, recognized Ivan's growing political influence and moved its see from Vladimir to Moscow.

As the star of the house of Moscow rose, there appeared signs of disintegration within the ranks of the Golden Horde. Competing khans ruptured the organization's unity, damaging its military efficiency. Eventually Sarai separated from Mongolia, and while the khanates scrambled for power, many Tartar warriors entered Kremlin service. By 1380, Dmitri, Grand Prince of Moscow, who had been delinquent in his tribute, felt strong enough to move against the Tartar army sent as a punitive force out of Sarai. His victory, like many subsequent ones against the Mongols, was not decisive; there was heavy loss of life, and two years later Moscow was burned, the entire principality pillaged, and Dmitri's son taken as hostage to the khan. But the myth of Tartar invincibility had been broken, and within eighty years, during the reign of Ivan III (1462–1505), the Tartars were gradually driven out of Russia.

When the vast Novgorod republic, last of the independent Russian principalities, had submitted to the Muscovy rules, Ivan, self-styled Tsar of Russia, was free to turn his attention to the West. When an emissary of Frederick III at Habsburg offered him a kingship and the honor of becoming the emperor's vassal, Ivan refused, declaring, "We are sovereign in our land from our earliest forefathers and do hold our commission from God himself." Opportunely, an ecclesiastical event of great consequence confirmed Ivan in his self-appointed role, and sanctified it. Greek Orthodoxy had formed an alliance with the Pope at the Council of Florence in 1439, and when, fourteen years later, Constantinople fell to the Turks, the Russian Church separated from Byzantium and proclaimed its most illustrious son as the true defender of the Orthodox faith. "The first was Rome, which was corrupted; the second was Byzantium, which betrayed Orthodoxy; the third is Moscow; a fourth there cannot be," the monk Filofey wrote to Ivan II. It was a doctrine that was to influence profoundly all future Russian thought.

The concept of Moscow as heir to the political and religious glory of Byzantium was tangibly endorsed when Ivan III married the Byzantine princess Zoë Palaeologa, orphaned niece of the Emperor Constantine. With her retinue, she brought to Moscow all the ritual splendor of her native court. To the crown of Vladimir was added the double-headed eagle of the Byzantine Empire. Elaborate court ceremony was instituted, and Italian architects, artists, and craftsmen were imported to build and decorate new stone palaces and churches.

But amid the grandeur, a love of cruelty and torture, bred among the upper classes, came to epitomize the age of Ivan IV (1533–1584). Better known in history, legend, and films as Ivan the Terrible, the Tsar turned his reign into a purge through tyranny and terror, directed against the boyars from whom he had suffered humiliation and abuse as a child. By systematic deportation, execution, and impoverishment, he sought to liquidate the hereditary aristocracy as a ruling class. His instrument was the army of cutthroats, the dread *oprichina*, whose black uniforms and black horses symbolized the destruction they dealt, and whose insignia—dogs' heads—designated them as devourers of Ivan's enemies and exterminators of the nobility. For their personal loyalty to the throne, they were given license to commit murder, rape, and extortion, to confiscate boyar properties after a pattern of atrocities reminiscent of a time three hundred years earlier, when Batu's henchmen scourged the land.

It was Ivan IV who, more than any of his predecessors, governed strictly by the Divine Right of Kings, bringing to its apogee the personal absolutism that had been gradually shaping the political ideology of the Kremlin. His rule, despotic and ruthless, was marked by acts of mad willfulness, one of which was to have grave consequences for Russia's immediate future. In a wild fit of rage, Ivan murdered his oldest son, thereby effectively extinguishing the royal line, for his younger son, Feodor, was an impotent simpleton. The murder left no successor to the throne after Ivan's death, and triggered a bitter attack on the government which brought the country to the verge of civil war.

The years 1598 (Feodor's death) to 1613 are known as the "Time of Troubles," a period of extraordinary national calamities. While two pretenders, the first backed by Polish supporters, vied for the Russian throne, there were successive crop failures, ensuing famine, and plague. Growing restrictions on the mobility of the peasants sparked open revolt in the rural areas; thousands of peasants fled, either to join the ranks of the pretender, or to the lower Volga where free communities of adventurers and fugitives were organizing Cossack strongholds. There a people's army was formed to march on Moscow, swelling with discontented elements on the way, until it reached the capital. At one critical moment, with a Polish regiment holding the Kremlin and a voluntary citizens' force besieging it, the rudderless nation was reeling toward anarchy, and the work of several centuries of consolidation appeared undone. Only the heroic efforts of a small band of patriots led by the mayor of Nizhni Novgorod, a butcher by trade, managed to restore order in Moscow and rid it of foreigners. Representatives from all classes in every Russian city were called together to elect a new sovereign, and in 1613, Michael Romanov became Tsar of Russia—and launched a dynasty which was to endure until 1917.

From the drama of historical fact developed the substance of the modern Russian state and its national characteristics as we know them today. The Tartars had imposed neither the language nor the culture of Mongolia upon their Russian vassals, nor did they attempt to abolish existing social and political institutions. Nevertheless, the changes wrought in Russian life as a consequence of the occupation were so profound that the civilization of Kievan Rus appears as a brief preface to the history of a Russia whose course was radically altered in 1240. During four hundred years (1240–1640) of rebuilding, consolidating, and expanding her territories, Russia was transformed economically from a martial, urban culture to an agricultural nation. Politically, where she had been a loose federation of semiautonomous principalities, she became a centralized, absolute monarchy. And socially, her boyars, freemen, and serfs split into rigid classes. Formerly, their rights and obligations had been commonly based, for the most part, on renewable contracts with their overlords. Now they formed a social structure which pivoted on compulsory and universal service to the state and total obedience to the head of state.

Kievan Rus had been vigilant against despotism, but all of

the old restrictions on power gradually disappeared in the new Russia. Nobles, burdened by Tartar levies or ruined by Tartar raids, forfeited their "right of departure with inheritance" from the prince's service, and placed themselves unconditionally under Muscovy protection. As towns decreased in size and number, the *veche*, a popular assembly at which all freemen could participate in principality affairs, dwindled in importance, and little by little, *veche* bells calling meetings in the public squares were silenced altogether. As a growing, agrarian land, the country was plagued by depopulation, and the agricultural worker was at a greater premium than the land itself. There had been fearful slaughter in foreign campaigns; conscription had taken heavy tolls; Tartar raids had carried off tens of thousands of children and young women to Eastern slave markets each year. Thus, ever heavier burdens of legal restriction shackled peasant to landowner, until in the sixteenth century, he had lost most of his civil rights and become a serf.

In the monumental task of freeing their lands from Tartar control, fortifying territories, and fighting off Western encroachers, the oppressed Russians demonstrated that much had been learned from the oppressor. The Mongolian scheme of universal conscription and a system of state-controlled taxation were grafted into Muscovite law. Russian commanders adapted for new use the familiar military techniques of the Mongols. In jurisprudence, torture as well as capital punishment, unknown in Kievan Rus, made their appearance. But the lesson most effectively learned and best retained was the concept of unlimited, unchecked autocracy. For numberless Russian princes who had been summoned to pay obeisance at Sarai, the court of the khan had served as an excellent training ground in the habits of naked despotism. Experienced in the success of such behavior, the princes of Moscow followed at home the example of the khan, practicing Mongolian methods in the collection of tribute and in setting standards for court servility. Foreign envoys in attendance on Ivan IV were astonished at the Tsar's display of petty tyranny, and at the slavish conduct of the boyars.

When the period of Mongolian domination officially ended in 1480, Russia could claim the status of an independent country. But to the Russian people, freedom from the Tartars was hardly liberation. By that time, just 240 years after the collapse of Kievan Rus, one bondage had replaced another, and all of Russian society had been pressed into lifelong servitude to the head of the Muscovite state. Toward the end of the eighteenth century, the landowning gentry did succeed in obtaining release from certain obligations to the throne, but in all other respects the habit of absolutism was now entrenched. For the Russian peasantry, enslavement was the habitual condition. Autocracy and serfdom, the two main pillars of the Russian nation, were to become the major issues in nineteenth-century literature.

CONSOLIDATION OF MUSCOVITE MENTALITY

Normal development of intellectual activity in Russia was retarded disastrously during the Mongolian rule. With the destruction of Kiev and the abandonment of the South, all contacts with Constantinople were severed, and the hostilities of western and northern neighbors encircled the Russian principalities with cultural isolation from the rest of Western Europe. Russia was thus barred from participation in the scholasticism of the Middle Ages, the Renaissance, the scientific revolution of the seventeenth century, the classicism of France. She was left to her own mental powers.

These were the more impoverished by the failure of the Church to maintain its intellectual leadership. It is true that chroniclers, briefly interrupted by the looting and burning of monasteries, resumed their record-making in towns that had survived the Tartars, and scribes continued to copy and recopy saints' lives, *patriki*, sermons, and the rest. But the major energies of the Church were channelled elsewhere. At the highest levels, it was engaged in developing the caesaro-papism policy at the Moscow court. The mass of its clergy, in the early dark decades of the subjugation, faced the immediate task of providing spiritual consolation to a stricken and outraged population. It was otherwise committed to bring the Christian faith into rural districts where pagan beliefs were still strong. Many young men were encouraged to take vows and pioneer their way into the northeastern wilderness and beyond the Volga, there to clear land, cultivate the soil, and establish monasteries where prayer, frugal living, and hard physical labor were the rule. They were followed by thousands of peasants who wished to escape the fear and violence at home, and who settled on tax-free Church lands around these religious centers.

By the sixteenth century, there were at least 150 such centers. One of the most active and successful abbots of the monastic movement was Sergey Radonezhsky, head of the fourteenth-century Troitsa Sergeyeva monastery. He was later canonized by the Russian Church. His "Life" propagates moral and religious fervor among the faithful, stressing the aspirations of the cloister: humility, mortification of the flesh, and prayer. Radonezhsky is somewhat of a lone figure, even in the field of ecclesiastical writings. Glorification of manual labor, added to physical isolation from urban life, were principal roadblocks to cultural development in this age, and may have accounted for the fact that the monasteries did not become centers of learning, nor attract great scholars, nor found educational orders as they had done in Western Europe. The monks, roughly shod and poorly clad, worked long, strenuous hours out of doors in primitive surroundings, side by side with the peasants. They had little time for intellectual pursuits, nor did they claim an interest in them. The sole art which flourished in these distant communities was iconography; indeed, the Russian icon, given impetus by the great master, the monk Andrey Rublev, reached its apogee in the fifteenth century.

For literature, it was a barren age indeed. Worthy of mention, however, are the chroniclers' reactions to the momentous events of the Tartar invasion and devastation. These were military tales extolling the heroism of communities which opposed the armies of the Horde, and are all somewhat stereotyped and similar. One of the best known and most dramatic of such "reports" is the story of the defense of Ryazan. The following passage is typical:

> And meeting the infidel Batu at the frontier of Ryazan, they
> began to fight with courage and fierceness. And it was a terrible
> and awe-inspiring fight and many of Batu's men fell in battle.
> And Batu himself, when he saw with what courage and fierce-
> ness the Ryazan warriors fought, became alarmed. But who

can withstand the anger of God? The armies of Batu were unconquerable and numberless. Every Ryazan warrior had to meet one thousand of the enemy, . . . and they fought with such courage and strength that the earth moaned and Batu's forces became alarmed and confused. . . . The powerful Tartars were just able to crush the Ryazan defenders. . . . The fearless warriors, and the glorious heroes, the pride of the Ryazan army, all suffered defeat and were slain on the battlefield. And Prince Oleg was taken prisoner. And all this occurred because God willed it as punishment for our sins.

The final rationalization of the tragedy in terms of Christian philosophy is the usual conclusion to every tale.

The momentous Kulikovo engagement in 1380 at the Don River gave the Russians their first victory against the Tartar army. It bore literary fruit as well. Best known is the poem *Zadonshchina* (*Deeds Beyond the Don*) by Sofonya of Ryazan. The work is not without artistic merit; it contains lyrical descriptions of the night before the battle and moves along in a coherent and logical fashion. But one cannot help contrasting it with the *Lay of the Host of Igor* which had great influence on the author. *Zadonshchina* may be called a "cento," because a great number of alliterative patterns, many lines of poetic imagery, fixed epithets, and even complete passages have been appropriated from the *Slovo*, but it is weak and unimaginative by comparison. Where some effort to make changes is apparent, the *Zadonshchina* suffers from overemphasis and overstatement. Compare, for example, Yaroslavna's lament (see page 13) with the following dirge of the women before they have learned the outcome of the battle:

> The wives and daughters of the princes and the boyars
>   Started to bewail the death of their men.
> Maria Dmitrievna, wife of Mikula,
> Cried into the early hour at the ramparts of Moscow:
> "O, swift River Don,
> Mountains fall away before you, and you
> Flow into the Kuman lands.
> O' carry back from there my prince, Mikula!"
> And Fedosia, the wife of Timofev Valuyevich, also wept
>   and cried:
>   "All gladness has forsaken the city of Moscow.
> I shall never see again my dear lord, Timofey Valuyevich."

And Marya, the wife of Andrey, and Xenya, the wife
of Mikhail,
Also lamented, ever since the early dawn.

The Marco Polo literary genre describing travel, imaginary
or real, was extremely prolific in the West during the Middle
Ages, but rare enough in Russia to give prominence to the one
extant account of a layman's trip to India. *Journey Beyond
Three Seas,* which somehow made its way into the *Moscow
Chronicle* in 1475, gives us the unrevised impressions of
Afanasy Nikitin, a merchant of Tver who sailed on business
through Persia to India. He spent three years there (1469–
1472) and died before reaching Smolensk on his way back to
Russia. His travel notations are artless and repetitive, but re-
freshingly personal. They reveal the mentality of an average
Russian of the period who misses his church holidays and ser-
vices in that "most un-Christian land," who is dazzled by the
oriental splendor of feasts and parades, astonished by the numbers of elephants and tigers, and shocked by the sight of women
with heads uncovered in public (a sinful sight in the streets of
Rus, then and even later).

In the sixteenth century, the Muscovite autocracy, having
merged Church and State, became the categorical imperative
of Russian society. The literature of that era both promotes
and reflects the intransigence, backwardness, and rigid orthodoxy of the times. Undoubtedly the most astringent and forceful writer of Ivan IV's reign is Ivan himself. In a long missive
sent to the head of St. Cyril's monastery, for example, the Tsar
flays the monks for their licentious behavior, spewing contempt
in superbly mock-servile rhetoric. To read his four letters to his
recalcitrant vassal Prince Andrey Kurbsky is to catch from
across the centuries the air of a passionate quarrel in which the
Tsar is winner by virtue of skillful polemic and pure vituperation.
The epistolary exchange between these two noble-born, learned
men is extremely curious. While Kurbsky is fighting to retain
his political primacy and ancient boyar privileges, Ivan justifies
the principles of autocracy and sets himself up as God's vicar
on earth, before whom all subjects are equally slaves to be
"caressed" or "executed" according to his will and pleasure.
Prince Kurbsky (ca. 1528–1583) was one of the best edu-

cated, most cultured boyars at the Moscow court; he had built himself a brilliant career as administrator, ambassador, and general. In 1563, when the Reign of Terror was in full sway, he was unfortunate enough to be defeated in battle, and fearing torture at home for his reversal, sought asylum with the enemy. From the comparative safety of Lithuania, he addressed several censorious epistles to Ivan and then wrote a prejudiced, partisan history of the Russian monarch. In restraint and elegance of style, his letters show considerable Western influence, and are in striking contrast to Ivan's florid phrases which mixed the cadenced dignity of Church Slavonic with street-language abuse. In a reply (which covers eighty-three modern printed pages) to Kurbsky's first letter, the Tsar directs a stream of invective at his refractory boyar, using as ammunition both common insults and Biblical judgments: "But the prophet David said, 'But unto the wicked God saith, What has thou to do to declare my statutes or that thou shouldst take my covenant in thy mouth?' . . . You are an adulterer not in the flesh; but an adulterer in treachery is like an adulterer in the flesh. So then you, too, have been a partaker with traitors, you filthy, rotten dog, you."

Ivan the Autocrat extended his royal prerogative in *patris potestas*, the principle which dominated family life of the middle and upper classes. The unassailable power of the Russian father was officially underwritten in a unique publication, the *Domostroy* (Manual of Household Management), probably composed under the direction of Ivan IV's friend and early spiritual advisor, the archpriest Sylvester. Among its detailed prescriptions for family conduct is the recommendation that any breach of patriarchal discipline by servant, child, or wife is to be "rewarded" with corporal punishment. The lord of the house is to administer the chastisement in private, with no onlookers, and he is to "handle the whip politely, holding both the culprit's hands, without indulging himself in his ire so that a minimum of disturbance and lasting bodily injury should occur." Admonitions concerning daily behavior, religious observances, respect for the master and the rearing of children crowd the sixty-four chapters of the *Domostroy*, but nowhere is there a single reference to the most rudimentary schooling for the young. Much of the document discloses by implication the extreme conservatism, intellectual insularity, and static mentality of the Muscovites, as well as the brutish coarseness of the times. Its guiding principle is the complete submission of all members of the household to its head, and its ultimate purpose is indoctrination, through acts of piety, toward abject, unquestioning obedience to the Muscovite state.

The *Domostroy* codifies domestic mores of sixteenth-century Russia. Two other encyclopedic works produced during Ivan's reign systematize the laws of Church and State, each, like the *Domostroy*, a final, didactic utterance on its respective subject. One, the *Saints' Calendar*, is a definitive compilation of all Russian religious writings; the other, called *The Book of Degrees of the Imperial Genealogy*, reworks the chronicles of old. The three together stand as an ironclad triumvirate intended to fix forever upon the Russian mind the endurance and power of the Third Rome. They came into existence because of, and for, a society now rigid in its cultural development, securely bastioned against further internal change.

LITERARY NOVELTIES—NATIVE AND BORROWED

Yet not long after these manifestos had been published and generally absorbed, the fortress that was medieval Muscovite culture quivered significantly under the onslaughts of three new, irresistible forces. Primary was the establishment of the first printing press in 1564. Then, during the brief reign of Dmitri, First Pretender during the Time of Troubles, Polish manners and Polish culture infiltrated the stolid, prescribed ways of Moscow life. And it was from Kiev, now governed by Poles and Lithuanians and resisting Catholic encroachment by reviving Orthodox scholasticism, that Moscow was to receive its final stimulus toward learning.

The Kiev Academy, founded in 1631 by the vigorous and learned Metropolitan Peter Mokhila, offered studies in Greek and Latin, serving as a model for the Slav-Greek-Latin School of Moscow inaugurated in 1687. Forty years earlier, influenced by the Patriarch Nikon, Tsar Alexis had invited Kievan scholars to his capital to help the inadequately taught Russian monks revise service books and make corrections from original Greek texts. None of the revisions was concerned with dogma, but public reaction to the "reforms" was immediate and violent. The Russian clergy was hostile to the scholarly newcomers; and for the lower priests, burghers, and peasants, the ancient rites and formulas of the Orthodox faith were sacred, of magical value, and not to be altered in any way.

The leader of the reactionary schismatics (*Raskolniki*) was the archpriest Avvakum. As a man he was fanatical, stubborn, of violent and uncontrollable temper, with a vocation for martyrdom. As a priest, he was exceedingly aware of his spiritual superiority and considered himself personally appointed by God to keep Russian Orthodoxy pure. He resisted the mandates of Nikon, who, as the Tsar's personal friend, was able to command his arrest and exile to Siberia. There the indefatigable "Old Believer" organized his followers and wrote didactic epistles to high-ranking churchmen, and to the Tsar himself. He also dictated, for "posterity's example," the first autobiography in Russian literature. Both letters and *Life* are conspicuous for their vilification of the "reformers" in language somewhat less than inhibited. The archpriest pronounces anathemas with the Biblical fervor and repetitiveness of the religious zealot.

Avvakum looms in Russian literature as a striking figure. He combines traditional modes of thinking with direct and pungent expression of such thought. His reactionary concepts are put down in vital phrases, drawn from the circles for which he was spokesman. The stately rhetoric of the churchman leaps to life in his indiscriminate use of the coarse, vivid idioms of peasant and burgher. His philippics recall the vigorous venom of Ivan IV, but unlike the Tsar's Avvakum's tirades are delivered for the preservation of the status quo. His writings are not only a passionate cry for the protection of ancient rituals; they are also a categorical denunciation of all that is new—things foreign smack of the devil, only Old Rus is truly Christian, and any change in Russian public or private life must be treated with deep suspicion and hostility. His attacks on the higher clergy and the reforms which they instituted led him to a martyr's death at the stake in 1681. He had fought a losing battle, for at the time of his death Russian society was becoming increasingly receptive to Western influence.

In the very heart of the State there had existed since the time of Ivan IV (ever in need of Western technicians and artillery men for his foreign wars) a large community of German, Swedish, and Dutch mercenaries, technicians, artisans, and some professional men. In a Moscow suburb allotted to them, they had attempted to reproduce their homelands. Along with technical skills and crafts, they had brought to Russia a taste for Western romances specializing in the lavishly sentimental, the fantastic, the farcical, and the crudely erotic. Young Russian boyars (particularly those serving at the Foreign Office), government scribes, literate men, and wealthy merchants, all were intrigued by this new kind of fiction, and it was translated in great quantities throughout the seventeenth century. Chivalric romances dating to the late Middle Ages and the early Renaissance described the adventures of knights who wandered through many lands, at last to be united with their beloved. These were very much in vogue. Among them, the history of *Apollon of Tyre*, *Peter of the Golden Keys*, *Basil the Golden-Haired*, *Bova Korolevich* (from the Carolingian romance *Bueves d'Anston*), and *Yeruslan Lazarevich*, of Persian ancestry, attained best-seller popularity and survived in chapbook form to the twentieth century. As they became more Russified, the courtly elements disappeared and the romances became pure fairy tales.

The translations and adaptations of these tales paved the way to a distinctly Russian literary genre called *povest*, a long short story which had a secular plot in a Russian setting and made a decisive break with earlier writings. Its main purpose was to entertain, though it contained occasional social criticism and satirical overtones. Free in style, it underlined its contemporary realism for the most part by use of the vernacular. Some stories did not escape the moralizing tendencies of Muscovite tradition, but in all there is a noticeable effort to shake off the old literary conventions and move in the direction of creative invention. *The Tale of Savva Grudtsyn*, written in Church Slavonic, is typically transitional. Among realistic scenes of drinking and wenching are interspersed moralistic asides on the destination of the hero's soul. The author is unable to consign the prodigal son, Savva, to either perdition or worldly success; snared again by the tradition of church-oriented writing, he saves Savva by sending him off to a monastery.

That the monastic life is the only salvation for a sinner is again the lesson of the verse tale, *Woe, Misfortune*, whose hero manages to escape his doom by taking vows. Disobeying the *Domostroy*-inspired admonitions of his parents, a youth leaves home and is lured through weakness into carousing and consequent destitution. His inability to cope with the world on his own is represented in a powerful figure of ill luck drawn from folklore; the figure is his alter ego and a symbol of his spiritual bankruptcy. The meter, the fixed epithets, and the repetitive refrains of this starkly dramatic story are all borrowed from devotional folk poetry. More novel in tone and temper is the *Tale of Frol Skobeyev, the Rogue*; the author takes obvious pleasure in the rascality of his hero, and there is no moral in the entire narrative. In fact, Frol's ascent of the social ladder by way of a wealthy nobleman's daughter, whom he seduces and subsequently marries in a clandestine ceremony, is recounted with considerable relish.

Another favorite, resembling Frol's adventures in its joyous disdain for conventional ethics and the occasional crudity of its colloquial idiom, is *The Story of the Merchant Karp Sutulov and His Wife*. Madame Sutulov manages to defend her virtue both slyly and profitably, besting a merchant, her confessor, and the bishop. Recalling the zestful intrigues of Boccaccio's *Decameron*, it is also a satire on ecclesiastical mores. Equally well known is *Shemyaka's Judgment*, which pillories the operations of a venal judge. Its very title has entered into the Russian language as a synonym for a court judgment tempered with bribery. Retold and rewritten in innumerable versions, this scathing tale was originally in verse, a form that had gained high popularity early in the century, and which may have been initiated by a nobleman, Ivanets Finnikov. In 1608, Finnikov wrote a long literary conceit in rhymed verse, satirizing common parlance. Called *A Letter to a Nobleman from a Nobleman*, it is full of puns, witticisms, sallies, and ribaldry. It launched a new literary fashion among younger Russian nobles, and there followed an epidemic of indiscriminate versification in the vernacular on all manner of social and amatory subjects.

With the arrival at the Moscow court of the West-Russian scholar Simeon Polotsky, the flood of versification reached its peak. Polotsky's language, a mixture of Muscovite and Kievan Church Slavonic, is surprisingly old-fashioned, but he transplanted to Russian verse the Polish form of a fixed number of syllables to each line with a break in the middle. Although this was suited more to Polish, with its constant accent, than to irregularly stressed Russian, the form remained a model for Russian poetry for more than eighty years. Even though Polotsky rates higher as a technician and teacher of poetry than as a creative artist, he has importance as the first prolific and systematic writer of poetry on worldly subjects, and his work reflects the Western trends emerging in Russian culture by the end of the seventeenth century.

The literature of the Land of Rus had been shaped by three titanic forces: Byzantine Orthodoxy, the Mongolian invasion, and the Muscovite hegemony. Now it was slowly disappearing, as a literature endemic to modern Russia emerged. The evolution would have probably come about naturally and in its own time. But it was given bold impetus by the advent of Peter the Great.

3 · Russia Goes to School in Europe

PERIOD OF APPRENTICESHIP

Peter's stupendous efforts to transform backward Byzantine Muscovy into a modern European state constitute some of the most dynamic pages of Russian history. To support his continual territorial wars with European powers, he needed an efficient chancellery, a first-class army and navy. He created them all, by reforms ranging from the cutting off of the nobility's beards and the transplanting of serfs to forced labor in munition plants to the founding of an Academy of Sciences.

Himself an eager and successful student of the exact sciences and technology, he had an immense respect for such learning, and he understood the vital role it played in the economic and political development of a modern nation. He invited hundreds of technological experts from Germany, Holland, England, and France to participate in his Westernizing campaign. He subsidized the training of young Russians at foreign universities and organized a program of "enlightenment" across his empire, centered around technical and practical achievement. Education for the upper and middle classes, which had been primarily religious, now became functional and secular. A nobleman's son was expected to channel his studies in preparation for an army or navy career. In 1700, a School of Mathematics and Navigation was founded in Moscow, and "cipher" schools were opened in principal cities where ten-to-fifteen-year-old boys, conscripted from merchants' families, were taught arithmetic, geometry, and trigonometry. (Of these fourteen hundred students only one hundred graduated; all the rest managed to run away.)

Printing, an unexploited potential for more than a century, began in earnest when the first Russian newspaper, a record of military and political events, made its appearance in 1702. More books were published in the first quarter of the eighteenth century than had been written during the previous two hundred years! Most of them were translations of scientific and technical material, or manuals and texts for the study of geography, history, military tactics, mathematics, and foreign languages. It was obvious that the cumbersome, ornate Church Slavonic could not easily be adapted to the functional new terminology, and Peter urged upon his translators the use of living, everyday Russian—at the literary level, then filled with many unassimilated words of Dutch, German, Polish, and Latin origin. Secular content was re-enforced by secular form when many Church Slavonic letters were changed to resemble Latin characters. The old alphabet was retained for Church needs, while the new "civilian" alphabet (slightly simplified in 1917) is still in use today.

The flood of printed matter, primarily technical and utilitarian in nature, turned up few examples of literature proper. There appeared some translations of antiquities—Aesop's *Fables*, Ovid's *Metamorphoses* (from a German text)—and in 1705, by order of the Tsar, there was published a curious collection titled *Symbala et Emblemata*. A series of pictures and mottoes, it acquainted Russians with the world of ancient mythology. Later in the century, during the Russian age of classicism, it was to become an invaluable handbook for writers and artists, and in 1788, it was reprinted with additional commentaries and lengthy footnotes.

The tales of the latter part of the seventeenth century were adaptations of Western romances and Russian *povesti* written by unknown Russian authors. These continued to divert literate and semiliterate readers, who read them during Peter's reign in widely circulated manuscript form. The story of the *Russian Sailor Vasily and the Beautiful Princess Irakliya of Florence* dates from the first decade of the eighteenth century and is noteworthy for its reflection of that period. As in

Savva and *Woe, Misfortune,* Vasily decides to break away from parental guidance, but unlike the earlier heroes, who are severely punished for this transgression, he manages to overcome all the calamities that befall him. His initiative, alertness and quick thinking all stand him in good stead—and are qualities which marked the character of Peter the Great; qualities that the Tsar was particularly anxious to cultivate in his subordinates. The love element in Vasily's adventure also assumes a more independent and Western flavor. In earlier stories, passion is synonymous with sin, or as in the episode of the rascal Frol, it is acceptable only as a means toward social success. Vasily, however, is purely and deeply in love with the princess and the lover's sensibilities are described with sympathy and at length.

Peter's urgent and uncompromising introduction of Western ideas, techniques, and manners was, in fact, a Russian "revolution from above." It precipitated European life into Russia. But, in the way of revolutions, it produced unforeseen and dangerous results. National unity, which centuries of Mongol rule and foreign invasion had only served to strengthen, was imperilled from within by Peter's cataclysmic reforms. There occurred a deep cleavage in Russian society. On the one side, the champions of New Russia, a small but powerful clique of ambitious young men—officers, adventurers, diplomats—were personally trained by Peter to propagate his reforms. Their fervent emulation of the West was equalled only by their contempt for all that was traditionally Muscovite or Orthodox. Opposed to these youthful rebels were the defenders of Old Russia, who believed that the sudden superimposition of alien modes of life was breaking the spirit of the people, and who therefore resisted Peter's revolutionary program and the methods used to implement it. Boyars who recognized (as did Ivan IV) the need for modernizing the nation's military operations with Western equipment and techniques were at the same time outraged by Peter's ruthless violation of religious observances and rules of family life. The Church was systematically debased and humiliated by a tsar who cared nothing for Orthodoxy, who abolished the patriarchate, founded a "holy Synod" after a Protestant model, and favored among his amusements unseemly parodies of religious ritual. All conservative Russians shuddered when Peter, upon his return from Europe, made German Christmas trees obligatory, forced his nobles to wear European dress, and commanded their daughters and wives to appear at "public assemblies" (to which he also invited his foreign companions, among them artisans, soldiers, and common workmen) where drinking, smoking, and dancing were the order of the day.

It is not surprising, therefore, that this period signals a widening rift between the educated nobility and the rest of the population. Toward the end of the century the split was decisive and complete. Nobles were forcibly removed from their country estates to serve in Peter's gigantic military or administrative complex. Further, they were taunted by their superior officers or by the Tsar himself into a total transformation of dress, language, and demeanor. They either travelled abroad themselves or sent their sons to Europe, as to a finishing school, whence these young scions returned more often than not with modish costumes, perukes, and Parisian accents, and with a sophisticated disdain for the barbaric manners of their own country. In Peter's barracks or government offices they associated constantly with foreigners, spoke languages other than their own, and in an atmosphere of indifference, if not contempt, for Orthodox ritual and dogma, they began to lose touch with their traditional heritage. They were, in effect, aliens in their Russian homeland.

A literary heritage common to nobility and peasantry made the estrangement between the two all the more dramatic. Long before Peter's time, serf and master alike had held common religious beliefs, shared a common ideology, had found solace and entertainment in Russia's oldest and greatest tradition, its oral literature. Once, children of both boyar and peasant listened to fairy tales whose origin was in the oldest of Russian folklore. On feast days, village boys and girls filled the manor courtyards with songs and dances, and at the master's behest, a peasant bard entertained, reciting archaic epic lays. But now the gentry were disassociating themselves from that common patrimony, and the great store of oral literature was left entirely in the keeping of the masses.

ORAL LITERATURE

The earliest purely Slavic poetry is to be found in the lamentations sung or recited by women during burial ceremonies. Structured on a pattern of incantations and questions, they varied according to the emotional improvisations of the mourners, who expressed their grief in language ranging from the most basic prose to lyricism of exquisite intensity. Yaroslavna's lament in the *Slovo* and the wailing of the wives in the *Deeds Beyond the Don* are based upon these ancient funerary dirges.

In the main, however, what has been handed down through centuries as the bulk of oral Russian literature are fairy tales, religious ballads, peasant songs, and epic lays.

FAIRY TALES

The Russian fairy tale shares with its West European counterpart the motifs of wish-fulfillment, escapism, and didacticism. Virtue is handsomely rewarded, evil is suitably punished. Thus, in spite of the wicked schemes perpetrated by his priviledged elders, the have-not younger child gains the prize in the end, through unexpected and supernatural means. In the sphere of fantasy, the Russian tale is more distinctive. Germanic, Oriental, and Slavic elements are all present, jostling indiscriminately. We may meet, for example, the famous monster Baba-Yaga, the child-eating old woman who lives alone in the depth of the woods in a sorcerer's hut which revolves on the legs of a hen. She is witchlike, Germanic in origin. But in the same story, we find a mythical bird of Persia, the exotic, crystal-eyed Fire Bird, each of whose feathers can illuminate an entire room. Or again, we encounter the purely Slavic spirit of the forest, green-eyed, green-bearded Leshi, who wears his left shoe on his right foot, buttons his coat the wrong way around, is as tall as a tree in the forest or as small as a leaf in the fields, and whose mission is to torment travellers and lead them astray.

RELIGIOUS BALLADS

Religion of the Middle Ages, in Russia as in Europe, encouraged pilgrimages to the Christian holy places. The Russian pilgrims were at first high-ranking churchmen, who, accompanied by retinues of attendants, visited Constantinople, Mount Athos, or the Holy Land. After the Tartar invasion, when egress was no longer possible, the class of pilgrim changed. A professional mendicant emerged from the oppressed and impoverished peasantry; he travelled from monastery to monastery, visited the holy shrines, and supported himself by begging. These wandering beggars were called *kaleki* (Latin *caligi*), after the type of sandal they generally wore. Current among the *kaleki* and part of their stock in trade was a vast repertory of religious ballads which they sang or recited while soliciting alms. Of very ancient origin, these ballads have their roots in the tales of the New Testament, in the Apocrypha, and in the Lives of the Saints. All are strongly rhythmical, many are composed in doggerel verse, and the language is in the main a rich mixture of Church Slavonic speech patterns and colorful vernacular. The themes are close to the intimate homespun theology of the Russian peasant, concerned as they are with pity for human suffering, God's compassion for His poor, and the personal intervention of Christ and His Mother in the lives of the lowly. Subject matter insured the popularity of these ballads, and among many perennial favorites, the *Song of Lazarus*, demonstrating God's love for the sick and homeless, is perhaps best known. It tells the story of two men, both named Lazarus; the one rich, enjoying the pleasures of this life, who denies entrance to the second, a poor, sick beggar at his gate. It is the latter who is received into the heavenly kingdom. Innumerable versions of each ballad still exist, for the *kaleki* remained a constant factor in Russian life until the Revolution, and their songs were passed by word of mouth to successive generations of singers and listeners.

PEASANT SONGS

Although the introduction of Christianity effectively smothered pagan practices in the towns, pre-Christian beliefs persevered in rural communities. The persistence of this "dual faith," or *dvoyeveriye*, was particularly evident in the cycles of seasonal and ceremonial songs of the peasants. When Orthodox feast days coincided with the old peasant festivals, elements from both traditions were vigorously evoked and woven into

both songs and ceremonies. At Christmas, for example, set at
the same time as the ancient winter solstice ritual to the sun
god Kalida, young peasant girls sitting around a fire in the snow
would chant:

> Hail to thee, holy Kalida,
> Born on Christmas eve.

On St. John's Eve, formerly sacred to the God of Water, Kupala,
the figures of the Baptist and the water god were fused, so that
on a midsummer night consecrated to them both, St. John was
invoked as "John Kupala."

Although the intrinsic meaning of these songs has long
been forgotten, they survive in the public holiday celebrations
as do other ancient songs connected with private ritual. Marriage
songs are, of course, among the oldest, and here also pagan
echoes are heard. In wedding songs, the newlyweds are addressed as: "lado" and "lada," meaning "lover, bridegroom"
and "bride, wife," respectively. In the mythology of the ancient
Slavs, "Lado" is the god of marriage, and "Lada" the goddess
of spring and love.

EPIC POEMS

In contrast to this village folklore, oral epic poems—the
byliny ("that which had been")—met the need for heroic
symbols. The *byliny* celebrate the deeds of warrior knights,
semimythical, semihistorical personages of a heroically recon-
structed past. They are generally divided into three cycles,
named for three cities: Moscow, Novgorod, and Kiev.

To the Moscow cycle belong the later poems, fewer in
number and centering around Ivan IV, Peter the Great, and
even more recent historical figures. Naturally enough, the group
of poems from the maritime trading center of Novgorod reflect
that city's interest in its favorite hero, both minstrel and wealthy
merchant, Sadko—also the name of an influential citizen of
Novgorod who founded a church in the twelfth century. Sadko's
adventures, folkloric in tone, full of boisterous humor and
magic-wand techniques, are the best known of the Novgorod
sagas. Having made a pact with the Sea King, but failing to
pay the tribute agreed upon, Sadko is forced to descend to the

bottom of the sea; there he must choose a bride from among the king's three hundred daughters, and play on his harp while the king dances, causing terrible storms which drown sailors and sink merchant ships. St. Nicholas steps in, compels Sadko to destroy his harp, and at last returns him safely to Novgorod.

The most important and numerous *byliny* belong to the Kievan cycle. We know that these poems were composed, probably by trained minstrels, between the tenth and thirteenth centuries, for they depict Christian Russia in continual clashes with pagan tribes, and their action is confined to towns prominent during the Kievan epoch (from which Moscow is still absent). The epics extol warrior knights, or *bogatyri* ("mighty men"), who rally around the Grand Prince Vladimir, much as the Knights of the Round Table pledged themselves to King Arthur and the enforcement of justice. Their exploits in defense of Rus and the Christian faith mirror the tense, stirring times of the country's early history.

Vladimir, a composite figure portrayed as both St. Vladimir, architect of Russian Christianity, and as the intellectual Vladimir Monomakh who died in 1125, appears in the Kievan *byliny* as a king or armchair general, setting the *bogatyri* on missions of derring-do. One of the most beloved of his paladins is Ilya of Murom, a peasant's son. Paralyzed until the age of thirty-three, Ilya is given a magic potion by three pilgrims, is cured, and instantly endowed with superhuman strength. He clears the land of fabulous monsters, slays thousands of raiding Tartars, relieves cities under siege. In one of his earliest and most memorable feats, he frees the beleaguered town of Chernigov by hacking his way through thrice forty-thousand soldiers. Then, upon learning that his way lies through a forest where the murderous Robber-Nightingale lies spread-eagled across seven oak trees in wait for the traveller, Ilya shoots him down, slings him across his saddle, and takes him to Vladimir's palace. There, sitting astride his great horse in front of the palace, Ilya cries out:

> O, Prince Vladimir, our little father,
> Are you needing any strong and mighty knights
> Who would bring honor and glory to you,

Our little father, and guard your royal city
And hack down the Tartars?

Second only to Ilya in valor are the warrior knights Dobrynya Nikitich and Alesha Popovich. In a late tenth-century
chronicle, Dobrynya is identified as Vladimir's uncle; in the
epic poems, he is Vladimir's nephew and steward, whose major
adventures include a fight with the mountain serpent, a battle
with the Amazons, and an encounter with the beautiful sorcer-
ess, Marina (who is in later versions confused with the Polish
wife of the first false Dmitri). Dobrynya is bewitched by
Marina, but, unlike her other victims, he frees himself through
a false promise and then strikes off her head with his sword.
Alesha is known as the dragon-slayer, but he is more frequently
alluded to as "Popovich" ("son of a priest") and seems to
generate dislike, as do priests and their families in many fairy
tales. His reputation is also that of a mischief maker whose
gibes offend guests at the festive board.

Personalities are shaped for each of the figures in the
Kievan epics. Vladimir is a kind and hospitable prince but a
somewhat timid one and not averse to fostering intrigue among
his retinue. Dobrynya is quick to anger and vengeful at times,
although he is also compassionate and deplores wanton bloodshed. Ilya remains the most modest and straightforward of the
knights, constant in the pursuit of his ideals. He reappears in
many later *byliny* as an "Old Cossack," that is, as a champion
of the common people, and sometimes as an "ataman," or
Cossack leader. In poems celebrating Stenka Razin's raids
against the boyars (to avenge tyrannized peasants in the sixteenth century), Ilya either comes to the assistance of the river
pirate and his band, or himself leads them, becoming Stenka
Razin. After a quarrel with Vladimir (recounted in a later poem
in which Ilya loses his usual composure and becomes disorderly
and abusive) Ilya gallops away from Kiev and consents to
return only on condition that all public taverns remain open
for twenty-four hours to serve the people as much free beer
and green wine as they choose to drink.

The spirit of an elemental, semibarbarous, but essentially
democratic life permeates this oral epic poetry. Romantic
glamour is noticeable by its absence; women play only bit parts

as witches, mothers, and faithful wives, or they are wooed roughly, sometimes taken by force. Marital infidelity is invariably punished with mutilation. The men's minds are uncomplicated, their humor naive, and their laughter large. Their chief pleasures, as in Scandinavian sagas, consist of great eating and hard drinking at the master's board, and boasting of manly prowess, horse, or sword.

The drama of the steppe with its endless plains furrowed by immense rivers haunts the Kievan *byliny*. In them "the mighty *bogatyr*, riding out onto the clear field" is ever on the alert against the sudden danger of the raiding enemy. Here early Russian history is crystallized in the attacks and counter-attacks of Vladimir's warriors defending the land against the encroaching "Tartar Terror," as all invaders of the Russian land were called—Poles, Lithuanians, pagan frontier tribes, and Mongol armies alike. These onslaughts attained fearful proportions and in the poems their perpetrators are often described as huge hawks or other birds of prey (like the Robber-Nightingale) which plummet with incredible, death-dealing swiftness, thus seeming to descend upon the Russians from above. Detailed and repetitive descriptions of these monsters reoccur. Another common but more artistic device builds suspense before the actual combat by magnifying the opponent's strength and minimizing that of the *bogatyr*. Ilya, for example, likes to dress as a "ragged *kaleka*," solicit alms, and listen in apparent fear to the boastful threats of his enemy until the very moment when he slays him, quickly and easily, in single combat.

Centering around one episode in the life of the hero, the poems vary in length from thirty to nine hundred lines, each containing an irregular number of syllables, three of them accented. The lines are free of assonance, alliteration, and rhyme, but they achieve a unity of structure by the simple repetition of the conjunction "and" together with interchangeable stylistic devices, such as fixed epithets, recurring gestures and speeches, and stock prologues. When they were first composed, they were probably chanted at the courts of the princes to the accompaniment of an ancient harp (*gusli*); to this day, the balalaika is often used to strike a few minor chords during the prologue

before the *skazitel* or *skazitelnitsa*—peasant narrators—begin
the recitative of the poem proper.

From as early as 1804 (when Kirsha Danilov's compilation
appeared) and into the last decade Russian scholars have been
collecting and are now recording these oral heroic poems. Some
four thousand have been unearthed, and others are still coming
to light in the remote Olonets and Archangel regions northeast
of Leningrad, particularly in the villages around Lake Onega.
How is it that only northern peasant bards have kept alive
the epic poems of heroic deeds accomplished in the south of
Russia, thousands of miles away, where nothing at all is known
of them? According to the most plausible conjectures, the tales
may have migrated in the thirteenth century with refugees from
devastated southern cities to the centers of the country north
and east. Still later, as new needs and new forms arose around
Moscow and the Church persecution of the *skomorokhi* (merry
jesters) sharpened, the refugees, who undoubtedly included
the *byliny* in their entertainments, travelled farther north along
popular fair circuits, and so transmitted their chants and recitations to peasant bards. It has been suggested that since the
Olonets peasants were not enserfed, there was more leisure
time for distractions, and oral literature could thus be more
easily maintained.

Opinions of the experts on the possible origins of the *byliny*
diverge in three directions. According to an early theory, they
are folk memories of the pagan Slavic pantheon. Perun, the
thunder god, becomes Ilya, whose horse represents the god's
chariot. Dobrynya, less aggressive than Ilya, develops out of the
Sun God, Kalida, in his passive aspect; and the Sea King, with
whom Sadko is involved, is quite obviously the god of the sea.
In 1868, the Russian philologist V. V. Stasov countered this
theory with the claim that these poems were mere transformations of Eastern epics. Tabulating adventures common to both
Russian and earlier Eastern heroes, he proposed, for example,
that Ilya is none other than Rustem of the Iranian legend, who
is also immobilized until the age of thirty, suddenly healed, and
strengthened by a vivifying draught. Further, the Hindu legend
of Krishna finds many echoes in the childhood and rearing of

Dobrynya. In contrast, the historical school asserts the autoch-
thonous origin of the sagas, finding them to be the embodiment
of the courtly ideals and heroic mood of early Rus, with allowance made for the exaggerations, dilutions, and supernatural
veneer which the *bylinys* have accumulated through the successive interpretations of countless peasant bards.

None of this evidence is as yet considered to be conclusive,
and it is highly probable that some part of each theory is true.
Be the origins what they may, the touchstone of popular
Russian imagination has transmuted the heroes of this primitive
epic poetry into national types, and the exotic foreign elements
have become mere ornamental motifs.

Much of the importance of these vast archives of living
oral literature lies in their obvious function as a repository of
national tradition. Transmitted by a semiliterate class, the
matter of the ballads, tales, proverbs, the epic poems, songs, and
incantations was readily available to sophisticated men of
letters.

Nineteenth-century writers—Puskin, Turgenev, Ostrovsky,
Gogol, Leskov, and Tolstoy—recognized the native genius of
this tradition, and in some of their works drew upon this great
treasure house of Russian national lore. The bulk of it, however,
remained a separate folk culture, unsifted and unrefined.

AGE OF CLASSICAL IMITATION

By the end of Peter's reign, Russia had come of age as a
modern European nation. As her first Western tsar, Peter had
established her course with a remarkably stable government
whose strength was to endure through the thirty-seven years of
political chaos following his death. The Tsar had left no heir,
nor had he appointed a successor. The autocracy was left to an
irresponsible, faction-torn nobility, whose highest members
filled the court with intrigue and strewed the path to the throne
with palace revolutions and assassinations. No fewer than three
empresses and three emperors reigned over Russia between
1725 and 1762, their claims to the throne so slender that only
well-rewarded partisans could effectively keep the crown from
other heads. Yet despite the wracking dissensions of the court,
the administrative, economic, and military machinery set in

motion by Peter the Great continued to function, almost autonomously, and in foreign trade, colonization, and most significantly in the aggressive expansion of her territories, Russia proved herself equal to the role of an emerging European power. By the end of the eighteenth century, the boundaries of her empire closely approximated those existing on the eve of World War I.

Under Peter's regime, upper-class Russians had been mobilized to serve the state in all branches of government, receiving promotions only on the basis of merit. But during the nearly four decades when conniver and pretender ruled the land, the nobility were released entirely from all obligation to the state—save that of supporting the current power on the throne. Taxed no longer, permitted to travel freely and even enter the service of a foreign prince, the Russian aristocracy had become by 1762 a truly leisured class for the first time in its history, Western in its tastes and influence.

The new social order had incalculable effect upon the development of Russian culture. The Imperial court at St. Petersburg had itself acquired a Western patina as the sybaritic Empresses Catherine I (1725–1727), Anna (1730–1740), and Elizabeth (1741–1762) surrounded themselves with luxuries from Europe. Effectively dominated by the fashions and philosophies of eighteenth-century France, the tone of European life permeated the stolidity of the Russian court, and now, in an atmosphere ripe for the innovations of fine arts, literature, and education, the most enlightened of the Westernizers set out to actively patronize the growth of European culture in the Russian homeland. At an academy for officer cadets, founded in 1730, liberal arts competed seriously with military science for recognition on the curriculum, and the students themselves published a literary magazine. The Academy of Sciences established at St. Petersburg a high school and university, where, in 1755, Russia's first popular scientific and literary journal was born on the university press. That same year, Empress Elizabeth granted Moscow University its charter, opening varied courses of learning to commoners and nobility alike. The University's activities included the production of a newspaper with a decidedly literary bent.

This learning-conscious period, full of enthusiasm for the newly introduced European studies, was surely the cradle of modern Russian literature. But the writings produced by the eighteenth century were hardly original, hardly creative. They were at first no more than slavish imitations of French forms, by authors for whom the masterpieces of French classicism established the canon of excellence. The first three major men of Russian letters, Kantemir, Trediakovsky, and Sumarokov, were convinced that Russian literary expression could be created only by copying French literary techniques, and they dedicated their lives to superimposing the popular European styles on Russian writing.

KANTEMIR (1708–1744)

Prince Antioch Kantemir was the son of a Moldavian king who had cast his fortunes with Peter the Great, establishing himself and his family as expatriates in Russia. The young Antioch grew up amid the humanistic revolutions of the Petrine era, and his education reflected all of Peter's aspirations for an enlightened Russia. Under the newly imported German professors, he achieved fluency in Greek, Latin, German, English, and French, and made intensive studies of antiquities and the exact sciences. During his first stay in France, the young prince met a number of outstanding French philosophers. He corresponded with Voltaire, and translated Montesquieu's *Persian Letters* of social criticism. It was not long before he was well known in the literary circles of Paris as an ardent, persuasive propagandist for the new Russian cultural order.

His major contribution to the literature of the period consists of nine satires, of which the last four were written in Paris, where he lived in "honorable exile" as a diplomatic attaché until his death. The first satire emerges as a commentary on Peter II's reign (1727–1729), castigating opposition to Petrine reforms and ridiculing the position of prominent boyars who were now openly condemning the new sciences. In the mode of Peter's reforms, the satire is specifically directed at certain members of the religious hierarchy. Titled *To My Mind*, Kantemir's work is a conscious imitation of the satires of the French writer Boileau, from whom the form and even the title, *À Son Esprit*, are borrowed. But for Russians, such barbed literary attack was entirely new, and delighted Westernizers eagerly joined the young poet in his indignation at religious hypocrisy, the complacent ignorance of tradition-bound nobles, the abuses of high-born privilege, the shallowness and foppishness of princelings who identified European education with the latest styles in costume and peruke. Steeped in the ideology of French classicism, Kantemir in his poetry appeals to his countrymen in the name of reason and self-control, rounding out his satirical verses with didactic instructions.

The satires were published in German and French shortly after Kantemir's death, but owing to the power of his enemies at home, they circulated in Russia only in manuscript form until the accession of Catherine II in 1762. During the eighteen years which elapsed between his death and the Russian edition, his poetry had become a literary anachronism. Written in syllabic verse, it seemed archaic when juxtaposed with the work of Trediakovsky and Lomonosov. Yet despite the heaviness of his language and style, Kantemir's place in Russian literature is secure on two counts: he pointed the direction which Russian men of letters were to take in their choice of French models; and, as the father of Russian literary satire, he paved the way for the work of Fonvizin, Krylov, and Gogol.

TREDIAKOVSKY (1703–1769)

Vasily Trediakovsky, son of a poor parish priest, made his way from distant Astrakhan to the Slavo-Greco-Latin Moscow Academy and then, in great privation, completed his education in Paris. Back in St. Petersburg, he became known first as a translator of fashionable gallant French poetry. He received a court appointment to compose eulogies for royal occasions; next, was made acting secretary, and later, professor of rhetoric at the Academy of Sciences. When this learned body met in 1735 to discuss problems of language and literature, Trediakovsky outlined a program of fundamental changes for lexicon, translation, and versification. Though his plan was not adopted by the Academicians, it formed the core of a literary activity to which Trediakovsky devoted the rest of his life.

Trediakovsky had, no less than Kantemir, absorbed the

tenets of French classicism. He was the first Russian poet to construct patriotic odes in the Pindaric manner. In 1766, he adapted Fénélon's *Télémaque* into Russian hexameters, and prefaced his own two volumes of verse with a translation of Boileau's famous codification of classical poetry, *Art poétique*. In his attempts to reform Russian versification, he was influenced by the French alexandrine, but he went far beyond mere imitation. He was the first to recognize the unsuitability of syllabic verse for the Russian language, and he put forward a system based on equal, bisyllabic metrical feet; that is, a regular sequence of alternating stressed and unstressed syllables, which was the rhythmical form of the Russian popular ballad.

Trediakovsky brought new freedom to the Russian literary language by purging it of Church Slavonic remnants which "sounded savage to his ear." He insisted that his translations show a closer relationship to the lively secular idiom, "as we ourselves speak it and hear it daily."

For his efforts, the lowborn and rather timid poet suffered humiliating abuse at court, ridiculed in that rude age as a verbal clown. His German colleagues, too—Academicians who had little interest in the Russification of literature—disparaged both him and his cause. Trediakovsky nevertheless persevered with his experiments, and it is almost tragic that, lacking creative talent, he generally failed to demonstrate the practicability of his aesthetic theories in his own poetry. His translations are unimaginative, often clumsy, and laborious. His work is significant, however, in that it broke new ground for the more gifted writers who followed him.

SUMAROKOV (1718–1777)

A Military Academy graduate with honors in French literature, Alexander Sumarokov claimed a family of ancient honorable lineage. His reputation as the first Russian gentleman to take up the writing profession was soon established by his frequent contributions of satirical, elegiac, and gallant verse to literary magazines. Some of his satires, twitting petty, ignorant bureaucrats, are exceptionally effective in their verve, tempo, and accurate aim, but his numerous articles on literary aesthetics amplify Trediakovsky's innovations with more zest than originality. Like his predecessor, Sumarokov sought to impose the rules of French classicism on Russian writing. In 1747, he put his theories to the test in a first play, *Khorev*. Written in punctilious imitation of the French tragic style, it was produced with great success by the cadets of the Military Academy, and the following year given in command performance before Empress Elizabeth.

When in 1756 the Russian theater was created by Senate decree, Sumarokov was offered the post of producer-director. In the absence of traditionally Russian plays to fill the repertory, he supplied a steady stream of his own tragedies and comedies, written in the manner of Racine, Corneille, and Molière. His labors earned him the right to be known as the Father of Russian Theater.

ORIGINS OF THE RUSSIAN THEATER

In Russia as in Western Europe, medieval drama grew out of liturgical rites; within the confines of the church building, the priests performed simple scenes related to the service proper. In the West, these dramatic presentations were rapidly secularized; Latin gave way to the vernacular, and the performances, no longer reserved for the congregation, were staged in front of the churches. Stimulated by private patronage and backed by guild participation, these elementary religious dramas developed into the great morality and mystery plays of the fifteenth century. No such parallel evolution occurred in Russia: the language of the Church was comprehensible to all, and dogmas could therefore be directly expounded within the framework of the service itself. Drama outside the Church received no religious sanction; it was, in fact, largely condemned by ecclesiastical authorities as immodest, unseemly, and devil-inspired.

If we are to exclude from history the village dramatics in song and dance which for the peasantry had marked seasonal changes since the pagan era, and itinerant companies of *skomorokhi* (from Byzantine Greek, "chief entertainer") or merry jesters whose comic turns, crude songs, puppets, and tame bears entertained country fair crowds across the land for centuries, true theatrical performances did not exist in Russia until the seventeenth century. Only then was the ice broken by the school dramas of the Kiev Academy. These were religious in content, long and declamatory, and considered to be supplementary training in poetics and rhetoric. Two of them, written in syllabic verse by Simeon Polotsky, were titled *On Nebuchadnezzar, the Golden Calf, and the Three Children Who Were Unscathed in the Furnace* and *The Comedy of the Parable of the Prodigal Son*. Happily, the solemnity and tedium of the productions were relieved by "interludes," short between-the-acts scenes running from parody of the drama itself to independent anecdote or spontaneous clowning in the colloquial idiom, reminiscent of the uninhibited pranks of the medieval *skomorokhi*.

When Tsar Alexis learned from his more emancipated boyars about the French plays they had seen abroad, he commanded Johann Gregory, amateur poet and minister of the Lutheran church in the foreign quarter of Moscow, to produce a play. Accordingly, on October 17, 1672, in a specially built wooden shed, Gregory staged the Biblical story of Esther with a cast of sixty-four, recruited mostly from among the sons of foreigners. The Tsar was the sole spectator, and so enthralled was he by the drama that he demanded the play to be given over and over again, while he remained in his seat, transfixed, for ten consecutive hours. Later, members of the court were invited to attend, the women peeping at the stage through screened partitions.

But there was no sequel to this venture. Orthodox Muscovites reacted with instant hostility to Gregory's cautiously pious play, branding it a sacrilegious Western import of a corrupt piece with the "accursed" alien faith, alien language, and alien manners of the foreign community.

A breakthrough to some form of professional theater was to have been expected of the Petrine epoch. In 1702, by order of the Tsar, a state theater was constructed on Red Square to lodge a German company directed by Johann Kunst. Kunst was also commanded to train Russian actors. As the Germans were not proficient in Russian, and the Russian trainees knew very little German, a state of bilingual confusion dominated rehearsals and performances, a condition in no wise alleviated by the repertory. The plays were poorly translated, second-rate English and German melodramas, and in the decadent Shakespearean tradition of the itinerant English companies then at the height of their popularity in Western Europe, Kunst charged his productions with abundant on-stage violence and stunning scenic effects, which contrasted oddly with the actors' studied "gallantry" of speech and delivery. Peter's theater, open to the public twice weekly, closed at the end of a year.

Further overtures on behalf of theater were made by both the Empresses Anna and Elizabeth, who invited foreign troupes to the St. Petersburg court. Anna favored German slapstick comedy performed by German actors; she imported an entire company from Leipzig. But the first bit of genuine sophistication in technique and dramatic art reached Russian salons via Italy. In 1731, the Neapolitan composer Francesco Araia brought to the Russian capital a large company of actors and singers for his production of an opera in which the "improvised" dialogue and subtle plot variations of the *commedia dell'arte* had their first Russian audience. Elizabeth's reign—for her entourage, a perpetual round of hunts, balls, masquerades, and diversions of all kinds—placed great emphasis on dramatics. Italian, German, and French companies vied for the pleasure-loving Empress' generous favors, and amateur theatricals sprang into fashion; courtiers themselves were producing plays staged at the Winter Palace.

Sumarokov, as we have already seen, was perhaps the best known of these gentlemen-playwrights. His nine tragedies and twelve comedies observe strictly the classical unities of time, place, and action; the "highness" of tragedy is kept distinctly separate from the "lowness" of comedy. In his comedies, Sumarokov treads the path blazed by Molière, personalizing in stereotypes from Russian life such universal vices as gluttony, hypocrisy, sloth. Caricatures are crudely but forcefully drawn, farcical interludes abound, and the action is held together with dialogue clever enough to entertain even today's reader. Sumarokov's tragedies were greatly admired by his contemporaries. Russian nobles were genuinely moved by the long, passionate harangues of his heroes evoking epic moments of Russian history. Declaiming in sonorous pentameter the responsibilities of an enlightened monarch to his vassal, and of vassal to retainer, the actors of a Sumarokov tragedy struck responsive chords in their court audiences. But the plots of the plays creak badly, and the characters, weakly motivated, do not come to life. Sumarokov's stage is merely a sounding box for antiphonal oratory in the manner of the classics, and the symmetry and balance of his dramas reproduce too patently the structure of French models. However, despite his creative limitations, his work has primary significance in the historical context of the Russian theater. During his lifetime, Russian drama achieved the status of an art.

LOMONOSOV (1711–1765)

Scientist, educator, philologist, man of letters, Lomonosov personifies Russia's enlightenment in the eighteenth century. There is a touch of greatness in his private and public story.

Armed with an insatiable lust for knowledge and a keen, retentive mind, Michael Lomonosov, son of a peasant fisherman, ran away from his village in the far north, near Archangel, when he was sixteen years old. He reached Moscow at last, and despite the barrier of his low birth, gained admittance to the Slavo-Greco-Latin Academy. Living on three kopecks a day (a purchasing power of about twenty cents), he studied for five years and finished at the top of his class. A scholarship took him next to the Academy of Sciences in St. Petersburg, and there he plunged into philological and natural sciences, learned French and German, and ultimately received a two-year grant to study in German universities. Upon his return to Russia in 1745, he was appointed professor of chemistry at the Academy itself.

His work now took on an encyclopedic quality of comprehensiveness. There was about it the same universality and urgency that had characterized the projects of Peter the Great. What the Russian sovereign had been to the practical life of Russia, Lomonosov was in the domain of intellectual endeavor. There was no existing branch of knowledge that did not interest him, and which as an ardent patriot he did not wish to develop in Russia, utilizing Russian resources. Himself a product of

German learning, he fought the German professorial control
of higher education, and succeeded in founding the University
of Moscow in 1755, where posts were open to qualified native
teachers. In the sciences—physics, chemistry, astronomy, metal-
lurgy—he conducted experiments little understood at the time;
he is today still known as an advanced precursor of physical
chemistry. In his scientific work, his textbooks, articles, speeches
pressing for the right to critical scientific inquiry, he personified
the technical institutes, laboratories, workshops, and teachers'
colleges lacking in his country. Alexander Pushkin called him
"our first Russian university."

In his own time, Lomonosov was best known as a court
poet whose grandiloquent odes on patriotic themes praised
Russian historical figures and military victories in vibrant metaphor. His eloquence approached intoxication when he described
natural phenomena and the infinite realms of science. But for
us, his poetry is more important as an illustration of his linguistic reforms. In versification he carried Trediakovsky's metrical
changes even further by the use of two-, three-, and four-syllable
iambics, thus creating a greater variety and flexibility in the
poetic line. He brought order to the chaotic coexistence of
Russian and Church Slavonic elements in the literary language.
Where Trediakovsky had proposed and theorized, Lomonosov
legislated. In his *Rhetoric* and *Grammar*—the latter, in 1755,
was the first Russian grammar—he fixed on a wide national
base the usage and syntax of Russian literary language. Russian
was then still pitted with chancellery jargon from the Petrine
era and contained many obsolete expressions of Church Slavonic, corrupted through daily oral use. These Lomonosov
attempted to eliminate. On the other hand, appreciating the
subtlety and strength of Church Slavonic syntax and the tested
power of its pictorial idiom, he encouraged a discriminating use
of it as a literary device. He set great store by his somewhat
pedantic system of style. The "noble style," replete with erudite
Church Slavonic, he reserved for heroic poetry and tragedy.
The "middle style," closer to pure Russian but avoiding the
colloquial, was to be used for dramatic productions, where there
was need for the lively spoken idiom to accompany action naturally. Finally, he designated the "low style" for the construc-

tion of farce and comedy, popular song and verse epigrams, letters to friends, and other ordinary communications requiring language closest to everyday speech.

Lomonosov was a pragmatist and an empiricist; he was also a man of some stubbornly held and passionate convictions. One of them, which motivated his solid pedagogical reforms and for which he is known as the founder of the Russian literary language, was his belief in the wealth and power of the native Russian idiom. His *Grammar* cites a cultural dictum of the Holy Roman Emperor, Charles V, who declared that he preferred to speak with God in Spanish, with friends in French, with enemies in German, and with women in Italian. To this Lomonosov adds: "If the Emperor had known Russian, he would have admitted that in Russian he could speak to everyone; in our language he would have found the sublimity of Spanish, the liveliness of French, the firmness of German, the delicacy of Italian, and besides, the wealth and taut brevity of Latin and Greek."

In such an affirmation, Lomonosov verges on linguistic chauvinism, and he was disproven time and again by the literary output of his own day. Russian literary language did not, in fact, achieve the qualities he attributed to it until several decades later, in the poetry of Alexander Pushkin. But what is certain is that without the reforms of Lomonosov and without his literary example, the Russian language would not have been ready for final transmutation at the hands of the first poetic genius of Russian letters.

4 · The Age of Catherine

THE AGE OF CATHERINE (1762–1796)

To its contemporaries, at home and abroad, the age of Catherine II was the most brilliant in Russian history. Able and unscrupulous diplomacy, the military genius of Russia's two great generals, Potemkin and Suvorov, and unprecedented territorial expansion elevated the Russian empire into the front rank of European nations. The splendor of the court at St. Petersburg rivalled that of Versailles, but it was above all the image of the Empress as the enlightened monarch par excellence that impressed liberal-minded men everywhere. No one labored more diligently to maintain this international image than Catherine herself for the major part of her long reign. Intelligent, ambitious, endowed with Peter's immense energy, insatiable curiosity, and desire to learn, she deemed herself the great Tsar's true heir. Upon his monument she had engraved the words, "From Peter the Great to Catherine the Second," and believed that she was, indeed, perpetuating his work of emancipating and civilizing Russia.

To us, her record seems less impressive. Deeds most renowned for their progressive liberalism in the eighteenth century now betray misjudgment, even frivolity. When, with her approval, the Royal Guard assassinated Peter III, her husband, and she, a young German princess, was proclaimed Empress of all Russia, Catherine was also placed in permanent debt to the aristocracy which had raised her to the throne. Just before his untimely death, Peter III had removed the nobility's last obli-

gation to the Crown—that of obligatory government service—
and Catherine, with undue willingness and haste, set about extending the privileges of the upper classes still further. To her
favorites and lovers (the latter numbering some fifty) she
deeded large grants of crown lands, complete with peasant
populations, and passed decrees which eventually gave landowners total control over their serfs.

If it was the Golden Age for the landed gentry, it was one
of iron for the peasantry. Under Catherine the serf lost all civil
status, including the right to complain against his master. He
was flogged at will; consigned, if rebellious, to forced labor.
Contemporary newspapers were filled with notices for the sale
and purchase of serfs. While the great figures in Russian society drew upon the apparently limitless wealth of their estates
(many owned thousands of serfs and 200,000-acre properties
were not uncommon), the great majority of the population
lived in bondage. Of Russia's 36 million, nearly 34 million were
enserfed. Heedless, nobles vied with their sovereign in emulating
the fashions of Western European courts, each seeking to outdo
the other with ever more ostentatious displays of culture. Occupied with private ballets, theaters, orchestras, libraries, and
conservatories, Catherine and her circle remained indifferent to
the frequent peasant revolts which punctuated the years between 1767 and 1772.

There had been some forty large uprisings by 1773. In
that year, Yemelian Pugachev, a former Don Cossack, assumed
the identity of the murdered Peter III, and as pretender to the
throne, vowed to seize control of the capital and abolish serfdom. Twenty per cent of the population joined his ragtag
forces to inaugurate a rebellion so vast, strong, and ardent as to
genuinely endanger Catherine's regime. Pugachev moved from
the industrial mines of the Ural toward Moscow, scorching the
countryside, looting, and killing landowners. His army swelled
with runaways from forced-labor camps, and it was only at
Moscow that he was halted. Handpicked royal troops de-
molished the rebels and bore their leader to the capital in an
iron cage.

The uprising left indelible memories of fear and hatred
among rich and poor alike, and for another century they

hovered over attempts at social and political reforms. Pugachev had received an excellent press in liberal quarters, but reaction from the throne was swift and vengeful. The alliance between Catherine and the nobility tightened with more despotic control of the empire, and was cemented even further when the French Revolution frightened all monarchs into rigid conservatism and implacable hostility toward the common people.

Nothing, however, prevented Catherine from posing as an emancipated humanitarian. Writing to Voltaire, she boasted that "if the Russian peasant wanted to, he could eat chicken any day of the week." Steeped in the work of the French encyclopedists, she composed a set of *Instructions,* 526 paragraphs patterned on Montesquieu's *The Spirit of Laws,* which was intended to replace the existing codification. She presented the document for a year's study to a nation-wide convocation of deputies representing all classes except the peasantry. Censored in France for its dangerous radicalism, it was soon removed from circulation in Russia, and with no action taken, the deputies were sent home under pretext of impending war with Turkey.

To literature, Catherine brought the same active interest, intellectual pretensions, and ostensible liberalism which marked the early years of her political and social philosophy. No sovereign before her had been so immersed in literary matters. She was a critic, a journalist, an author. Rising at seven in the morning, she would light her own fire and spend several hours alone at her desk in literary efforts which apparently gave her spiritual relief. She maintained a steady correspondence with the leading thinkers of her day—Voltaire, Diderot, Grimm—and her letters indicate wide, careful reading and an easy relationship to the whole cultural life of her age. She wrote fables in French, composed, in somewhat ungrammatical Russian, several satirical comedies in the style of Molière, and in 1769, launched a satirical journal under the transparent pseudonym of a secretary.

Neither original nor powerful enough to survive contemporary interest, Catherine's writings nevertheless served to raise the status of literature from mere entertainment to a major intellectual industry. Her work inadvertently served the cause of education as well. Advanced scientific and social ideas from France, absorbed and ardently propagated by the young empress, were taken up by the aristocracy, and a demand for more education was met by the establishment of several Institutes of Learning for young ladies of the nobility. By 1769, there were 316 elementary and secondary schools, with an enrollment of 18,000. Fourteen years later, the Academy of Russian Language and Literature was founded, and its director, Princess Dashkova, Catherine's closest friend and intellectual equal, established a literary magazine as the Academy's official publication, welcoming contributions from new poets and prose writers.

Under a royal decree authorizing the operation of privately owned printing presses throughout Russia, all forms of literary activity burgeoned. Scores of periodicals made their appearance in St. Petersburg and Moscow. Western European authors, ancient and contemporary, were translated with greater frequency, and, correspondingly, Russian works were more plentiful. After 1762, five or more times as many volumes appeared as had been printed in each previous decade. In Kantemir's time a mere ten to twenty creative writers had kept him company; in the *Historical Lexicon About Russian Writers*, compiled by Novikov in 1772, over 250 living writers were listed.

Despite its reliance on pseudoclassical forms, Russian literature during the last third of the century was revitalized by new talent and new concepts. Mainly satirical in tone, it drew to some extent upon the language of popular tradition. In content, it reflected the newly emerging stream of protest against the glaring abuses in Russian society. Literary art in general, throughout the eighteenth-century world, was evaluated in the light of prescribed moral criteria. Artistic merit was identified with moral purpose, each work judged according to its beneficent influence on the mind and heart. European literature, boiling with ideas for reform in education and government, was now filled with criticism of all that suggested the traditional. Russian writers followed suit, and began a scrutiny of problems at home. The odes of the court poet Derzhavin, strictly classical in style, describe the atmosphere at court and criticize the entourage of the Empress, but the solemnity of the lines does not always conceal what the poet called "smiling satire." Novikov's satirical commentary and Fonvizin's comedies obliquely denounce certain vicious aspects of Russian life, and Radishchev's mock travelogue is a powerful, direct accusation. It was a new trend in Russian literature, satirical in form, earnest in purpose.

DERZHAVIN (1743–1816)—POET LAUREATE

For more than thirty years, Gavrila Derzhavin towered in Russian literature as its most eloquent and talented poet. Born in the province of Kazan, his father an impoverished squire, he received a mediocre secondary-school education, learning German but neither French nor Latin. Later, he served as a private in the army for ten years before he attained an officer's rank. After distinguishing himself in the suppression of the Pugachev rebellion, he returned to civil service in St. Petersburg, where he devoted himself to poetry. He was, on his own, gaining something of a writer's reputation, when in 1782 Princess Dashkova discovered his ode to the Empress, *Felitsa*. Published in the *Literary Magazine*, it made the poet's name a byword in court circles overnight.

Derzhavin had portrayed Catherine as an intelligent, straightforward, unselfish woman, surrounded by a self-indulgent, negligent, intellectually limited entourage. Catherine was, of course, enchanted, and showered the poet with gifts and high posts. He became governor of Olonets, then of Tambor, and was finally appointed Catherine's own secretary in charge of receiving petitions. In each of these capacities, however, Derzhavin failed miserably, despite his energy and real administrative ability, managing to quarrel noisily, even scandalously, with his immediate superiors. An intractable personal integrity, uncompromising convictions about duty, truth, justice, and honor, and a self-righteous, high-tempered manner did nothing to endear the poet to Russian bureaucrats, who were repeatedly disconcerted by a man who practiced what they were supposed to preach and what they were content to leave undone.

After Catherine's death, Alexander I made a final effort

on Derzhavin's behalf, appointing the poet laureate Minister of Justice. But his increasing conservatism and tactlessness jarred the emperor's liberal cabinet, and he was allowed to retire in 1803.

The contradictions of Derzhavin's personality—he was on the one hand an honored and popular literary figure, and on the other, an irascible, difficult official—are reflected with curious consistency in the content and style of his poetry. Like Lomonosov, he composed his most celebrated odes in high style, eulogizing the monarchy by sounding the patriotic motifs of Russian military histories and valorous deeds of its great men. But unlike his great predecessor, and in sharp contrast to the lofty tones and grandiloquent abstractions of the pseudo-classical style, Derzhavin gave the ode new dimensions by the addition of satire and realism, composed in language far less formal than the form had hitherto required. Mingling the comic and the heroic, juxtaposing daily idiom and highflown metaphor, he effected a break with the strict rule of French classicism which had straitjacketed Russian writers for more than fifty years.

The mixture of the sublime and the satirical, of powerful invective and lowly jibe, is to be found in a great number of his poems, from sacred odes to the most lighthearted of Anacreontic lyrics. For that reason, Pushkin was prompted to exclaim that Derzhavin's work was one-fourth gold and three-fourths lead. Much of his poetry seems inflated now, the sentiments outworn, the rich oratory the worse for repetition, as though the poet never tired of thinking "greatly," and writing "greatly," about subjects that he was convinced were "great." There is, nevertheless, pure gold in Derzhavin's descriptions of movement and light and color. With unsurpassed richness, he paints worlds afire with precious stones and metals, as in these famous lines from *The Waterfall*:

> Lo! like a glorious pile of diamonds bright,
> Built on the steadfast cliffs, the waterfall
> Pours forth its gems of pearl and silver light:
> They sink, they rise, and sparkling, cover all
> With infinite refulgence, while its song
> Sublime as thunder rolls the woods along . . .

NOVIKOV (1744–1818)

The imagery of protest, fleeting and oblique in Derzhavin's poetry, became the central ingredient of the new satirical journals which prospered briefly from 1769 to 1774. Catherine herself launched the fashion by supervising, in her liberal years, the publication of a periodical called *All Kinds of Things*. It was obviously modelled on the English *Spectator*, large portions of which were then being translated in the *St. Petersburg Gazette*. The Empress used Addison's playful tone of censure to expose the foibles of her entourage. The ignorance and callousness of the aristocracy, its prejudices, and its slavish, grotesque imitation of French manners were favorite topics.

Full of generally harmless, good-humored court gossip, the "satirical" style grew in popularity, and encouraged by "Grand-mother"("Babushka" in Russian—Catherine's pseudonym), others joined the literary frolic. With the appearance in 1769 of *The Drone* (the name a satirical allusion to Sumarokov's *The Industrious Bee*), then of *The Painter* (1773) and *The Purse* (1774), what had been a game for the elite exploded into serious public satire. The three journals were published and substantially authored by Nikolay Novikov. Where Catherine's criticism had not exceeded censure of manners and safely mocked universal human failings, Novikov bit deeply into fundamental questions, using as his vehicle answers, given under several pseudonyms, to letters from anonymous readers. His attacks focussed on the cancer of Russian life, serfdom. It was not to be expected that "Babushka" would long tolerate the daring young editor's sharp exposure of noblemen delinquent in their treatment of serfs. As letters in *All Kinds of Things* appeared more and more frequently, with their veiled threats growing stronger, Novikov suspended one magazine after another, finally withdrawing from journalism entirely.

He was one of the most outstanding men of his time. Of a moderately well-to-do family, he was dismissed early from the Moscow University high school for "indolence and excessive absence," spent several years in the army, and at the All Deputies Congress was appointed secretary to the "middle-condition" groups. Here the twenty-three-year-old Novikov recorded statistics concerning the semiliterate, semi-independent Russian caught between the downright misery of the peasants and the cruelty of their masters. Much of his civic action may be explained in terms of that experience.

Upon the dissolution of the Congress, he left government service and plunged into journalism. There, as we have seen, he waged a persistent if losing battle with his sovereign in an attempt to rouse educated Russians to the dire need for social reform. At that time, too, he edited the first systematic survey of Russian writers. In 1777, he moved to Moscow, became a Freemason, and made arrangements with his friend and fellow Mason, Mikhail Kheraskov, director of the University of Moscow, to rent the university press. He launched a vast publishing business, and in ten years turned out more books than had ever before been printed in Russia. His purpose was very much less personal profit than public enlightenment. He opened bookstores in all the larger provincial towns, insured regular deliveries of literary materials, founded a children's periodical, and provided texts to elementary schools which he established with donations from philanthropic Masons. Almost singlehandedly, he not only met the demand for books across the land, but created a steady reading public.

Freemasonry at that time had incorporated into its doctrine the Rosicrucian-like aspects of English Deism, which tended to counteract the rationalism of Voltaire and the encyclopedists. Novikov's expression of such ideas in some of his publications unfortunately caught Catherine's attention. At the peak of her reaction to the French Revolution, she suspected all secret societies, and the Freemasons in particular, of conspiring to overthrow her regime. In a maneuver both hypocritical and naive, she first approached the Metropolitan, asking him to examine Novikov's religious attitudes. The head of the Russian church vowed that Russia needed more Christians of Novikov's piety, but Catherine arrested the publisher nevertheless, confiscated his property, and imprisoned him in the Schlüsselburg fortress. Novikov was very harshly treated there and when he was pardoned four years later by Tsar Paul, he left the prison ill and penniless, his crusading spirit extinguished. He did not return to public life.

FONVIZIN (1744–1792)

If great satire depends upon caricature which develops into a living portrait through verbal play, gesture, and situation, then one of the most rewarding and enduring forms of satire has been achieved in the works of such dramatists as Aristophanes, Molière, the Danish playwright Holberg, and the Russian Denis Fonvizin.

Nobly born, Fonvizin received an excellent education, learned several languages, and left his native Moscow quite early for the glittering capital. His connections with the moneyed social set won him a job as secretary to Count Panin, an enlightened aristocrat who deplored Catherine's increasing despotism and the license of her court favorites. Panin was tutor to the Grand Duke Paul, and in the manner of Fénélon, he attempted to imbue his royal pupil with concepts of a more rational, constructive government, one which would execute laws justly and practice restraint in its treatment of the serfs and lower classes. Panin's hope for clemency in the person of a genuinely virtuous monarch is clearly reflected in the speeches of the benevolent Uncle Starodum (Old-Fashioned Thinker), the most positive personality in Fonvizin's second and most famous play, *Junior*. But Fonvizin himself was not convinced that a return to pre-Petrine days would be welcome. His first comedy, *Brigadier* (1768) mocked the generation of the fathers as well as of the sons, burlesquing the dull relics of the "good old Muscovy" days and their flighty offspring for whom a few French words, an elegant and a quick trip to Paris, constituted a satisfactory modern education. The *Brigadier* characters are completely Russian, speaking in wholly suitable dialogue, but the play is grounded in lumbering action. Not until *Junior*, written in 1782, did Fonvizin learn to construct a dramatic sequence.

Original in neither subject nor plot, both of these satirical comedies are based on the classical tug of war between virtue and vice, the action delayed by much discourse. *Junior*, however, the first Russian comedy of merit, earned Fonvizin a lasting place among Russian playwrights as an able, relentless satirist and a master of characterization. In scenes from the family life of Mr. and Mrs. Simpleton, small provincial landlords, Fonvizin aims his arrows at the crassness and smug ignorance of the Russian lower gentry, their barbarous manners, their brutish cruelty to servants. The henpecked husband, the dominant wife and doting mother are caricatured with monumental excellence in dialogue which rings with laughter, but Fonvizin concentrates most on the adolescent son. Uneducated, coarse, and stupid, "Mitrofanushka" has come to stand for any illiterate nobleman's heir.

Having laughed to tears over *Junior*, General Potemkin advised Fonvizin to either die or stop writing. The casually cruel remark was prophetic. For the remainder of his life, the dramatist travelled in Europe for his health, his only literary contribution during those ten years his elegantly styled *Letters from France*. They are filled with pious hopes that Russia might never experience the French centralized system of taxation by legalized extortion.

Although he ranked first in the art of dramatic satire, Fonvizin did not stand alone. Most notable of those who shared his success on stage was Vasily Kapnist (1757–1823). Based on his own experience in a law suit, Kapnist's most prominent play, *Chicanery*, is a lively, bitter satire on the administration of justice in the provinces, and the overall corruption of court officials. The happy ending, as true justice intervenes, a device used by both Kapnist and Fonvizin, was to influence Gogol in the composition of his greatest comedy, *The Inspector-General* (*Revizor*), as popular in the nineteenth-century as *Junior* was in the eighteenth.

KRYLOV (1769–1844)

Second only to the ode, the fable was the most popular literary genre of the eighteenth-century. Hardly a writer of note did not try his hand at the composition of fables, satirical, realistic, or lyrical, but all were eclipsed by one of the world's great fabulists, Ivan Krylov. Krylov was one of those rare Russians who enjoyed great literary fame during his lifetime. His fat, indolent figure was a familiar sight at court and in the salons of St. Petersburg, where recitations of his fables were much in demand. When published, always in large editions, they were translated immediately into other European languages.

Little is known about Krylov's beginnings. The son of a poor army officer who had risen from the ranks, he was exposed to very little formal learning, and at fourteen, was working in a government office and writing his first comic opera. In 1792, he came into brief fame for several virgorously satirical portraits, the best of them concerning a squire who, like Skotinin of Fonvizin's *Junior*, cared more for his hogs than for people. These pieces appeared in the *Spectator*, and in the *St. Petersburg Mercury*, both of which Krylov edited. Soon afterward, when he published a savagely satirical article, he was obliged to liquidate the *Mercury*, and for twelve years he was absent from the literary scene. It was rumored that he had become a tutor in the provinces, that he lived parasitically in the houses of great noblemen, that he spent most of his time gambling, for which he had a great propensity.

In 1805, he returned to the capital with a knowledge of French, German, and Greek. He translated La Fontaine and wrote two moderately successful comedies lampooning Russian women's craze for French fashions. The plays read like adaptations of Molière's *Les Précieuses Ridicules*. Four years later, 23 of Krylov's fables were published and he was instantly famous in a manner previously unknown in Russia. He was read and quoted everywhere; each of his editions, enlarged with new fables, was an immediate sellout. By 1824, he had composed 140 fables, in the following twelve years, 53. When he was accused of laziness, he answered that he preferred to be blamed for writing too little than for writing too much.

Some seventy of his animal fables are clearly adapted from Aesop and La Fontaine, but even these are completely Russian in tone, flavor, and language. It is difficult to settle on the one element that gives Krylov's fables their supreme quality. Is it the language, written as it had been only spoken before, alive, gay, spontaneous, each word irreplaceably right, the last moralizing lines so pithy that many of them have become proverbs? Is it the style, declarative rather than descriptive, its dramatic effect heightened by the utmost verbal economy and deliberate omissions, the seemingly effortless rhymes, at once lilting and trenchant? Is it, finally, the satire itself, sly, delicate, and restrained, a perfectly mature aesthetic form in the hands of a master? The content of the fables is immensely varied and defies classification. Whether a tiny dramatic episode bears reference to current politics (the Napoleonic Wars, 1812–1814) or begins with a classical allusion, it is one of the universal human pretensions that invariably emerges as the target of Krylov's keen satire, be it vanity, greed, social ambition, hypocrisy, megalomania, or any other foible—the reader may have his choice. The morals of these small masterpieces are grounded in common sense. Like Molière, Krylov was a classicist in his sanely balanced view of life. His philosophy as a Russian is also conservative and realistic, even somewhat archaic. He seems constantly to be urging that it is wise to "leave well enough alone" and avoid all manner of exaggeration—in appetite, in behavior, in work, in play, in virtue. Ironically, this man of wisdom was also a great lover of rich foods, and met his end from overeating partridges.

RADISHCHEV (1749–1802)

Known to all educated Russians as the author of one book, *A Journey from St. Petersburg to Moscow* (1790), Alexander Radishchev remains the eighteenth century's most controversial figure. To Communists and the more radically minded intelligentsia, he stands as the first spokesman for revolution and as a martyr to the cause. More conservative opinion places him among the liberals of his own day, a typical product of enlightenment but less sophisticated and less cautious than Novikov or Count Panin in expressing his ideas.

There was no suggestion during Radishchev's adolescence or early manhood of the disaster he was to bring upon himself. Like the sons of many privileged noblemen, he was sent by the empress with twelve other young men to complete his studies in Germany at the University of Leipzig. There he read deeply in the works of Helvetius, Rousseau, and Raynal, all promulgators of the natural rights of man. Young Radishchev was especially impressed by Abbé Raynal's descriptions, in his *Histoire des deux Indes,* of atrocities committed against Indians by their European conquerors. Radishchev must have recalled the accounts he had heard time and again, from his father's own well-treated serfs, of injury and injustice dealt the peasants of neighboring estates. Upon his return from Germany, he received a post at the customs office, and, like Novikov, was able to learn first-hand how the lowly lived: peasants, tradesmen, low-ranking officials alike.

Because it was useful in his job, Radishchev learned English, and so became acquainted with the works of Richardson and Sterne. In 1790, he printed on his own private press the famous *Journey,* distributing to his friends its twenty-five chapters, each named for one of the towns situated between Moscow and St. Petersburg. Picaresque in form, it is reminiscent of Sterne's *Sentimental Journey,* but it is far less a travelogue than an inventory of serfdom's evils. In its emotionally charged scenes, it is not unlike the more eloquent passages of *Uncle Tom's Cabin.* Intensely moved by the unrelieved suffering his travels reveal, the narrator tells of forced recruitment, of families separated at the auction block, of the endless, sadistic flogging of male and female servants, of sixty peasant girls raped by one landowner (whom Catherine identified in the margin of her copy), and above all of the dead-end despair of these victims, shackled without recourse to justice.

Radishchev proposed no revolutionary measures for the abolition of serfdom. He appealed, rather, to the consciences of his peers, urging that "this monster of 1,000 snouts" be revealed to Catherine, whom he sincerely believed to be ignorant of existing conditions. Though his style is awkward and heavy with long passages of exclamatory, sentimental rhetoric, his message was blunt and clear. Condemning autocracy in repeated praise for the newly formed democracy of the United States, he called for the exposure of administrative and judiciary corruption, declaring that political freedom must be granted to all of Her Majesty's subjects.

Curiously enough, this attack on all political institutions was passed by the censor; Radishchev had deftly branded censorship in the *Journey* itself: "If any man takes exception to printed lines, he makes us suspect that what is printed is true, and he himself is as he stands in print." But Catherine was not deceived. She had read the work—was reported to have exclaimed, "But he is worse than Pugachev! He praises Franklin!"—and promptly wrote a sharp criticism of it. Radishchev was arrested and sentenced to death, but by "special clemency" of the empress was sent in chains to Siberia instead, to live out his life at hard labor. He was freed in 1801 by the liberal Alexander I, who even appointed him to the Committee of the Review of the Legal Code. But Radishchev, broken in health, felt himself out of touch with the new literary men who ridiculed his old-fashioned humanitarianism, and in a fit of nervous melancholy, he committed suicide.

A Journey from St. Petersburg to Moscow was printed by Herzen in London in 1854, but it was not published in Russia till 1901. However, it did go through many clandestine editions and despite Catherine, Radishchev, called "the foe of slavery" by Pushkin, was an influential force far into the nineteenth century's radicalism.

KARAMZIN (1766–1826)

Literature was ill-served in the old empress' last reactionary years. Pseudoclassical forms, though still favored at court, had become sterile and dull, casualties of censorship. The moment for Russian reaction against classicism was at hand, and because it had arrived in Europe a few decades earlier, a larger, more literate public waited for a new kind of reading entertainment. Nikolay Karamzin provided it. His break with the classical tradition was complete, and although he was not a creative writer, nor a particularly original one, the times made his formula for fiction overwhelmingly successful. He popularized in Russia the literature of the new sensibility, of the triumph of sentiment over reason, which German and English writers—young Goethe and Herder, the poets Macpherson, Thomson, and Young, the novelists Richardson and Sterne—had introduced in the West.

A pensive lad, given to daydreaming alone on his father's Simbirsk estate, whose lands stretched to the Volga's banks, he received a good education in Moscow, specializing in languages. The curriculum was dominated by the sentimental pietism of the German poet-moralist Hellert, whom the school's director admired deeply. Hardly prepared for civic duties, Karamzin became an officer; when lack of funds forced him to leave his regiment, he returned home to what might have been, but for I. N. Turgenev, the indolent life of a country squire. Turgenev, a wealthy Freemason, persuaded Karamzin to go back to Moscow and work for Novikov's publications. While he was greatly influenced by Novikov's idealistic, cosmopolitan views, Karamzin did not become a Mason, nor did he develop the publisher's interest in civic affairs. He contributed short, moralizing stories to Novikov's *Children's Magazine*, and began enthusiastic readings in the works of Herder, Richardson, Sterne, and Rousseau. He translated Thomson's *Seasons*.

His translation of Shakespeare's *Julius Caesar*, the first in Russian, was published in 1787, with a glowing foreword in which Karamzin called Shakespeare a "magnificent interpreter of human nature" and a "great psychologist of the heart." It was a view which differed radically from the prevailing opinion of the English dramatist; inspired by Voltaire, Sumarokov had found in Shakespeare only "barbaric violence, coarseness, and disorder."

In 1789, Karamzin visited Switzerland, Germany, England, and France, keeping daily notes during the eighteen months of his stay abroad. On his return, he established *The Moscow Journal* and published in it his notes. *Letters of a Russian Traveler* (1791–1792) not only established his reputation, but launched a new movement in Russian literature. Where other Russian writers had admired, imitated, or, like Fonvizin, found chauvinistic reason to criticize Western Europe, Karamzin wrote with the objectivity of a visitor in conscious kinship with the culture of the West. Places of interest are described vividly and compared with care: "Here in London everything is clean; in Paris, which is immense, everything is dirty, and luxury jostles penury at every turn. There I saw hovels out of which crawl ragged, pale-faced humans; here, Health and Contentment walk out of small brick houses with a seemly and complacent air." Still, Karamzin liked the French, their courtesy and impulsiveness, their ability to enjoy themselves. "The French character is best expressed in its love for the theater. To know a German, you must see him in his study; an Englishman, at the Stock Exchange; and a Frenchman, at the theater."

The *Letters* avoid controversial topics—in deference to Catherine's censors, the revolutionary fire ablaze in Paris at the time of Karamzin's visit is not even mentioned—but, urbane and impartially curious, they resemble the smoothly spun documentaries of our own day but for a tone of sentimental romanticism as ludicrous to us as it was new and exciting to Karamzin's contemporaries. For the author, the notes were less an account of what he had seen than a record of the emotions that had assaulted him in foreign surroundings, especially in the contemplation of nature. Like Jean-Jacques Rousseau in his *Confessions*, Karamzin revealed, and invited his readers to share, a passionate interest in the world of the senses, displaying boundless tolerance for actions which, in moments of extreme emotional tension, spring spontaneously from the heart.

His insistent emphasis on the emotional is nowhere more clearly seen than in *Poor Liza* (1792), Karamzin's earliest and best known story. A model for all his others (*Natalya; The Boyar's Daughter; Burgomistress Marfa*), it is based on the old melodrama of sophisticated seducer and pure young girl, who, abandoned by her lover, commits suicide. The serf-girl Liza falls in love with Erast, a young officer from the city who returns her love. Their tenderly passionate meetings in the environs of Moscow might have continued forever had he not gambled away his fortune at cards and therefore been forced to leave Liza and marry a wealthy widow.

Social-protest writers like Novikov and Radishchev must have found it something of a mockery that literature's first portrayal of the Russian peasant was tinged with rosy romanticism. Liza's father is a "rather well-to-do rural dweller" (Karamzin's euphemism for serf) whose success is laid to the fact that he "liked to work, tilled the soil ably, and didn't drink." The rustic heroine is as well-spoken and well-mannered as any young noblewoman, and there seems to exist no obstacle in that Russian feudal society to her permanent union with a noble-born lover. Elsewhere, Karamzin does acknowledge the abuses of serfdom, but with the typically optimistic conclusion that "in every situation man may gather roses of pleasure," and that "a peasant in his stinking hut may be happier than the nobleman who resorts to the most refined luxuries to alleviate the boredom of his life." The degeneracy of the aristocracy, whose energies and abilities were dissipated in idleness, in the fruitless pursuit of education, and in the political games of bureaucracy, is a theme stated for the first time in Russian literature by Karamzin. It was to become a major thesis in nineteenth-century fiction. Erast, that happy-go-lucky bane of "Poor Liza's" life, may be considered the ancestor of Pushkin's Eugene Onegin and Lermontov's Pechorin; and Karamzin's influence would touch Turgenev in the creation of the "superfluous man" and Tolstoy, in the "guilt-laden landowner."

Karamzin brought much that was stylistically new to Russian literature. His stories, not overly original in plot, were concerned with single episodes only, and displayed a unity not heretofore achieved. Also, they involved readers in an unprecedented way. Karamzin invited his public to muse with him on the flow of events in his stories, which were supposedly drawn from real life. Within the framework of the fictional adventure another fiction was, perpetuated—that the stories were, in fact, true. It is clear that Karamzin successfully hoodwinked his readers: the pond near Moscow where the unfortunate Liza supposedly drowned became a site of romantic pilgrimage for a generation of Karamzin fans.

But Karamzin's greatest contribution to the new literature of sentiment was his language. He cleared it entirely of Church Slavonic, discarding the Lomonosov canon of three styles, and evolving a limpid prose patterned on the graceful conversation of society drawing rooms. He made the literary idiom more flexible by adapting the simpler construction and shorter sentences of English and French. He did not hesitate to introduce Gallicisms, translate French words literally, or coin new ones by forcing Russian roots to carry new burdens of meaning. These radical changes were violently opposed by academicians, who saw the gap between a cultured minority and the illiterate masses widening even further, but most writers seized eagerly on the more serviceable language.

By 1803, Karamzin had become the influential editor of *The Messenger of Europe*, which he had founded and which remained the most prominent periodical of literary criticism until 1917. He retired from literature to concentrate on historical research and shape the story of Russia's past from documents in archives, private libraries, and monasteries. Twelve years of labor resulted in the first eight volumes of *The History of the Russian Empire*, in which he glamorized the evolution of the Russian state in a subjective, extremely sentimental, but eloquent biography of the tsars. That much of the material had been prepared by earlier historians (Müller, Schlötzer, Stritter, Shcherbatov), and that little space is given to the social and economic growth of Russia was of little consequence to Karamzin's contemporaries, generally ignorant of their historical past. Published at a propitious moment, in 1818 after the Napoleonic Wars and the Congress of Vienna, the monumental *History* was read with the pride of a nation at the peak of its national consciousness. In less than twenty-five days, the entire edition of ten thousand was sold out.

SUMMARY OF THE EIGHTEENTH CENTURY

To read *The Story of the Russian Sailor*, one of the most popular fiction pieces of Peter's day, and follow it immediately with Radishchev's *Journey from St. Petersburg to Moscow*, is to realize what astounding progress Russian literature made in some seventy years.

Peter's annihilation of the Church's social and political power must be assessed as both the beginning and the turning point of Russian letters, for by it the centuries-old religious monopoly over learning crumbled, and there rose in its stead a practice as destructive as it has been long-lived. Russian literature, secularized, continued to perform its ancient function, the glorification of the mighty, a task set by the clerics of the Middle Ages in Russia and in the West. But there was one significant difference: the monarchy, albeit eulogized in the "ecstatic" poetry of its men of letters, exercised over Russian writers a constant and arbitrary control, either through formal censorship or more intangible marks of censure and disfavor.

The rise of literary strictures may be attributed to the closer contact between writers and rulers established after the Petrine era. Peter's brilliance in technological achievement was equalled by his fundamental indifference to the aesthetic aspects of European culture. His immediate successors, however, were almost without exception women who had a taste for luxury and concerned themselves with the literary, plastic, and performing arts. Men successful in literary pursuits who pleased and continued to please the sovereign were granted favors and rewarded with lavish gifts and profitable government appointments. Since writing was not yet lucrative, nor even considered a profession, most educated Russians with a bent for writing served their country, first of all, as officials, diplomats, and officers.

The Empress Catherine II was herself the most illustrious practitioner of this unwritten law. She liked to write; she did write. She was, however, the sovereign ruler of a very large country, and could devote only a dilletante's attention to artistic disciplines. In compensation, therefore, she encouraged literary talent to partake of court splendors. Thus it happened that a small, extremely brilliant coterie of sophisticated and highly educated Russians from the governing classes, many of whom were also gifted and prolific men of letters, gave her reign distinction. With Catherine as the central luminary, it was a group in which any cultivated Frenchman could feel, mentally and socially, very much at home. Yet it must be remembered that the members of this circle were, for the most part, grandsons of the Muscovite nobility, nurtured on the ideology of the *Domostroy*.

Such an advance was extraordinarily rapid in the history of Western civilization, but the price paid for it was exhorbitantly high. Russian literature in the eighteenth century was Russian in name only. It was constructed out of foreign borrowings, and struck no root in native soil. Toward the end of the era, some small awareness of Russia's indigenous oral tradition could be noted in scholarly research of the *byliny*, in the famous manuscript find of the *Lay of the Host of Igor*, in the discovery of folk songs that were beginning to find their way into song books. But these were transient and peripheral interests. The main body of materials used by writers was based largely on classical mythology as adapted by seventeenth- and eighteenth-century French writers for their own purposes. The forms, the genres, the literary movements and methods were almost entirely Western European, primarily French, in origin.

The French influence, prevalent in every European country, dominated Russian intellectual life of the post-Petrine era. French, not Russian, was taught first, and early, to children of the upper classes; it was the language of the court, of diplomacy, of higher army echelons, of private correspondence, and of memoirs. Imported as briskly as any commodity, French artists and artisans poured into the capital for more than a hundred years; cooks and lackeys, singers, dancers and musicians, teachers and governesses, the latter often taken to the provinces as instructors in deportment and French a-b-c's, shaped Russian social and cultural mores. A Russian nobleman's most prized possession was his library of French works; before his children had learned to spell in Russian, their taste for reading was awakened and satisfied by French authors. Thus, in Pushkin's *Eugene Onegin*, a girl of the provinces composes her first love letter in French; in one of his short stories, *The Queen of Spades*, an old countess begs her nephew for a few French novels, and when he suggests that she read some Russian books, she replies, "Are there any?"

That Russian aristocrats, who formed the major part of the reading public, preferred the French literature on which they had been raised to any writings natively Russian may account for the relatively insignificant circulation of this type of reading matter in Russia as late as the end of the century. At the height of its popularity, for example, Novikov's *Drone* did not exceed a sale of fifteen hundred for any one issue. *The Moscow Journal*, which Karamzin had sought to popularize with his *Letters of a Russian Traveller*, was discontinued after two years for lack of capital, its subscriptions numbering only five hundred.

Toward the end of the century, the men who were advancing the cause of Russian letters found themselves in a paradoxical situation. In one accelerated thrust of history, they had been emancipated from the narrowly religious medievalism of the Muscovite mentality. Once anonymous bookmen, they were now established writers. In their society now existed the instruments necessary to stimulate and sponsor the writer's art: private printing presses, schools, academies, university centers, scholarships, theaters, and, formed by newspapers and magazines, an emerging public opinion. On the other hand, the Russian writer still wore the livery of a foreign potentate; he still took his schooling from the Parnassus of Western culture, paying obeisance to foreign canons of taste, foreign ideas, and foreign literary forms. Only satirists had been able to give their work a native Russian flavor, dealing with specific social abuses existing within the Russian feudal system.

To the modern literary critic, the eighteenth century seems a gigantic experimental laboratory where imported literary concepts were studied with reverence and tested with care in the creation of Russian poetry and prose. It is to be noted that almost every important writer of the epoch was also a theoretician, a literary scholar and critic as well as an artist. Inevitably, as must happen when imitation becomes slavish, the student rebelled against his foreign teacher. Thus the eighteenth century witnesses Lomonosov's feud with German academicians; the satirists ridicule the Gallomania of the social set; and in one of philology's most vituperative denunciations, Shishkov, the grammarian president of the Academy of Russian Language and Literature, leads the attack on Karamzin's new literary idiom.

Of all the experiments conducted in that period, the greatest single achievement was in the field of language. From Trediakovsky to Karamzin, writers had struggled with their unwieldy legacy of Church Slavonic, ill suited to the expression of new ideas and a foreign aesthetic. The cornerstone of reform is Lomonosov's, but Karamzin alone is to be credited with shaping literary Russian into a beautiful and flexible instrument, ready for burnishing in the hands of its great master, Alexander Pushkin.

5 · The Golden Age of Russian Letters

PAUL I (1796–1801)

The enduring illusion of those who entrust themselves to an autocracy is that a newly installed ruler is certain to be preferable to his predecessor. But when Catherine's forty-two-year-old son succeeded to the throne, only apprehension swept Russia.

A physically ugly, coarse-mannered, brutish man, Paul I had been slighted by his mother, kept virtual prisoner in a St. Petersburg suburb, where he nourished a passionate admiration for the Prussian king, Frederick II, by furiously drilling and parading his tiny military escort. When he became emperor at last, he poured his rancor into a policy of revenge, undoing with single-minded urgency all that Catherine had done. His vendetta found expression in a range of extremes, from the grotesque to the impetuous. Having exhumed his father's coffin, he directed that it be placed beside Catherine's grave, ordering that the military procession be led by Count Orlov, reputedly among those who had murdered Peter III. He granted freedom to hundreds of political prisoners, and won the over-all hostility of the upper classes by curtailing the right of noblemen to withdraw at will from government service.

Though Paul was not without intelligence and a strong interest in affairs of state, he infuriated the aristocracy even further when, by errant treaties with Napoleon, he closed the English market for Russian hemp and timber, primary export products of the nobles' estates. It was the palace guard, however, which suffered the greatest humiliation. No longer exempt from corporal punishment, they were dealt with cruelly for the slightest infringement of the odiously detailed regulations drawn up personally by the Tsar.

In the last years of his reign, he was encircled by hatred. Many of his entourage, familiar with his sadism and monstrous fits of temper, seriously thought him insane. For the last time, the royal guard exercised their prerogative of palace revolution—in the future, Russian tsars were to be assassinated publicly, in the streets—and, with the implicit consent of Paul's son and heir, Alexander, the Emperor was strangled, in the night of March 23, 1801, with an officer's scarf.

ALEXANDER I (1801–1825)

Much was expected of Alexander I after the oppressive reign of Paul. His Swiss tutor, the Republican La Harpe, had, under the imperial nose, filled the boy with abstract concepts of liberty and equality, and though Alexander's notion of freedom was at best unstructured, it was known that now, as tsar, he favored constitutional government and the abolition of serfdom. Unaware of what was to come, liberal Russians rejoiced during the first years of his reign, seeing promise of great reforms yeasting in the capital.

Like an American president who was to hold office 159 years later, the twenty-four-year-old Alexander radiated youth, vitality, receptivity to change. Handsome and charming, unfailingly courteous, he possessed a rare ability for suasion; his interlocutors left him each content that he alone had the Tsar's sympathy and support. Moreover, like the Kennedy of another time and place, Alexander began his sovereignty with a brain trust, gathering into St. Petersburg young men of progressive mind, poised to effect a new order. Alexander himself often presided over meetings of this aristocratic assembly, called to debate proposals for changes within Russia's involuted political structure.

But the hopeful vision of true reform dwindled and dispersed strangely. Within eight years of Alexander's accession, one of his most farsighted and intelligent administrators,

Michael Speransky, had completed for the Tsar an ambitious scheme to curb the power of the monarchy. Speransky proposed a system of law that would separate judicial, legislative, and executive functions, to be supported by a semi-independent parliament elected from among the propertied, serfs excluded. Action on the liberal proposal foundered. Several minor measures to improve the condition of the serfs were passed: they could no longer be advertised as salable chattels; they could not be forced into penal servitude; nor could they be emancipated without provision of land. The right to inherited land was now granted to all free classes, state peasantry included. But this was token action, far removed from Alexander's implicit promise to destroy feudalism. An undisciplined theoretician, the Tsar seemed unwilling or unable to face the reality of wholesale reforms even in blueprint. Vacillation, indefinitely prolonged, took the place of final imperial decisions.

While wavering and procrastination undermined all hope of serious internal reform, Russia was well served by Alexander's elusive, not to say invisible foreign policy. For it, Napoleon had dubbed him the "wily Byzantine," and because of it, Russia was spared continuous war with France. It did not, however, prevent the invasion of Russia by French troops in 1812, nor did it hinder the burning of Moscow.

The destruction of Russia's ancient city, whether by accident or design, had an extraordinary effect upon Alexander. Whatever remained of his youthful evangelical fervor was now turned toward self-aggrandizement in a tragicomic way. Harassed by the Russian weather and guerrilla fighters from the rural population, Napoleon's invincible Grande Armée had broken and withdrawn in due haste. But Alexander, like a reincarnation of his imperious grandmother, issued forth from the flames of Moscow to emerge in Paris, there to proclaim himself savior of Europe—hardly by virtue of any tough policy of diplomatic or military strategy against Napoleon. By calculation or in self-delusion—history has not yet penetrated the mystery of the man—Alexander moved to solidify his position at the Congress of Vienna. Thereafter, his energies were sunk into his role as leader and light of the Holy Alliance of Russia with Austria, Prussia, and England. In June,

1815, he met in midnight interview with Julie de Krudener, currently fashionable in international circles as a mystic and seer, and endowed with considerable psychic powers. She apparently focussed the Tsar's wandering thoughts, for under her influence he, too, became a mystic, directing the sovereigns of Europe to abide by the Christian principles of "holy faith, love, justice, and peace."

Metternich and Talleyrand, obdurate cynics of diplomacy, could find nothing but "nonsense" in Alexander's new-found mysticism, and while the Tsar may have sincerely believed it could only better international pacts, his pietistic obsession led to disaster at home.

Intent upon his chimerical pursuits in Europe, he left the actual administration of Russian affairs to conservatives and religious bigots. Count Alexis Arakcheyev, risen through the ranks of the army to become Alexander's chamberlain, set about inexorably to oil and buttress the machinery of despotism. With the Tsar's blessing, he established and administered with intense brutality the military colonies which Alexander had hoped would support and enlarge his already huge standing army. At once soldiers and farmers, the colonists lived every phase of their dreary lives under Arakcheyev's Tartarian rule, bearing children as the law dictated, tilling soil to the sound of military drums, drilling as peasant regiments child and man. Revolts were quickly put down by an efficient punishment for which Arakcheyev was to be remembered in the Russian army for fifty years—the Green Birch. Insurgents were condemned to navigate an avenue formed by army comrades (from 250 to 500 men) wielding raw birch switches, which, under threat of like treatment, each man used with maximum force against the condemned.

"Reforms" in the Arakcheyev manner did not stop at the entrenchment of slavery. Just as Arakcheyev had by coercion put teeth into the military maws of Russia, another of Alexander's deputies stripped Russian education of any potential for enlightenment. Prince A. Golitsyn, Minister of Education, launched a wholesale purge of schools and universities, ferreting out with the enthusiasm of a McCarthy history and philosophy departments suspected of liberal tendencies. These

were placed entirely under bureaucratic control. Further, he
instituted a system of effective if capricious censorship, aug-
menting studies in science with "theological aids," expanding
the blackout measures to grotesque degree; a pamphlet on
poisonous mushrooms, for example, was banned because
"mushrooms are eaten in quantity during Lent."

THE DECEMBRISTS

If Napoleon's march into Russia had indirectly caused
Alexander's withdrawal from the duties of sovereignty, it was
even more significantly responsible for the most useless tragedy
of Russia's nineteenth-century revolutionary movement.

For many of his high-ranking young officers, Alexander's
entry into Paris in 1815 had been a rude awakening. Already
fluent in the French language, they were now able to observe
at first hand how a broad spectrum of French society lived
in freedom. What they saw was in sharp contrast to what
they knew to be true of despotic Russia, and their sympathy
for their oppressed countrymen was roused as never before.
Returning to "Arakcheyevnian" Russia from his enlightened
French quarters, one such disenchanted officer noted in his
memoirs that as he landed, crowds of peasants, gathered to
welcome the soldiers home, had been dispersed by the whips
of the police.

Urged by their sense of wrong, the more thoughtful scions
of the Russian nobility—among them some of the oldest aristocratic names in the country—formed in 1816 the "Union of
Salvation." Their objectives were to abolish serfdom and establish a constitutional government, reforms which, though
no more than those promised by Alexander some fifteen years
earlier, were now the meat of high treason. Expanding and
recasting its program, the Union went underground, and in
1822 split into the Northern Society and the Southern. The
latter, directed by Paul Pestel, had sharpened its projects
for reformation and now demanded outright assassination of
the Emperor, with autocracy to be obliterated by a republic
based on universal suffrage. From 1823 to 1825, the Society
held clandestine meetings, distributed inflammatory propa-

ganda, sought new recruits—there were never more than three hundred, most of them junior officers—and agreed at last to strike the coup in May, 1826, when the Tsar, reviewing troops in the south, could be more easily assassinated. The troops were never reviewed. In November, 1825, Alexander joined his mistress at a resort on the Sea of Azov, and, quite suddenly, died there—though a rumor persisted for over a century that he had simply disappeared to become a religious hermit, one Feodor Kuzmich, who lived in Western Siberia until his death in 1864. To quell the story, Alexander's coffin, at rest in the capital fortress of St. Peter and St. Paul, was opened in the 1920's—and found empty.

While title to the throne wavered between Alexander's two brothers, Constantine and Nicholas, the conspiracy foundered. Caught without plans and uncertain of their following, Pestel and his sympathizers agonized through the three-week interregnum until Nicholas finally proclaimed his accession. On December 14, the more prominent leaders of the movement assembled in protest before the palace, where Nicholas was receiving oaths of allegiance. Amid the insurgents' cries for a constitution—their uncomprehending army thought their leaders were shouting for Constantine's wife (the Russian word for "constitution" having a feminine ending) and so cheered accordingly—a shot was fired accidentally and the military governor of the capital was killed. Nicholas moved instantly. The demonstrators were cannonaded, their leaders were arrested and for several months interrogated personally by the new Tsar. Five were sentenced to death by quartering, thirty were to be decapitated, hundreds to be exiled in Siberia.

Though the savage sentences were later commuted to death by hanging, capital punishment had become so rare an occurrence in Russian life that the country was convulsed by pity and horror. The young civic-minded aristocrats who had been martyred on the people's behalf were raised to the status of legendary heroes. Known as the Decembrists for the date of their insurrection, they were to be invoked by revolutionaries for the next hundred years. Nor were they to be forgotten by Nicholas I.

NICHOLAS I (1826–1855)

As a man's approach to love or war may be shaped by his first experience of either, so the reign of Nicholas I was molded by his first bloody act as emperor. Shocked by the extent of the rebellion which his interrogation of the Decembrists had revealed, he set out to cleanse Russia of all subversive elements, and before he died in 1855, he had secured and tightened the bands of tyranny forged under Alexander.

Incurably suspicious, not only of his subjects but of his administrators as well, Nicholas arrogated to himself all responsibilities of government. Upon the already top-heavy apparatus of a swollen bureaucracy he superimposed his own private imperial chancellery, formerly concerned with personal matters or questions of state. It was now elevated to a position of central authority, its most powerful institution the infamous Third Section. Predecessor to the totalitarian secret police of today, it functioned independently of other government departments or controls, its sole purpose being to discover and destroy that which smacked of liberalism. In all that was individual or spontaneous, all that did not conform exactly to official views, it detected sedition.

The rule of conformity extended to education as well. Though Nicholas himself branded serfdom the evil of Russia, he feared the potential of enlightened masses. Secondary and higher education was restricted, therefore, to children of the nobility, and under rigid governmental control, schools and universities offered little more than natural sciences and theology, the latter mandatory for all students. Purged of "dangerous" influences from Europe, the curricula symbolized the narrowness and inflexibility of Nicholas' design for Russia. She was internally what she seemed to be to her neighbors, a prison administered with cruel discipline by a martinet whose love of parades was equalled only by his devotion to bureaucracy.

In thirty years, Russia, far from joining the progressive revolutionary movements of Europe, had slipped fifty years into her past under the banner of "Orthodoxy, Autocracy, and Nationalism." The French Revolution of 1848, which so roused the Tsar that he was only just prevented from marching 400,000 troops into Paris, merely served to cement and expand the resources of coercion and repression. Any thoughts of feudal reform that Nicholas might have entertained he now abandoned with finality. As earnest a man of action as Alexander had been a dreamer, he died, possibly by suicide, at the height of the Crimean War, straining to win with the lumbering bureaucratic monster in which he had placed his hope.

Engulfed by the intellectual darkness which had fallen at the close of the Napoleonic Wars, smothered by bureaucratic tyranny, and bedevilled by police supervision, which all Russians lived in dread of, Russia could not have been expected to claim artistic laurels. Yet under the Romanovs, new currents in philosophy filled the air, and Russia's literary greatness not only grew but flowered in full. Alexander's reign saw the Golden Age of poetry, and the rise of Pushkin's literary genius. Under Nicholas, Russian intellectuals began their extraordinary debate on all social and philosophical questions fundamental to Russia's statehood. These last Romanov years of official persecution produced some of the greatest writers in the ranks of serious world literature: Turgenev, Gogol, Tolstoy.

LITERARY CLIMATE OF THE NINETEENTH CENTURY

It is difficult to determine whether the sparkle and vigor of Russia's literary life in the early nineteenth century is due more to a phenomenal production of poetry or to the passionate polemics that poetry inspired. At universities and preparatory schools, at military academies and in government offices, all who aspired to any degree of fame sought it in the writing of verse. Poetry was printed or circulated in manuscript to be read and ardently discussed in literary societies and innumerable reading clubs. In St. Petersburg and Moscow, weekly or monthly reviews mushroomed to accommodate the overflow of literary criticism.

Discussion centered on the "new idiom" versus the "old." Younger writers supported Karamzin's linguistic reforms; they were bitterly opposed by champions of the Church Slavonic tradition, whose spokesman was Alexander Shishkov, president of the Academy of Russian Language and Literature and a philologist in his own right. Shishkov sparked the controversy in 1803 with a public declaration that new writers who refused to employ Church Slavonic expressions were, in fact, reflecting the destructive influence of French revolutionary ideas in Russian life. Illogical and typically Russian in its fusion of literature and politics, the statement provoked fervent and lengthy rebuttals on both sides. Literate Russians followed the debates in the press with as much avidity as today's tabloid reader searches his paper for latest details of a sensational murder trial.

In 1811, die-hard conservatives formed a Society of the Lovers of Russian Speech. Meeting in Derzhavin's formal St. Petersburg drawing room, academicians, dignitaries, and semi-retired literary men of Catherine's time delivered speeches to stately, bemedalled old officers, high government officials, and society ladies, all seated in hierarchical order among the pillars and potted palms. The fame of these archconservatives was established four years later, not, certainly, by the decorous tedium of their lectures, but by the creation of the Arzamas Club, a band of aristocratic Bohemians gathered to parody the society. Composed of devotees of wine, women, and song, practitioners of light verse, the group included Prince Vyazemsky, Count Bludov, Andrey Turgenev, Batyushkov, and Vasily Pushkin. The name "Arzamas" had been chosen for its lampooning value; it was the name of a small Russian town renowned for its geese, and the club's dinners usually ended with a roast goose. Each member received a nickname—Cassandra, Laura, Aeolian Harp, Old Woman—and when, in its second year, Arzamas accepted a young man named Alexander Pushkin, just out of preparatory school, he was called "The Cricket" for the frequency of his scalding contributions to the riotous evenings.

Arzamas sessions were conducted as spontaneous burlesques of the protocol-regulated society meetings, the "enemy's" more ludicrous practices parodied with exuberant wordplay, mimicry, and farcical asides. A new club member, having undergone a travestied Masonic ritual of initiation, was required, in the manner of academic tradition, to eulogize his dead predecessor. In the absence of one, contemporary literary personages were caricatured with merciless wit. It was inspired buffoonery of the highest order, a sophisticated game of words, nothing more. Innocent of political convictions, these young aristocrats were drawn together by common aesthetic tastes to share a gaiety and warmth of fellowship which none would know again. When Nikolay Turgenev, Nikolay Muravyov, and Mikhail Orlov—poets who were later to join the Decembrists—attempted to inject matters of social protest into Arzamas discussions, there was dissension among the members and the club soon dissolved. Its liberalism had been of a purely literary nature, and chief among their idols was Zhukovsky, acknowledged leader of the Karamzin school.

ZHUKOVSKY (1783–1852)

Justly recognized as the architect of Russia's Golden Age of Literature, Vasily Zhukovsky was the first to infuse its poetry with purely personal feeling. Prior to him the classical ode had dominated the field in an impersonal display of eulogy and abstraction. The intimate, lyrical poem did not exist. It was popularized and given indisputable authority by Zhukovsky, whose subject matter, style, and diction were to be a major influence in the poetry of the century.

Fluent in five European languages, it was Zhukovsky who introduced German and English romantics to an enthusiastic Russian public. A master of the demanding craft of translation, he transformed the difficulties of versification and idiom into an act of inspired recreation. In Zhukovsky's Russian, the poems of Gray, Thomson, and Scott, Southey, Byron, Moore, and Uhland, Bürger, Schiller, and Goethe, frequently surpass their originals. It is, perhaps, for this service that Zhukovsky must be most applauded.

In 1802, when his translation of Gray's *Elegy* appeared in Karamzin's *Messenger of Europe*, Zhukovsky's career was launched. He soon became known for his own elegies, a genre in which he excelled. Composed with careful inventiveness, they abound in the dreamy melancholy, the sensuous languor, and occasional gothic horror of all romantic poetry. What is distinctively Zhukovsky's own, and gives his work its particular sweetness, is a blend of irregular rhyme and pure, melodious diction.

He used the Western themes of unrequited love or lost friendship with special poignancy in his own verse. Of a melancholy bent himself, he had experienced a tragic love affair with his half-sister's daughter, whom he was not permitted to marry. That sorrow may have been responsible for the tone of faint religiosity and gentle resignation that hovers over his lyrics, which repeatedly and obstinately evoke joys that are no more, or mourn the transcience of all things. Such wistful sentiments were new to Russians; Zhukovsky was widely read, quoted, and adored—which may have caused Vyazemsky to exclaim, "May God preserve Zhukovsky from happiness! Happiness would break his lyre's most beautiful string!"

His life was, in fact, unusually sunny. Although he was the natural son of a wealthy Tula landowner and a captive Turkish girl, he was adopted and given the literary and musical instruction characteristic of a privileged education. A gentle, sweet-tempered boy, affectionate and kind, he had a gift for lasting and loyal attachments, which extended from his family circle to the great of Moscow. Karamzin's protégé, he was from 1810 to 1812 his successor as editor of *The Messenger of Europe*. As his literary fame grew, his circle extended to St. Petersburg; he was a member (though less active than most) of Arzamas, and unwittingly fraternized with many of those who were to become Decembrists. A brief flirtation with civil service and six months of noncombat duty during the Napoleonic campaign convinced him that writing was his métier, but that writing could not provide him with sufficient income. When his first two volumes of poetry were published in 1815, they bore a respectful dedication to Alexander, suggesting with great tact that a writer's laurels were as useful to his country as any soldier's, and should be suitably rewarded. He was granted a yearly pension of 4,000 rubles.

In 1818, when his Arzamas companions were either dedicating themselves to underground politics or were being exiled for sedition, Zhukovsky was befriended at court. He became the Dowager Queen's reader, and soon afterward was appointed tutor to the future Tsar Alexander II, upon whom he exerted a strong liberalizing influence. He remained with the royal family until his retirement in 1841, writing almost nothing. He was mourned as though dead by a public who, with the young Pushkin, believed that

> The captivating sweetness of his verse
> The centuries' enviable distance will traverse.

BATYUSHKOV (1787–1855)

At the moment that Zhukovsky was repudiating the world of letters for life at court, Russian literature was losing another, equally gifted poet, Constantine Batyushkov, victim of an inherited mental disorder which darkened his mind for the last thirty years of his life.

That Batyushkov has earned an important place in Russian poetry is certain. Often compared with the full-time romantic, Zhukovsky, he was less a romanticist than a classicist who knew how to convey the pleasures of contemplating beauty in the ancient world. Emulated by his contemporaries, he influenced the poets of the next generation as well. The clarity and lightness of his lines are evident in Pushkin's early lyrics, and it was the fifteen-year-old Pushkin, writing a school verse filled with classical allusions, who was asute enough to name Batyushkov the "Russian Parny."

The first French poet whom Batyushkov translated, Evariste Désiré de Parny (1753–1814), was a transitional figure. He was partial to romantic elegies, but a terse form and love of the sensual gave much of his poetry the sculptured substance of the classics. A disciple of Voltaire, he worked into his poems his scorn for all mythologies, Christianity included. His voluptuous descriptions of frivolous doings on Olympus were greatly admired by Russian poets of the eighteen twenties, although in translation, many artful details had been deleted by the censor. Parny's impact on Batyushkov is clear. Between 1805 and 1817, he wrote many lyrics which, melodious and romantic enough in tone, are primarily classical in inspiration. His dominant themes are epicurean, concerned with the enjoyment of life and of the erotic, though these are frequently cloaked in Zhukovsky's tones of melancholy and disillusionment.

OZEROV (1770–1816)

Something of the same mixture of classic and romantic characterizes the work of Vladislav Ozerov. His three tragedies, *Fingal, Dmitri of the Don*, and *Polyxene*, were very popular between 1804 and 1809, largely, perhaps, because of Catherine Semenova's great talent for tragic acting. Constructed on the French classical pattern, they were bathed in fashionable sentimentality. Dmitri's patriotic tirades, for example, drew wild applause from spectators who, on another stage, watched Napoleon's advances across Europe.

Only one comedy survived the first decades of the nineteenth century. Composed by Alexander Griboyedov in 1822–1823, it was called *The Misfortune of Being Clever*, and is the wittiest of all the great comedies in Russian dramatic literature.

GRIBOYEDOV (1795–1829)

A superlatively educated nobleman, an able diplomat, and the author of one immortal play, Alexander Griboyedov filled his brief life with brilliant accomplishments. He graduated from the University of Moscow with high honors in three disciplines: science, philosophy, and law. Appointed to the Foreign Office in St. Petersburg, he indulged his passion for the theater by joining forces with Prince Shakhovskoy, a tireless producer of comic and lyric operas and ballets. For Shakhovskoy and Katenin, another minor but prolific playwright, Griboyedov wrote, translated, and staged plays. He was also an active member of Shishkov's conservative literary society, yet he managed to earn promotions for solid achievement in his government job.

In 1818, he was sent to Persia as secretary to the Russian mission, and although he hated the country and its people, he mastered its language and made a serious study of the Middle East. In 1826, he was charged with treason for his association with members of the Decembrist group. His self-defense so impressed his superiors that he was not only freed but promoted into the bargain. In 1828, during his negotiations for a treaty with Persia, its provisions decidedly in Russia's favor, he was offered the post of Persian ambassador. He wished to retire to a life of writing, but surrendered to his mother's insistence that he remain in service, and with deep foreboding he bid his friends goodbye. "It will be a matter of knives," he predicted. The treaty, to be executed in Teheran, called for the release of Christian women from Persian harems, a demand which, as Griboyedov had foreseen, the Persians considered excessive for religious reasons. While treaty negotiations were being pressed, rebellion mounted, and on January 30, 1829, a mob stormed the Russian legation. Though the Cossack guard held off attackers twenty times their number for a whole afternoon, all of the Russians, save one who fled the building, were massacred. Griboyedov died fighting; his mutilated body was dragged through the streets and was later identified only by a finger which had been disfigured in a duel.

Griboyedov's letters, models of a concise and caustic epistolary art, reveal this active, successful man to be a Hamlet of discontent. He was frustrated by the pettiness and hypocrisy of his social circle. He scorned the servility of officials and their sinecured complacence. Indignant, abusive, rebellious by turn, he longed for a freer, bolder, more intelligent shaping of the world, and into Chatsky, hero of *The Misfortune of Being Clever*, he poured his restless aspirations. He had begun the play in 1816. He finished it in 1823, and it was first performed in 1825. Not until forty years later was it published; but censorship could not prevent the circulation of countless manuscripts. In *Misfortune*, the public had instantly recognized a masterpiece.

Chatsky is the first of many maladjusted characters in Russian literature. A passive rebel, he is the victim of a deep split in Russian society, of allegiance divided between Alexander's increasingly reactionary regime and the revolutionary spirit of the Decembrists. Returning to Moscow from a three-year trip abroad, Chatsky spends a day in the house of Famusov, a high-ranking official. Straightforward, intelligent, educated, and eager to serve, Chatsky is repelled by his peers' dishonesty and distrust of "book learning," their corruption and habitual fawning before rank and wealth. One estrangement follows another, as he discovers that his childhood sweetheart, Sophie Famusov, has fallen in love with her father's secretary, an ambitious nobody who exploits her for his own advancement. Sophie and her father greet Chatsky's criticism and liberal ideas with mockery and indifference; to be rid of him, they spread rumors of his madness, and the young man departs, outraged and frustrated, in despair.

With such a plot, one might hesitate to call *The Misfortune of Being Clever* a comedy. But Griboyedov's characters and dialogue are creations of a triumphant wit. While he observed the classical unities of action, time, and place, Griboyedov, like Fonvizin, stressed the development of character through dialogue. Judging by hostile reactions in certain Moscow drawing rooms, he grafted from life: Famusov, amorous and proper, a pillar of convention; his irreproachably subservient assistant, Molchalin; the smooth-faced swindler, Zagoretsky; Repetilov, alcoholic and garrulous, a compulsive joiner of secret societies. These and a score of others are animated universal types, and provide one reason why the play is still a feature of the Russian repertoire. Language provides another. Griboyedov used the irregular iambics of La Fontaine's rhymed verse, which Krylov had adapted for his fables. In this intricate, demanding form, he created by the exclusive use of the spoken Moscow dialect the most spontaneous and effective dialogue ever heard on the Russian stage. Nothing since has equalled its great liveliness, zest, and movement. Ironies and witticisms without number fall effortlessly into rhyme, with the economy and neatness of proverbs. Indeed, Pushkin, reading the play for the first time, prophesied that a good half of its lines would become proverbs, familiar to every educated Russian. His prophecy was to hold true not only for Griboyedov, but for himself.

PUSHKIN (1799–1837)

Ask a non-Russian to name the greatest among Russian writers, and he will at once think of Tolstoy, Dostoyevsky, or both. But a Russian will answer "Pushkin," as unhesitatingly as the English-speaking name Shakespeare sovereign of English literature. For Russians, Pushkin is a comrade in life, a poet whose prodigious output has given them countless lines and couplets to quote as epigrams, whose stanzas, recited with universal familiarity and pleasure, crystallize Russian life in the language of the people. A Russian will add, too, that Pushkin is little appreciated by the non-Russian world, because he is essentially untranslatable: his virtue lies in an organic bond between thought and expression, in a language of complete simplicity, lucid and unadorned.

For the historian studying the broad canvas of Russian literature, Pushkin's greatness lies in his dual role of synthesizer and creator. Like Dante, born astride two eras, with one foot in the Dark Ages and the other in the Renaissance, Pushkin was a bridge into a new age of Russian literature. And he was the age itself. With the apparently effortless achievement of genius, he carried Russian letters from a state of imitative brilliance to one of illustrious originality. Before him, Russian writers had heeded their lessons from the West. After him, writers were to develop upon Pushkin's foundations a national literature of international significance. But it was Pushkin himself, influencing his own countrymen, who paid in full Russia's cultural debt to the West.

Heritage: 1799–1820

Born on the eve of a new century, Alexander Pushkin lived as a paradox in a time of paradox. He was by birth a creature of conflicting opposites. From his father he inherited a name six hundred years old, hallowed in earliest Russian records of feudal military aristocracy, and of it Pushkin was unfeigningly proud. He was by temperament passionate, uncontrolled, candid, and vulnerably open-hearted—his mother's bequests from a lineage begun by Abram Hannibal, son of an Abyssinian prince captured by the Turks and sent as a gift by the Sultan to Peter the Great, to whom he owed his education and marriage to a boyar's daughter.

Saturated in the frivolous, Frenchified culture of Moscow's middling nobility, living richly and close on the income of dwindling estates, Pushkin's parents found the oldest of their three children unmanageable, apparently dull, alien, and ugly with his tightly curled dark hair, swarthy skin, and thick lips. Eager to be rid of him, they placed the eleven-year-old Alexander in the Lyceum of the Tsarskoye Selo just outside the capital, calling upon the influence of Alexander Turgenev (son of the Mason who had directed Karamzin to Novikov's publishing house) to get the boy into the freshman class of thirty. Planned by the Tsar as a model school for the preparation of future statesmen and government officials, the Lyceum offered a curriculum of encyclopedic breadth, though subjects were treated somewhat superficially. During the three years of secondary schooling and three of university training, the boys were taught humanities, languages, jurisprudence, and natural sciences. Corporal punishment forbidden, they were vagabond students at best, learning more from stolen excursions into the city than from classroom drills.

Mediocre in all subjects but Russian literature and French, Pushkin so excelled in the latter that his classmates called him "Frenchman." He had had extraordinary preparation: except for his Grandmother Hannibal and the servants, his family had spoken only French, and, free of even rudimentary supervision, the boy had read voraciously from his father's eclectic library. By the time he was eleven, he had devoured eighteenth-century French classics, the lighter novels, and even fashionable pornography. Drawn most to the wittier, more irreverent poets— Piron, Gresset, and Parny—he idolized Voltaire. Among the ancients he admired Catullus and Propertius; from them he absorbed the realistic view of carnal love which was to persist throughout his life.

In his father's house, Pushkin mingled with the literary great of the day—Karamzin and Zhukovsky were frequent visitors—and as a nine-year-old had written verses in French. He soon demonstrated to the Lyceum boys an even more exceptional accomplishment, for he filled the school's literary magazines with poems revealing an extraordinary facility for rhyme. Pushkin's years at the Lyceum were, despite lack of discipline, a time of fruitful assimilation. The poems written during that period emulate the fluid elegance of Zhukovsky and the purity of diction and sense of classic balance mastered by Batyushkov. Before he left the Lyceum, which for six years had been a home and a refuge from home, his work was published. Graduated in 1817, with a purely nominal government appointment, he plunged into the dissipated life of St. Petersburg in company with the most brilliant and world-weary of the young aristocracy. He drank, he gambled, he loved, he duelled.

He also wrote poetry. Already a sure craftsman, Pushkin now gathered the components of a formula for his art: a classic restraint, a language without ornament, economy of expression, an unerring sense of *le mot juste*. At nineteen, his genius for poetry was unmistakable, the Pushkin signature instantly recognizable in a blend of taste, purity, flexibility, and control. But his originality erupted in other ways, always different, always present, fresh and new. The six cantos of *Ruslan and Lyudmila* (1820), his first long poem, Pushkin based partly on a chapbook adventure, partly on medieval lore and fairy tales: the princess-heroine, kidnapped from her bridegroom knight, is catapulted into a series of romantic adventures. Reminiscent of Zhukovsky's medieval ballads, the poem's mock epic tones relate it even more strongly to Voltaire's *Maid of Orleans*, but it is unmistakably Pushkin's own. In verses enchantingly fluid and clear, he snips the placid story line with ironic digressions and comic descriptions. It was an instant success, enjoyed for its swift, airy fantasy as a sophisticated public might enjoy a beautiful ballet. Pushkin's name was secure: to the young poet, Zhukovsky sent his portrait, inscribed, "To a victorious pupil from a vanquished master."

He was acquiring another sort of fame at the same time. As a schoolboy he had revelled in ideas of constitutional reform, promulgated by Hussar officers recently returned from France to quarters near Tsarskoye Selo. He had been particularly influenced by one of these "rebels," Chaadayev, whose philosophy proclaimed the individual's right to social and political criticism. Living as a fashionable rake, Pushkin was open to even stronger radical influences. As he breathed, he wrote. His few "civic-minded" odes to freedom and the sanctity of law over autocracy passed unnoticed, but with more pointed and widely circulated epigrams against Arakcheyev, Golitzyn, and even the Tsar himself, he placed himself in lasting disrepute with reactionary circles. In 1820, Alexander ordered his exile to a monastery on the White Sea, and only the intercession of

Karamzin, Turgenev, and Zhukovsky mitigated the sentence to exile in the South.

Though *Ruslan and Lyudmila* was about to be published, Pushkin was not sorry to leave turbulent St. Petersburg, where his excesses had led to illness, a bout with typhoid, and, apparently, a hopelessly unrequited love affair. But from the date of the Tsar's wrath, Pushkin was a marked man, for the rest of his life "on parole," under police surveillance, restricted in his movements, in his associations, even in his work. He was never permitted to leave Russia, a blow to the young nobleman whose compulsion to experience all kinds of life would surely have taken him to Europe—there, perhaps, to have spent his powers wantonly. His bitterness at this restriction never eased; he wrote, "The devil must have willed it so, that I should have been born Pushkin, talented, intelligent—and in Russia."

Nevertheless, that he accomplished his greatest work in enforced solitude seems evidence enough that state-imposed strictures worked more for him than against. Intellectually a titan of rationalism—disciplined, steady, and dispassionate—Pushkin was emotionally as candid as a child, confiding and uncritical, easily led and influenced. Lacking the built-in stabilizers of personality, he required artificial controls to preserve a balance from which he could write, and Tsar Alexander unwittingly provided the straightjacket that allowed the Pushkin genius to function.

Far from the conviviality and intellectual companionship he craved, Pushkin, alone in the south of Russia, understood something of himself for the first time. To Chaadayev in 1821 he wrote of the beneficence of his exile:

> In solitude, my wayward genius
> Has come to love the quiet of reflection.
> I discipline my day; make friends with order
> And learn to stay my passing thoughts;
> Attempt to make amends in freedom and in peace
> For years of stormy youth, misspent. . . .

"The Russian Byron": 1820–1824

Pushkin discovered in the Crimea an exotic land still glittering with ruined Tartar palaces, the Caucasian ranges bristling with hostile Circassian tribes. Intoxicated by the romance of a semibarbaric people and by the dusky splendor of sea, steppe, and mountains, he now, at precisely the most appropriate time, read Byron for the first time, inescapably identifying in the Byronic hero his own estrangement from society. Influenced by the *Oriental Tales, The Corsair,* and *Childe Harold,* he explored new ground for four years, writing three narrative poems: *The Caucasian Prisoner* (1822), *The Fountain of Bakhchisaray* (1824), and *The Gypsies* (1824).

The Fountain of Bakhchisaray, based on a local legend, is largely impressionistic; against the dark brilliance of the Crimean night, Pushkin draws the dramatic conflict between two captive women, a chaste, Polish Christian girl and the Oriental queen of a Tartar khan's harem. In both of the other poems, however, his emphasis is special. His heroes are disenchanted products of a corrupt society, fleeing civilization in the tradition of the Byronic hero. The Caucasian prisoner, in the poem so titled, a Russian never otherwise named, is captive of a mountain tribe. Weary with living and unrequited loving, he cannot respond to the love of a Circassian girl, who nevertheless frees him before she drowns herself, a victim of the Russian's inflexible individuality.

The Gypsies, a longer poem, is stripped of description and confined to terse dialogue, which alone discloses the action. Characters are more fully developed, and in content and form the poem is more mature than its predecessor. Like the Caucasian prisoner, Aleko of *The Gypsies* is a solitary refugee from his past, seeking a free life among the "children of nature." When his mistress, the gypsy Zemfira, discards him for a lad of the tribe, Aleko, raging, kills them both; for his unbridled passion he is banished from the camp by Zemfira's father. Through the old gypsy, Pushkin judges the undisciplined rebel against society as cursed by the contradictions of his own nature, betraying and destroying those he touches. To sharpen his moral—remarkable for its presence at all in romantic poetry —Pushkin demonstrates that Aleko, too egocentric for his own society, is a destructive element in a primitive, less demanding milieu as well.

In these "southern" poems, Pushkin developed and matured as a romantic poet; but characteristically, as he mastered the new form he left it to explore and develop another. No hero of Byron's had posed a moral problem concerning human responsibility in any society. Absorbed in the character, so like himself, which he had created, and unsatisfied with his exploration of it in *The Gypsies,* Pushkin turned in 1823 to the first chapter of *Eugene Onegin,* intending to study the Aleko personality in a familiar, contemporary setting. He was as yet unaware that he had reached a sharp turning point in his artistic career, and, as it developed, in his life.

In Kishinev, the small, southern outpost town of his exile, Pushkin lived no less profligately than he had in St. Petersburg; the bazaar-like quality of the Crimea was a lure, an irritant. Amid a surfeit of opportunity, he squandered his health and money among various Greek and Moldavian ladies, while he wrote frantically to friends in the north of his need to escape. He was at last transferred to the cosmopolitan center of Odessa, which boasted European drawing rooms and an opera house, and, as governor, Count Vorontsov, a cultured Anglophile in whose office Pushkin was to work. They were instant antagonists: unimpressed by Pushkin's venerable name and recent fame, Vorontsov treated the young poet as an inferior, and Pushkin, nettled, responded in kind, complicating matters by falling hopelessly—and harmlessly—in love with the Countess. Though Pushkin was deeply involved with Amelia Riznich, wife of a Dalmatian merchant, Vorontsov's suspicions increased, and his opportunity came when, almost by accident, one of Pushkin's letters was intercepted. In that period of clerical authority it was incriminating enough that Pushkin should have written of "an intelligent atheist" whom he had met, "whose beliefs, not as agreeable as is usually imagined, are unfortunately likelier than any others." He was immediately expelled from service and ordered to his mother's estate in Mikhailovskoye, where he was to remain "subject to supervision of local ecclesiastical and civil authorities."

A Meeting with the People: 1824–1826

"Sad was my arrival," wrote Pushkin, of his depressing return to the North in September of 1824. His father thought him a dangerous rebel, watched him, and read his mail to "assist" the local police. After three months of intolerable quarrelling, the family moved and left him alone at Mikhailovskoye, where in two years he produced twice as much as he had in southern exile.

He wrote friends in Moscow of his rigid program of study, intended to fill the gaps in "my rotten education." From them he ordered German, English, and Italian classics, European histories, current literature, and memoirs. Hundreds of annotated volumes attest to the magnitude and intensity of his study. It seems natural that the last two volumes of Karamzin's history should lure him into Russia's past. Particularly engrossed by the tensions between historical forces and human individuality, he now wrote *Boris Godunov* (1825), in conscious imitation of Shakespeare's chronicle plays, hoping that the form would obliterate once and for all the French classicism that had hampered the development of Russian theater.

The play contains twenty-six scenes, in which there are powerful dramatic monologues in blank verse, and a tavern sequence to rival any of Falstaff's bawdy perfection. The unhappy Tsar, racked by guilt and his lust for power, is magnificently portrayed. But the drama which Moussorgsky was to use so successfully as the libretto for his opera made poor material for the stage, persistent changes of locale and tone disrupting the dramatic progression and destroying the unity of the whole.

Boris Godunov is nevertheless one of Pushkin's most significant contributions to Russian literature, for it recognizes and stresses the power of a faceless, formless mass of common people to alter the course of history. Pushkin's interest in the Russian people, its oral literature, and its place in the national life marks a new stage in the evolution of his art. His years at Mikhailovskoye put him in touch for the first time with the people of his own northern country—and for Pushkin, merely to touch was to assimilate—whose peasant ways he absorbed in long walks and rides in the country, and in days at the market fairs. He listened attentively to the ancient chants of blind *kaleki* (thereby causing the local police to suspect him of mutineering among the townsfolk), and from his old nurse,

Arina Rodionovna, heard countless versions of folk legends. She and her culture were to be immortalized in *Eugene Onegin*. The portions of the novel written at Mikhailovskoye are studded with information about Russian country life, festivals, superstitions, and ancient lore common to the lower provincial gentry and their serfs. It is in the landscape of central Russia, lush with elms, oaks, birches, and gentle meadows furrowed by streams, that Pushkin places his heroine, a provincial lass who reads French and English novels, who cannot spell in her own language, but who, "she knows not why, is Russian in her soul." The poetry of this period, too, reflects Pushkin's closeness to the people. *The Bridegroom*, his first attempt to tell a fairy story in verse, is written in the style and tone of surviving popular legends. When he had finished *Songs About Stenka Razin*, he wrote to his brother that he found in the sixteenth-century Volga pirate "the one poetical image in the saga of our common people."

New Fetters: 1826–1831

At the death of Alexander I, Pushkin dared hope his term of estrangement ended, and pressed friends to intercede with Nicholas. The canny Tsar, his reign begun in bloodshed, was not loath to divert public opinion in his favor by recalling the country's greatest poet, and a courier was dispatched to escort the prodigal son to St. Petersburg. With barely time to burn compromising papers and stuff his travelling pouch with writings, the apprehensive poet arrived, mud-spattered and weary after frequent changes of post horses, to be ushered at once into the Highest Presence for an hour-long interview.

Nicholas received him with gracious benevolence, chiding him gently for his offensive conduct, inquiring solicitously why he published so little. Disarmed by the formidable Romanov charm, Pushkin blamed the restrictions of censorship, and when the monarch pledged that he alone would supervise the poet's work, Pushkin knew the exhilaration of a freed man. His illusion, bolstered by the accolades of an adoring public, was soon shattered, as he discovered that the Emperor's personal patronage meant line-by-line scrutiny of all that he wrote. So stringent was imperial control that a semiprivate reading of *Boris Godunov*, not yet submitted to the Tsar, brought immediate reproof from Russia's highest, most efficient political censor, the head of the Third Section. His writing continued nonetheless, largely within the framework of history. He planned and wrote several chapters of a novel, *The Arab of Peter the Great*, which, with his great-grandfather Hannibal as the central figure, was to draw parallels between the turbulence of that time and the revolutionary undercurrents of his own. His admiration for Peter led him to write his first long historical poem, *Poltava* (1829), telling of Peter's heroic victory, despite treason in his ranks, over Charles XII of Sweden. Free of digression, the verse swells and resounds with the thunder of battle, eclipsing the romance between the traitorous Hetman Mazeppa and his goddaughter, Maria, with which the poem begins. For Pushkin, it achieved a new level of Miltonic objectivity.

His life he continued to live hotly, obsessed now with gambling away the gold his poetry won. Yet he was restless and unhappy in drifting, longed to settle down, and vowed to friends that he would marry the most beautiful girl in Russia. He met her. Nathalie Goncharova was sixteen in 1829, one of three marriageable daughters in an impoverished family of noble lineage. A dazzling beauty, she was expected to make a brilliant match; Pushkin was at first rejected, then, a year later, when no better prospect had appeared, was accepted. His father, approving, settled upon him a small estate near Nizhni Novgorod, at Boldino, and the bridgegroom went there to take possession and, to defray the expenses of marriage, mortgage the property. During the transaction, the countryside was struck by cholera, and for three fretful months Pushkin was imprisoned by quarantine. They were the most creative months of his life.

At Boldino

For eight years Pushkin had labored with *Eugene Onegin*, and now, in twelve weeks, he completed it. A novel in verse, it progressed through eight chapters of fifty stanzas each, a total of 5,249 lines, to emerge as literature's first novel of modern realism, and a new art form. Pushkin had first conceived it as an episodic satire in conscious imitation of *Don Juan;* but as his contemporary hero developed under the same "premature aging of the heart" which had plagued Aleko of *The Gypsies,* the work assumed a seriousness and an organic unity completely foreign to Byron's poem. It became instead a sharply brilliant profile of Russia's town-and-country society in the 1820's.

The opening scenes in aristocratic St. Petersburg bubble with the outrageous gaiety of Arzamas sessions, as in endless rounds of balls, ballets, and private supper parties, Onegin, an eighteen-year-old dandy, very much like his creator, fills his days and nights with the "monotonous variety" of amatory and epicurean pleasures. Unlike Pushkin, however, he wearies of them early, and plunges into ennui. An uncle's bequest takes him to the country, where, "like a faithful wife," boredom pursues him in book-lined solitude. There his neighbor, Vladimir Lensky, a young romantic poet, gains him entree to the hospitality of a local squire, whose eldest daughter, Tatiana, falls in love with the disenchanted, cynical Onegin. Her naive declaration, in one of fiction's most poignant love letters, elicits from Eugene a dry, moralizing rejection, and after a senseless duel in which he kills Lensky, Onegin departs for travels in Europe. Tatiana, meanwhile, in one of her walks in the country, comes by chance upon his house, and is admitted to his library. From marginal notes in his books, she learns of his spiritual exhaustion, discovering him to be an able, intelligent man whose education and social position have fitted him only for a useless, sterile life. Several years later, Onegin returns to the capital and meets Tatiana once more, now married to wealth and rank, a poised and beautiful woman of society whom he barely recognizes as the erstwhile provincial Miss. He conceives a desperate passion for her and believes himself rebuffed, until one day he finds her weeping over one of his many ardent letters. In this final scene, Tatiana acknowledges her love, then dismisses Onegin with lines that are perhaps the best known in all Russian poetry:

> I have been given to another
> And I'll be true to him forever.

Just as Eugene Onegin is the ancestor of the "superfluous hero" in the works of Lermontov, Herzen, and Turgenev, so Tatiana's steadfast moral courage has inspired the unswerving natures of numberless Russian heroines, particularly in the novels of Turgenev. The muffled ending of the book reaches out to influence as well Grigorovich and Chekhov, and, in the twentieth century, Ivan Bunin. Pushkin's realism, happily called poetic, pervades Russian fiction for over a century, though it is quite different from the dissecting realism of Flaubert, or from the "slice-of-life" novels so prevalent in France and England in the late nineteenth century. Pushkin's characters are in life-size focus. They move and act naturally in their own atmosphere, individuals created by suggestion or lyrical asides. Tatiana grows to maturity in front of us, and although we never know the color of her eyes or of her hair, we understand her better than we do ourselves through an indirect, poetically eloquent impression—of a dream she had, of a walk she took, of books that crowd her bedside table.

Very few poets have attempted—and none, successfully—to emulate the intricate fourteen-line *Onegin* stanza. In three quatrains of varying rhyme schemes and a neatly crowning couplet, it offers the balance, harmony, and sense of satisfactory completion associated with the sonnet. In it, Pushkin was able to introduce and elaborate any one mood or thought, summarizing it in crisp, epigrammatic fashion. He used his invention to utmost advantage, as in this stanza from the first chapter of *Onegin* which summarizes with delightful wit and brevity his hero's childhood. Capital letters beginning a line note masculine rhymes; lower-case letter beginning a line denotes feminine.

> fresh from a blameless state career,
> His father lived on IOU's,
> he used to give three balls a year,
> Until he had no more to lose.
> fate treated young Onegin gently:
> "madame" first watched him competently,
> From her "Monsieur" received the child;
> The boy was likable, though wild.
> "Monsieur," a poor "abbé" from Paris,
> To spare the youngster undue strain,
> Would teach him in a playful vein,

With moral strictures rarely harass,
Reprove him mildly for each lark,
And walk him in the Summer Park.*

Much of Pushkin's critical commentary between 1826 and
1830 concerns the state of Russian literary language. He believed it stifled by the demands of verse, and because poetry was
too indirect and concentrated, its appeal too restricted for changing literary tastes, he felt with other critics that the day for
prose had come. Accordingly, he experimented with storytelling
for its own sake, writing five short stories known as the *Belkin
Tales*, adventures from contemporary life ostensibly witnessed
and reported by one Ivan Belkin, a provincial squire. With the
perseverance of an apprentice, Pushkin strove for and mastered
all the self-set goals of the new "naked art." His prose narrative
is swiftly paced, urged toward its conclusion with short, pungent
sentences free of adornment in dialogue as well as in exposi-
tion. "Little" people are his heroes—a maidservant, a craftsman,
a station master—whose doings escape the melodramatic or
sentimental by dint of the narrator's sympathetic humanity.
Gogol and the young Dostoyevsky were to learn much from
these brief masterpieces, the most perfect of which is the
perennially popular *Queen of Spades* (1834). Carried by a taut
prose through the Hoffmannesque labyrinths of the story, the
hero, crazed, is an early kinsman to the hallucinators of Dostoyevsky.

The months at Boldino produced as well some thirty lyrics,
a spate of literary criticism, and *Four Small Tragedies*, which
Pushkin called experiments in dramatic composition: *The Miser
Knight, The Feast During the Plague, The Stone Guest*, and
Mozart and Salieri. Each miniature tragedy pivots on one passion (lust, envy, avarice, man's defiance of death). In dramatic
monologues rivaling Shakespeare's for emotional power and
complexity, Pushkin probes man's inner world, building scenes
of extraordinary suspense and demonstrating yet another side
of his genius, the ability to create effective drama. Each tiny
play, stripped to its tragic essence, is universal in meaning; yet
characters in their native English, Spanish, or Italian settings

* *Eugene Onegin*, by Alexander Pushkin, translated by Walter Arndt (New
York, E. P. Dutton, 1963. © 1963 by Walter Arndt.

retain their distinctive nationalities, a reminder of how vividly Pushkin comprehended worlds he had not seen.

Last Years

His own world splintered, then shattered. His marriage, outwardly happy, fettered him to the throne and burdened his purse. Nathalie, as vacuous as she was beautiful, gambolled at court, and to assure her presence there, Nicholas appointed Pushkin Gentleman of the Chamber, a demeaning office which Pushkin's friend Prince Vyazemsky had held at the age of eighteen. Though he received unprecedented sums for his poetry (five gold rubles a line), Pushkin was hard pressed by the demands of too opulent a life, of a retinue of three children, housemaids, tutors, and relatives, by the frivolity of a wife whom he could not bear to deny. In spite of these private pressures, he attempted to establish a literary review that would be authoritative and objective, free of pedantry and "vulgar journalism." Prevented at first by the ban of censorship, he at last launched *The Contemporary*, which was to succeed only later, under other editors.

He wrote. His interest in Russian oral literature undiminished, he adapted in 1834 several fairy tales from Arina Rodionovna's store; they hold honored place in all anthologies. Granted access to the national archives, he studied documents of the Pugachev revolt for a two-volume account (one, a text; the other, notes) in order that nameless Russian millions might be accorded a rare breakthrough into recorded history. He sought to give the rebellion immediacy and eloquence in a short historical novel, *The Captain's Daughter* (1833–1834), in which the fortitude and heroism of the common people in time of upheaval is paid tribute.

The Bronze Horseman (1833) is his last long poem, and his greatest. Recreating the disastrous flood of St. Petersburg in 1824, Pushkin writes of a lowly clerk, Eugene, who has seen his sweetheart swept away by the raging waters. Demented, he wanders about the capital, to come at last before the palace. Confronting the mighty bronze equestrian figure of Peter the Great, he curses the Tsar for having founded the city on perilous marshland. Turning away in despair, he hears the great bronze hooves pursuing him as he flees through the streets, screaming in terror. In an allegory rare for its descriptive power, Eugene embodies all victims of an implacable State. Pushkin does not try to resolve that peculiarly Russian dilemma, the tragedy of ruler versus ruled; but *The Bronze Horseman* is a memorial to his prophetic vision across nineteenth-century tyranny to the totalitarian Russia of our own time.

Pushkin was now at odds with all circles. He was hounded by creditors, baited at court as the accommodating husband of a flirtatious belle, and ridiculed as a literary conservative by a new generation of critics. He saw, perhaps, that his day was over, but with the dispassionate eye he had always turned upon his work, he was able to evaluate his career. The lyrical *A Monument to Myself* begins,

> I have created a monument to myself
> Not shaped by human hands
> To which the people's path will not be overgrown.

The measured balance and common sense of his poetry did not exist in his personal life. Nathalie, ever flattered by persistent attentions, did nothing to discourage the scandalous advances of a French baron, George d'Anthès, and the enraged Pushkin challenged him to a duel. D'Anthès drew the first shot, and Pushkin was cruelly wounded. For two days, he bore his pain with stoicism, "so as not to unduly alarm" his wife, and on January 29, 1837, died.

The century was drawing to a close before the magnitude of Pushkin's contribution to Russian letters was fully comprehended. In Russia, his feats of literary synthesis and his originality were recognized with wonder, and foreign critics who had not followed his career were thunderstruck to discover that overnight, it seemed, Russian literature had been transformed from a lengthy, imitative adolescence to a confidently mature national art. Evolving steadily, Pushkin's work had encompassed and surpassed the achievement of several generations of writers. Until 1820, he wrote under the influence of Zhukovsky and Batyushkov, having assimilated the culture of seventeenth- and eighteenth-century France in the preromanticism of the first, and the classical forms and themes of the second. His brief infatuation with the Byronic hero introduced still another new strain to Russian literature, one that was to be altered forever by the creation of a singularly Russian personality, perfected in *Eugene Onegin*. The realism of that novel he attempted to develop and strengthen in his last "prose" period, imbuing his stories with a compassion that was later to distinguish all serious Russian fiction.

From his letters, notes, and drafts, we know that Pushkin was aware of his accomplishment, at least in part. He did not minimize, for example, the importance of his explorations in oral tradition, or his persistent efforts to shape the Russian language; his fusion of popular parlance and the elegant idiom of Karamzin is the language of educated Russians today. But for all his kaleidoscopic genius, Pushkin's consummate gift was that of a poet. His production of lyrics did not slacken until the early 1830's, and the poems maintain a consistently high level of excellence. Some five hundred shorter poems attest to the precision of his art and the wealth of his imagination; no Russian is without his favorite among them. Perfectly constructed, each is a marvel of harmony; language, form, and content are fused in a culmination of the Pushkin style. They are of the substance of all great poetry—love, death, parting, friendship, slight joys or deep suffering; whatever is timeless, Pushkin celebrated with the "divine indiscrimination" of Shakespeare.

AFTER PUSHKIN

In Gogol's arresting metaphor, Pushkin's creativity "was a fire tossed out of the sky, from which lesser poets of his day, like candles, became alight." To read the delicate Anacreontic lyrics of Baratynsky (1800–1844), who was later to write deeply pessimistic poems on the futility of human effort; to detect the social protest in the poems of the Decembrist Ryleyev (1795–1826); or to appreciate the verbal brilliance of Yazykov (1803–1846), is to realize the extent of Pushkin's impact on the writers of his own generation. Each poet, though he eventually developed his own style, had begun by emulating Pushkin's.

None, however, has greater claim as Pushkin's direct heir than Michael Lermontov (1814–1841). His literary fame began with the appearance of his *Death of a Poet*, a blunt denunciation of the circumstances surrounding Pushkin's death. He had written the poem immediately after Pushkin's fatal duel, and accused "murdering" authorities of negligence in permitting the duel to occur. Poetry and political agitation were, in bureaucratic language, becoming synonymous at that time; the twenty-three-year-old officer was expelled from the Guards, court-martialled, and sent off into front-line fighting in the Caucasus with another regiment.

Lermontov found relief from social pressure in the grandeur of Georgia's snowcapped peaks and stretches of virgin forest. Like Pushkin, he was excited by the air of danger surrounding native villages nestled in the semitropical vegetation of the steppe, or along narrow gorges where the dry, warm air was extraordinarily transparent. In this majestic scenery, he began work on two long narrative poems, *The Novice* (1840) and *The Demon* (1839). For sustained power and brilliance of imagery they are unequalled in Russian poetry. Both are tautly structured on one theme, the need to escape society, and are all the more dramatic for their settings in the spectacular land of Georgia.

The more interesting story of the two is that of *The Novice*. A young Circassian boy, captured by Russians and left at a monastery to recover from an illness, grows up among the monks, secretly longing for his native village. Dimly rebellious against his keepers, he flees into the mountains, hoping to find his own people and "press his heart against someone who, to him, is not a stranger." For three exultant days he tastes liberty, braving torrents and fighting a wild tiger—only to hear again, as he falls unconscious from his wounds, the tolling of the monastery bells which tell him that he had been wandering about in a circle. The story is told as though the dying youth was reconstructing for an old monk those few moments of freedom.

In *The Demon*, Lermontov infuses an overworked theme with new passion. In his love for a mortal girl, Satan is moved to cry out for liberation from the curse of tedium under which he exists for eternity. But the moment passes; his closeness to truth and light recedes as the girl perishes under his kiss, and her soul is carried away from him to heaven.

Both poems reflect the spiritual malaise which tormented

Lermontov throughout his brief life. The society which had bred him he found intolerable; sardonically, he had symbolized the antireligious currents of his time in the monastery of *The Novice*. He cultivated early the habit of solitude, but deliberate isolation, too, oppressed him, and like the Demon, he sought relief in numerous love affairs and perverse manners calculated to arouse antagonism. The Byronic pose protrudes in most of his poetry, with the exception of a few lyrical masterpieces which most Russians know by heart: *Angel, A Sail, Alone, I Go Out on the Road, My Country*. In these poems, he seems to attain a reconciliation with life, but in the main, his verse disgorges sentiments of frustration, estrangement, futility, and regret.

From the beginning his life seems to have been oriented toward moral bankruptcy and despair. His father, descended from George Learmont, a Scottish missionary who had fought with the Russians during the seventeenth century, was a small landowner who had married above his station. When his mother died, the boy was wrenched from his father to be reared in plenty by his grandmother. The ensuing family quarrels were as much a part of Michael's childhood as his excellent Franco-German education and the pampering he received from a bevy of female relatives. As a vain, selfish, and self-centered boy of thirteen, he entered the communal life of the Moscow University preparatory school. Later he was expelled from the university itself for having disputed violently with one of his teachers.

He had learned English during these years, and read voraciously in the works of Byron and Shelley. He remained aloof, however, from the many philosopical and literary societies active at the university, some dominated by Herzen and his group of Utopian socialists, others by the "frenzied Vissarion," Belinsky. Though Belinsky's debates nightly shook the walls of the famous Room #11, Lermontov, next door, was unmoved. Leaving Moscow for the St. Petersburg Cadet School of the Guards, he plunged into the customary dissipations of his class, attracting a kind of fame with his pornographic verses. Awkward in manner and painfully conscious of his unattractive looks (he was short and thickset, with wide shoulders and bowed legs, his wide, dark eyes disconcertingly immobile), he was nevertheless a very successful Don Juan. He was too successful; the one girl he truly loved jilted him to marry another. His year in exile did nothing to divert his bent for self-dramatization. His return as a celebrity to fashionable drawing rooms was marked by ill-tempered sarcasm and deliberate rudeness. But Belinsky, then principal critic for *Notes from the Fatherland,* to which Lermontov contributed occasionally, observed that in private conversation the poet was charming, lucid, and unaffected.

Neither Lermontov's youthful dramas nor the lyrics he wrote for the better part of his life evidence true originality. The themes are Byronic, and his style, though balanced, clear, and more mellifluous than Pushkin's, borrows from Zhukovsky, depending for effect on imagery. The poems are saturated with Lermontov's complete and sincere absorption with himself. Even in the swollen rhetoric of lines bursting with romanticism, the poet's psyche is apparent: society appears as a hindrance, a menace to happiness, a subject to be treated with hostility and contempt.

Lermontov seemed to be less interested in writing than in his mundane conquests and escapades. In 1840, a dispute with the French Ambassador's son ended in a duel, and again Lermontov was dispatched to the Caucasus. Apparently in an attempt to subdue the difficult junior officer, the Tsar had ordered Lermontov to the Tenginsky regiment, then holding an isolated fortress against massive Moslem attack. Through a bureaucratic error, Lermontov was sent further west, and when he distinguished himself in fighting there, a recommendation for honors was ignored in St. Petersburg. After a short Moscow leave, he was instead given another dangerous assignment. En route, he stopped for a brief rest at Piatigorsk, a Caucasian spa, and there met a former classmate, Major Martynov. Both courted the same girl, and Martynov, provoked by the poet's jibes, challenged him to a duel. Lermontov was killed outright in his twenty-seventh year.

He had anticipated the circumstances of the duel and the duel itself in a novel, *The Hero of Our Time* (1840), but with the difference that the protagonist of the novel, Pechorin, had fired the fatal shot. It is tempting to trace Pechorin's literary lineage to the earlier romantic heroes of Europe. He resembles

Chateaubriand's René, for example, travelling with the same abandon, falling in love with a native girl to the same destructive end, as had the restless character of *The Genius of Christianity*. Or he is very like Lovelace, who, in Richardson's *Clarissa Harlowe*, works havoc for the sake of diversion. But these are only distant relatives; Pechorin's immediate predecessor is Eugene Onegin. Onegin, a harmless drifter who indulges his world-weariness in more or less free expression, is the "superfluous man" of pre-Decembrist years. Pechorin, child of the dreary barracks regime of Nicholas I, has no outlet for his discontent. He suffocates in the humdrum world of officialdom; his frustration becomes bile, then deliberate destructiveness. The difference between the two characters is not only a matter of personality, but of the decade in which each finds himself.

With no precedent for a prose novel, Lermontov developed the Pechorin character by writing *The Hero of Our Time* in a combination of travelogue, straight narration (like Pushkin's *Belkin Tales*), and diary form. Five of Pechorin's adventures in the Caucasus are thus related from three separate points of view: that of the omniscient author-narrator, that of Pechorin's immediate superior, and finally, of Pechorin himself. The result is Russian fiction's first psychological character study, constructed with sound logic and in prose which shows no trace of burning midnight oil.

In quite a different vein is *The Merchant of Kalashnikov* (1837), an epic poem reflecting current interest in national folklore. The Kirsha Danilov collection of seventy *byliny* had been reprinted for the third time in 1818, and Lermontov probably studied it closely. *The Merchant* is true in meter, language, and spirit to the Muscovite narratives of Ivan the Terrible's day. Lermontov may have been thinking of Pushkin's encounter with d'Anthès when he elected to base his story on a Russian folk opera. The valiant merchant, knowing that the tsar's law decrees death to any who defy his guards, engages nevertheless in a public fight with one who has threatened his wife's virtue. Set in the rhythmic measure of the *byliny*, the poem flows with the wide authentic richness of an ancient people's lay.

Lermontov's association with Russian oral tradition was that of a sensitive observer; his *Merchant* is a skillful adaptation from the tradition—it is not of the tradition itself. In the work of Alexey Koltsov (1809–1842), the opposite is true. The son of a cattle dealer in South Central Russia, Koltsov has been called the "Russian Burns." His poetry comes directly from the literature of peasant songs. More sentimental than the poems of Burns, his best known lyrics sing of seasonal changes and of the beauty and limitlessness of the steppe. There are love lyrics as well, in which a woman's voice recites the folk pleasures of peasant life. In great favor with the literati of Moscow, these melodious poems were the last romantic echoes of an age of literature which flourished in the shadow of Alexander Pushkin.

6 · New Ideologies

Trail Blazers to the Revolution

BETWEEN RUSSIAN REALITY AND GERMAN IDEALISM

From its beginnings, Russian literature had reflected Russian history. In the nineteenth century, it was to become a force in the shaping of history. It was to guide the same political and social movements from which it sprang, developing so close to the politics of the time that one could not speak of the one without understanding the other. Both literature and politics were to exert Russia's most profound influence on the culture of the West.

The intellectual mood of Russia was changed by the abortive Decembrist revolt. The aristocracy, scintillating in Pushkin's generation, declined in the torpor of manor life or faded into the cautious conformity of bureaucratic officialdom. The court divested itself of intellectual interests, and the center of society and learning shifted to Moscow. Radiating from the university were numerous private circles where students of the middle nobility and the lower gentry mingled with the sons of wealthy merchants and members of the liberal professions. These progressive young men, united by a certain "classlessness" of sympathy, rapidly became known as the "intelligentsia," a new cultural elite whose energies were born of frustration.

They were outcasts, fugitives from the iron regime of Nicholas, a tiny, subversive element sandwiched between the great, illiterate mass of people on the one side, and, on the other, official Russia, ever on the alert against them. Preferring starvation to material success in a society they detested, they lived precariously on family allowances, on tutoring or translating fees, on what could be earned by writing for the frequently suppressed journals of Moscow. Their lives were dedicated to philosophical debate on the future of Russia. They saw her as a barbaric nation, retarded both socially and intellectually. Ninety per cent of her people remained passively illiterate, shackled by feudalism. While her men of letters had repudiated Western culture, no native aesthetic had risen to replace outworn imitations. But though the intelligentsia were haunted by Russia's cultural emptiness, they could devise no practical means for her deliverance. They were "rootless men, living on ideas alone," said Dostoyevsky, and they lived, therefore, in a social vacuum.

Their mental and moral despair was given voice in 1836, when Peter Chaadayev's *Philosophical Letter* appeared in the *Moscow Telescope*. Herzen likened it to "a shot that rang out in a dark night; it forced all to awaken." Its impact on educated Russians was great enough for the *Telescope* to be suppressed, its editor exiled, and the censor who had permitted publication dismissed. Chaadayev was declared officially insane and placed under medical care in his own home.

As a young officer in the Napoleonic campaigns he had talked to the youthful Pushkin of individual liberty and free public opinion, Western concepts of government which even during his association with the Decembrists he believed doomed in Russia. He had written his views privately in 1829. Published seven years later in the potent *Letter*, they accurately expressed the prevailing mood of the educated.

> The history of other nations is that of their emancipation. Russian history is that of serfdom and autocracy. . . . Alone of all the peoples of the world, we have not given anything to the world, and we have not learned anything from it. . . . There is something in our blood that repels all true progress.

Though he thought of Russia as "a blank piece of paper on which to write the word 'Europe,'" Chaadayev nevertheless predicted that Russia could only benefit by steady learning from the West. He thereby clarified two positions in Russian thought, precipitating a debate between Westerners and Slavophils which has persisted to the present day. Such famous exponents of Slavophilism as the humanitarian Khomyakov (1804–1860), Ivan Kireyevsky (1806–1856), founder of the movement, and the later, more militant publicists, Konstantin (1817–1860) and Ivan Aksakov (1823–1886), shared Chaadayev's hatred of Nicholas' regime and with him urged the abolition of serfdom. Unlike him, however, they believed in Russia's moral supremacy over the "decadent" West, identifying in her anxious imitation of Europe the source of all Russian ills. Her only hope, they argued, lay in the deep strength of the Russian people and in the purity of the Orthodox faith. It rested with her oldest form of government, the peasant commune (*mir*), (administered by village elders elected by the entire male population), to transport Russia beyond the currents of corruption, coercion, and exploitation common to Western materialism. The *mir* alone was flexible enough to preserve her complex traditions and her thousand-year-old rural way of life.

The Slavophils tended to oversimplify and sentimentalize the problems of ninteenth-century Russia. Justly, by Slavophil standards, Ivan Aksakov, a brilliant journalist and landowner of parochial mind, could champion in the late 1850's the cause of pan-Slavism, calling for Russian solidarity with all neighboring Slavic peoples as a means to Balkan liberation.

Both Slavophil and Westerner agreed, however, that Russian culture could be revitalized only if her standard of living was raised. Paradoxically, they looked to German philosophy for directives. Men like Herder, Fichte, Schelling, and Hegel were attempting to recreate a spirit of medieval unity in a world increasingly mechanized by the revelations of eighteenth-century science. Their theories exalted man as the "finite center" or "fragment" of an absolute cosmic entity. Not static, as envisaged in traditional Christian dogma, this absolute entity was dynamic, the essence of ceaseless movement, development, growth. It could, according to Schelling, be measured only by a certain intensive intuition of the imagination. According to Schiller, that privileged imagination belonged to "noble souls," artists whose depth and excellence were judged by how perfectly they expressed their finite visions of the infinite. The duty of all men was to detect and define the march of history by identifying themselves with the "larger organism" toward which history moved. For Herder, this organism was spiritual culture. For Fichte and Hegel, it was represented in national states.

In the West, such lofty abstractions were to be tested in the habitually skeptical climate of controversy and debate. Russian intellectuals, however, innocent of a native tradition in philosophy, accepted the German ideas without reservation or criticism. The German concept of universal movement and growth consoled the intelligentsia for their own social stagnation, justifying further their withdrawal from practical life in order to cultivate understanding of the universal "essence." That a nation could be conceived as a growing part of a universal whole gave impetus to their desire for an identifiably Russian culture. But Schelling's aesthetic dictum of 1807 was the greatest ideological spellbinder of all. "The artist must not subordinate himself slavishly to reality and try to reproduce it. Rather he must withdraw from it so as to develop within himself individual forces and return to reality to enrich it with his own strength a thousandfold." To many young Russians wasting in self-imposed isolation, the commandment gave direction and a heightened sense of vocation.

The danger of these ideas lay less in their content—they were to lose all popularity in Russia by the 1850's—than in the method by which they were interpreted and developed. Established in emotional generalizations, they reached exalted conclusions by force of reason without regard for reality. Already intoxicated by abstractions, the Russian intelligentsia were swept ever higher and farther from reality in the spirals of German romanticism. Intransigent, they became dogmatists, then spokesmen of a fanaticism that was to distinguish all radical Russian thought and culminate in the intellect of Lenin.

LITERARY EVANGELISM

Characterized by the extremes of intellectual wealth and physical poverty, the intelligentsia could have been represented by no more suitable a man than Vissarion Belinsky (1811–

1848). Raised in the squalor of a small village near Moscow, where his father, a former ship's doctor, practiced medicine and alcoholism, Belinsky entered the University of Moscow at state expense. He read widely and feverishly, debated endlessly and vociferously, but at the end of three years was expelled. He was a less than average student and had written a play attacking serfdom. In 1834, having become a journalist for the *Moscow Telescope*, he published his *Literary Musings*, and gained a reputation as a bold, pugnacious avant-garde critic. Two years later, Chaadayev's *Letter* appeared, the *Telescope* was suppressed, and Belinsky was scratching a living as tutor and writer of textbooks. At last, in 1839, he was invited to become chief literary critic for the influential St. Petersburg weekly, *Notes from the Fatherland*. He was wretchedly paid, and the northern climate of the capital hastened his death from tuberculosis, but his articles sent circulation figures soaring; students waited at Moscow coffee houses for deliveries of the thick journal, eager to read "what Belinsky was up to this week." In 1846, he was writing as well for the *Contemporary*, newly purchased by Panayev and the poet Nekrasov.

A year later, Belinsky went abroad for his health, and there, free of censorship, wrote his famous letter to Gogol. It castigated the tsarist regime and censured Gogol's preoccupation with faith and mysticism in the face of Russia's need for social justice and individual freedom. Circulated throughout Russia in handwritten copies, the letter became the credo of the progressive intelligentsia; in 1856, Ivan Aksakov wrote his father that "there was not a single high school teacher in the provincial cities who did not know the letter by heart." Police authorities knew the letter well enough. When Belinsky returned to Russia, he was in danger "of being taken off to rot in the fortress," and had he not died of his lifelong illness, he would undoubtedly have been imprisoned.

A penniless outcast, poorly educated, Belinsky was to become the most influential of Russian intellects. Turgenev rightly called him the central figure of his age, and in the Soviet Union he is invoked second only to Lenin as "a great teacher." Not surprisingly, Western biographers, writing of him with respect and exasperation, fail to agree on his definitive role in

Russian life. For his uncompromising nature and the fierceness of his debates, Belinsky was known as "furious Vissarion." But he was intellectually fickle. In private disputes, letters, articles, and philosophical "book reviews," he leaped from one ideological enthusiasm to another without pause for consistency. Each of his currently favorite theories he accepted eagerly and totally, be it Hegel's dialectic of history, Schelling's concept of national character, or Fichte's position on individualistic self-assertion. Each argument was discarded as Belinsky wearied of it, and he was the first to admit his incurable vacillation.

He was in no doubt, however, about his function as literary legislator. To his criticism he brought the highest sense of personal commitment, an unswerving love for letters, and an incorruptible judgment that was to inspire Russian literary canon for the remainder of the century. It was he who first assessed Pushkin's genius and the originality of Lermontov; who detected the rising stars of Turgenev, Goncharov, and Dostoyevsky, though he lived to read only their earliest works. But his most resounding judgments defined the role literature was to play in Russian culture.

Ruthlessly censored in the press, criticism of the State had long since been channelled into more discreet paths. "All our moral interests," wrote Belinsky, "all our spiritual life have hitherto been and will, still for a long time to come, be concentrated in literature; it is the vital spring from which all human sentiments and conceptions percolate into society." Thus, he bestowed upon literature the burden of social and moral reform in Russia. His own task, as literary critic, was to discover and promote artistic talent, serving as intermediary between society and the artistic imagination, which, of necessity, outstripped society. As he worked for the liberal *Contemporary*, he came to believe that creative writing was not only the refined articulation of national life, but the actual shaping of its aspirations as well. The writer, therefore, could no longer create only from his private vision; he had to imbue his work with criticism of existing evils, acting as society's conscience and source of enlightenment: "He who deprives art of its rights to serve social interests debases the reader instead of elevating him."

Few writers protested that Belinsky had sullied the purity

of art. Most approached their work with a new sense of social responsibility, building into Russian literature the distinctive features that have surprised foreign readers: the moral overtones, the high seriousness, the emphasis on ideas. While Belinsky was responsive to the "intangible magic" of art, his first commitment, keeping faith with the intelligentsia, was to wage battle against Russia's spiritual stagnation. He prepared the soil for dragons' teeth, for the century was to produce militant writers who would distort his views.

In at least two ways, Belinsky rendered great disservice to the literature he loved so well. Engrossed in the "what" of literature, he neglected the "how"; matters of form, style, or structure rarely appeared in his critiques. His own style was execrable; ponderous and involved, it had an unhappy influence on the Russian prose that followed. Even more serious, a kind of blight fell upon Russian literature when it became principally a vehicle for social reform. Art for art's sake rejected, writing lost the fresh exuberance and creative frivolity that had coursed through the work of Pushkin.

Perhaps history's most enduring impression of Belinsky is of his dedication to his chosen work. He had insisted that the writer never permit his talent to become subsidiary, a separate part of his life. His own commitment was given with an energy Alexander Herzen was to remember long after Belinsky's death:

> When he was touched to the quick, when his cherished convictions were challenged, when the muscles of his cheeks began to quiver and his voice trembled, then he was worth seeing. He pounced on his opponent like a panther; he tore him to pieces, made him look ridiculous or pitiful, and incidentally developed his own thought with extraordinary force, with extraordinary poetry. This discussion would often end with blood coming from the sick man's throat; pale, gasping, his eyes fixed upon the man with whom he was speaking, he would lift his handkerchief to his mouth with shaking hand and stop, deeply mortified, crushed by his physical weakness. How I loved and pitied him at those moments!

HERZEN (1812–1870):THE ARISTOCRATIC REBEL

If Herzen's autobiography, in which the portrait of Belinsky appears, had been his only work, literature would be indebted to him for the century's most remarkable memoirs. *My Past and Thoughts*, written between 1853 and 1861, is crowded with colorful impressions of the fulminating mid-century years. There are free-wheeling reports of moods, ideas, conversations, and meetings between the era's most prominent personalities: Nicholas Stankevich, idolized by apostles of German metaphysics in the 1830's; Michael Bakunin, international anarchist; Granovsky, the Hegelian historian; Garibaldi, Carlyle, Mazzini; Michelet, Victor Hugo. But Alexander Herzen, who shared with Belinsky the intellectual leadership of the intelligentsia, left so distinct a mark on Russian political and social thought that his writing tends to be obscured by the power and perseverance of his actions.

Natural son of a wealthy Moscow nobleman, he was sentimentally named (Herzen—"Little heart") in memory of his young German mother. He was spared the erratic education common to his class; his tutors, one a French political exile, the other, a member of the classless intelligentsia, saw to it that he read Pushkin's antiautocracy poems, and in general oriented him toward political and social humanism. At the University of Moscow he was the first to study the French precursors of socialism, and was known for his dialectical fireworks and a vigorous, original interpretation of politics. After a short term in civil service, he was, of course, arrested for holding "revolutionary" opinions. He was exiled to serve in remote provincial towns, once for six months, again for a year.

He attempted to write fiction, and did publish several short stories, and, in 1846, a novel, *Whose Fault?*, which showed the influence of Belinsky. His philosophical articles, far more interesting, defined categorically the differences between Westerner and Slavophil, and revealed a growing hatred of autocracy. As the endless abstractions of the intelligentsia's debates began to pall, Herzen's longing to see the "development of philosophy into life" surged. Stifled by the compulsory inaction of his circle, he identified hope with the revolutionary currents then flooding Western Europe. In 1846, he inherited his father's large fortune, and after great difficulty, obtained a passport. On the eve of the 1848 revolution in France, his two carriages crossed the Russian frontier with his family, retainers, and goods. He entered Paris "as if entering Jerusalem or Holy Rome."

But in May and June of 1848, the bourgeoisie routed the socialist forces in Paris, and France was swiftly reorganized into a Second Empire. It was a blow to Herzen, the heavier for the deaths at sea of his mother and youngest son, and for his wife's love affair with a young German poet, her subsequent breakdown, and early death. Then, Herzen saw "life as devastated, crushed at the meeting of two historic worlds." He blamed the bourgeoisie for the destruction of the individual: freedom was enslaved by the compulsive drive for gain. Leaping to the extremes so characteristic of the Russian mind, Herzen came to the conviction that Europe, caught in a materialistic stranglehold, was no longer capable of moral or social rebirth. Indeed, she was destined to a kind of spiritual death. Ivan Karamazov, Dostoyevsky's nineteenth-century hero, was to call Europe a graveyard; and in the twentieth century, Khrushchev was to give grim assurance that Soviets would bury capitalism.

Where, then, pondered Herzen, could social reform be effected? America, young and still uncorrupted, was nevertheless a child of Europe, heir to Anglo-Saxon traditions and prejudices. Only primitive Russia was as yet free: "In our naturalness of peasant life, in our fluid and unorganized economic and judiciary concepts, in our weak sense of property, in the fact that we have no middle class, and in our remarkable ability to assimilate foreign ideas, we have an advantage over those countries that are fully established and exhausted." Could not a man of good will and resolute purpose, working freely as an émigré, stir a sleeping potential and enlist forces for reformation within Russia herself? So Herzen defined his mission. Establishing the Free Russian Press in London, he launched a twenty-three-year campaign of anti-tsarist propaganda that was to baffle the censors.

Two journals provided his ammunition. In 1855, *The Polar Star*, named for the shortlived Decembrist periodical, made its first appearance. Limited to discussion of general issues in Russian government, it was supplemented in 1857 by an even more popular weekly, *Kolokol (The Bell)*, in which specific abuses were detailed. Both were smuggled regularly into Russia and read everywhere, from Moscow to small Siberian outposts. Each week, *Kolokol* made its way to the Tsar, who read it so carefully that when a counterfeit copy was once substituted for an issue implicating several high officials, the Emperor called immediately for the genuine copy. Herzen himself became a legend in Russia.

His purpose was to arouse the independent spirit of the landowners and the initiative of the intelligentsia, in order to develop an articulate body of public opinion committed to peasant reform. His London-based attacks were, as he well knew, perfectly timed. Alexander II had ascended the throne in 1855, when Russia, defeated in the Crimea, was reeling under staggering human and financial losses. Russians of all classes were beginning to see that Nicholas had bequeathed them thirty years of useless regimentation and a monolithic government riddled with corruption and incompetence. Violence, particularly among the restive rural masses, was dangerously near; even the thirty-seven-year-old Alexander, cast in his father's despotic mold, understood that the peasantry must be appeased with some kind of reform measure. "It is better to abolish serfdom from above than wait to have it abolish itself from below," he told the nobility of Moscow in 1856. On February 19, 1861, some two years before Lincoln freed American slaves, Alexander officially abolished serfdom in Russia.

For five years preceding the Great Reform Bill, Herzen urged his Russian readers toward action, tracing Russia's history of failure to secure meaningful social legislation, and drawing a course for emancipation. He counselled the establishment of a decentralized, agrarian communism. The framework for it already existed in the *artel*, a union of tradesmen, and in the village commune, the *mir*, sustained by communally held land and governed by village elders. With the help of European technology, Herzen argued, agriculture and small-scale industries could be strengthened in Russia without creating the urban complexes of the West. Founded on cooperation rather than competition, the *artel* and the *mir* would insure individual freedom and preserve fundamental "humanity"— present primarily, Herzen believed, in Russia's uncorrupted peasantry.

Scattered throughout the twenty-two volumes of his writings, especially in his correspondence with Mazzini, Michelet, and Turgenev, are evaluations of the Russian "muzhik"—his apathy, inefficiency, even his "imbecility"—which belie Herzen's faith in the potential of the Russian common man. His optimism may have sprung from the length and distance of his exile, or his doubts may have vanished when Baron von Haxthausen, a Westphalian agronomist who had made extensive trips throughout Russia, returned to Europe to project peasant communes as an important unit of local government. Or, Herzen may simply have created a peasant mystique to fill the void left by the "setting sun of the West." After 1848, he bent his energies toward the resurrection of his country, hoping, building, promoting in a vacuum, the lot of even the most informed and zealous émigré. The "lure of distance. space, open conflict and free speech" had driven him from Russia. "I was seeking an independent arena," he wrote. "I longed to try my powers in freedom." He was determined that all Russians should do likewise. What he failed to recognize, or willed to disbelieve, was that the Russian serf of the nineteenth century, liberated though he might be, could afford no such luxury of freedom.

The peasant wanted what his leaders had prepared him to expect of the Great Reform Bill: unqualified ownership of his own land, with all the privileges of independent ownership. He received, instead, a second-class citizenship. Free to engage in business, to marry at will, to own property and take action at law, he was yet bound to the village commune, economically dependent upon his master. He was given land—"beggars' allotments," picked from his master's least valuable acreage—less than half of what he had formerly cultivated for his own use. Now, far from owning land privately, he had to yield it to the commune for periodic redistribution; this land was to be redeemed from the landlord by payments extending over forty-nine years. The allotments were poor and small; balanced farming, impossible; the land itself frequently worth only a fraction of the payments made for it. The peasant was ultimately forced to rent his land at whatever price was asked, or work out his redemption payments on his landlord's own estate. Nor were all peasants so fortunate. By 1878, only 50 per cent of the emancipated serfs had received adequate land endowments; the rest barely subsisted. Some four million house serfs, freed without provision of land, became rootless paupers, unable to leave the commune for work elsewhere, save by permission of the *mir* assembly. While passports from the commune might be granted, payment of taxes and debts were still exacted; failure to pay justified flogging. Payment systems were revised, but peasant debts mounted hopelessly. Not until the great revolt in 1905 were they cancelled. Meanwhile, during the last decades of the century, Russian living standards declined apace with the improvements of life in Europe.

The reformers had failed. Their plans for the village commune had not provided for natural increases of the rural population. The *mir*, founded on custom and solidified in tradition, was unable to equip its communities for agricultural improvement. Nor could landowners supply the required methods and means; by mid-century, 43 per cent of them were burdened by heavily mortgaged estates. The reformers had failed to translate theory into workable reality. But the communal plan itself had been based on an error. It had been argued that the *mir* would protect the rights of the peasant, and instead, it had destroyed what little independence he had once possessed; his land belonged to the commune, and his obligation to the commune robbed him of initiative to develop the land.

Herzen soon understood that emancipation had solved few of serfdom's ancient problems. Between 1861 and 1863, *Kolokol* editorials reflected the dismay of the intelligentsia, as the new law was greeted with bitterness, disputation, and violence in village, town, and city courts. But it was beyond the power of an émigré organ to clarify the complex issues of regional life in Russia. The popularity of *Kolokol* declined, then virtually disappeared when fiercely nationalistic Russians read Herzen's articles in support of Polish independence. Herzen closed the

Free Russian Press, moved to Geneva, and published *Kolokol* only sporadically until his death, in 1870.

RADICALISM ON THE MARCH

Herzen's spectacular fame ended abruptly, but his philosophy of social reform inspired a new commitment to the success of the peasant commune. The intelligentsia of the 1860's and '70's shared his belief that Western democracies were an urban phenomenon; irrelevant to agrarian Russia, they were to be distrusted. Socialist doctrines could be imposed only through revolution, and revolution could be effected only by "going to the people." Thus, *v narod* ("to the people") became the battlecry of the *Narodniki* (Populists), whose crusade to educate the common people for revolution is one of the most extravagantly idealistic of modern times.

Alexander II unwittingly created the movement. When protests and demonstrations erupted after the emancipation, the government responded, predictably, with mass arrests, exiles, and imprisonments. When a single student, inspired to independent revolt, shot at the emperor in 1866, schools and universities were once more purged of sedition; discipline was intensified, inspections tightened, expulsions increased. The intellectual climate of the 1830's and '40's returned as great numbers of young men and women, cut off from professional careers, were forced into penury and idleness.

Unlike their predecessors, the new intelligentsia scorned the lofty aesthetics of Schelling and Fichte. Saturated in the writings of Chernyshevsky and Dobrolyubov, champions of the natural sciences, they were, to a man, utilitarians, pragmatic activists. They conceived a way to transform Russian society. Some two thousand young Russians were enlisted: students (among them, women who had met revolutionary exiles abroad, while seeking the medical education denied them at home), repentant noblemen trying to "expiate the sin of serfdom," teachers, emancipated officials of the lower ranks. Singly and in groups, these volunteers set out to teach the gospel of social revolution to the Russian masses.

They put on peasant dress, shared the wretched lodgings and poor food of the lowest mill and field workers; the success of their mission depended on establishing a common meeting ground. They had gone prepared with illegally printed pamphlets expounding the theories of such socialists as Proudhon, Lassalle, Lavrov, and Louis Blanc. Their language as well as their ideas were incomprehensible to the peasants. By the end of the "mad summer" of 1874, when hundreds of the intelligentsia had flocked to help victims of famine in the Volga region, more than fifteen hundred of the young volunteers were in the hands of the police, many of them betrayed by suspicious, resentful peasants.

The failure of the venture convinced a more radical element of the intelligentsia that autocracy could be overthrown only by a secret organization whose spies were trained to terrorize. Such an organization was formed under the name "Land and Liberty," its purpose molded by the writings of the anarchist Michael Bakunin, a former collaborator of Herzen's and a professional promoter of revolutions. So successful was the conspiracy—railroads were dynamited, bombs exploded, and high officials assassinated—that police power, already strengthened to deal with the comparatively peaceful Populists, was redoubled to destroy the Radicals. On both sides, any means for coercion was considered legitimate; the entire level of political life in Russia sank to a depth from which it has not yet recovered.

In March, 1881, the terrorist goal was reached. A bomb was thrown into Alexander's carriage, and the "Liberator Tsar" was dead. Victory was short-lived. The conspirators had not foreseen the accession of the reactionary Alexander III. The revolution they had anticipated was not to come until 1917.

THE LITERATURE OF RADICAL REFORM

Two men emerged as codifiers of radical thought in the nineteenth century: Nikolay Chernyshevsky (1828–1899), and Nikolay Dobrolyubov (1836–1861). Both were influenced by Herzen, and like him, both were steeped in the literature of French socialism. Unlike the aristocratic Herzen, however, both came from provincial, ecclesiastical stock. They had become atheists, yet each retained an ascetic, somewhat puritan temperament, a quality that was to distinguish Populist leaders. Men of their age, in sympathy with advancing scientific materialism, they were to fill their programs for reform with the utilitarian concepts of John Stuart Mill and Jeremy Bentham. Chernyshevsky was by far the more profound thinker of the two. A scholar, he drew upon an encyclopedic knowledge of history, economics, and philosophy for his plan of reform through the peasant commune. Like others before him, he cloaked his revolutionary ideas in literary criticism, and as chief critic for the *Contemporary* scorned all endeavor that did not emphasize Russia's urgent political needs. Uncompromising by nature and in his beliefs, he was ill-suited to objective analysis of imaginative works of art. In his Master's dissertation (*The Aesthetic Relations of Art and Reality*, written in 1855), he had defined art as handmaiden to civic action, whose duty was to reproduce reality much as a photograph catches a sitter's likeness. Art, he argued, must be literal and practical if it would enrich and improve lives. Chernyshevsky apparently saw no absurdity in his explanation that a marine painting was valuable because it showed the sea to natives of Central Russia who lived too far away to see it for themselves. The pragmatic approach to literature was solidified in his *Studies of the Age of Gogol*, a lengthy survey shot through with scientific and sociological jargon. In it, Chernyshevsky dethroned all writers prior to Belinsky and Gogol; a characteristic review of Turgenev's *Asya*, a poetic story of frustrated love, urged Russians to "forget all these erotic questions! They do not suit today's reader who is absorbed in problems of judiciary and administrative improvement, of financial reform and the abolition of serfdom."

As his influence on the radical intelligentsia grew, Chernyshevsky relinquished his *Contemporary* column to Dobrolyubov, and in 1857 began writing specifically of reform. Expert in literary camouflage though he was, he was finally arrested in 1862. Awaiting judgment in the Fortress of Peter and Paul—he was sentenced to fourteen years of Siberian exile—he wrote a novel, *What is to be Done?* (1863), which was to fire another generation of radical Russian youth. Lenin was to remember the book as a major element in his revolutionary education: "For months I literally lived with Chernyshevsky's heroes. Rakhmetov was my particular favorite. I set myself the goal . . . to be like this irreproachable man." It is precisely the "irreproachableness" of Chernyshevsky's fiercely ascetic hero that gives the book a wooden, dreamlike quality, much like that of a didactic fairy tale without charm or mystery. Rakhmetov tests his endurance by sleeping on a plank studded with nails; he arises "bloodied but happy." Other characters display similar nobility of character, civil purposefulness, and self-sacrifice; one man even feigns suicide so that his wife might marry another whom she truly loves. Chernyshevsky believed that his novel would put the "frivolous fiction" of his day to shame. But *What is to be Done?* is far less a work of serious fiction than a catalogue of the author's favorite causes and ideas. The emancipation of women, the priority of morality over self-interest, cooperation between employer and employee, the doctrine of man's perfectibility—all are affirmed by serene and confident characters, precursors of the positive images in official Soviet fiction, and, more immediately, of Nikolay Dobrolyubov's "new men."

During his brief but highly successful career as a literary critic, Dobrolyubov evaluated literature as an "auxiliary force, whose importance is in its propaganda and whose merit is determined by what it propagates." Like Chernyshevsky, he denied literature the independence and creativity of art; writers were to portray reality, but, insisted Dobrolyubov, only that reality which could be useful to modern Russians. Four of his best known essays, including the often quoted *What is Oblomovism?* decry the purposeless life reflected in the works of Pushkin, Lermontov, Turgenev, and Goncharov. The "superfluous man" had once, perhaps, successfully argued the case for reform in Russia, but the day of his effectiveness was over. Now let literature come forth with a new hero, constructive in his bent for civic affairs. The evangelical call had been sounded by Belinsky, but where Belinsky had urged writers to accept a general burden of reform, Dobrolyubov dictated the very matter of literature. In the creation of a new breed of strong, positive men, he postulated, writers would lead

Russia to her socialist future. Dobrolyubov's youth, his righteous anger, his fidelity to Chernyshevsky's principles endeared him to his readers. His untimely death at twenty-five only strengthened the magnetic appeal of his writings for the radical intelligentsia.

The radical movement in literature was to take one more step toward extremism in the nineteenth century. It remained for Dmitri Pisarev (1840–1868) to reject the arts entirely. Of gentle birth, independently wealthy, Pisarev belonged to that group of postreform nihilists, or, as they called themselves, "thinking realists," dedicated in their disenchantment to the greater glory of natural sciences, skills, and professions. The humanities were dead; aesthetics, literature, classical history were all forms of "sybaritic self-indulgence."

As chief spokesman for this ultimate utilitarian stand, Pisarev granted art a place in Russian life only insofar as it was able to educate a scientifically oriented intelligentsia. It served no other useful purpose, as he sought to prove in his *Destruction of Aesthetics*, articles written while he served a four-year prison term for having printed radical propaganda. Poetry, he wrote, was beneath contempt; it had lulled the best Russian minds. Shakespeare's tragedies were of less value than a pair of boots; boots could, at least, be worn. Pushkin's works, extolled by Belinsky only twenty years before, were now the target of the young critic's most brilliant and vicious attacks. In violent, uncontrolled language, Pisarev—and, indeed, the majority of radical journalists from the 1840's on—was Belinsky's direct heir. Belinsky's coarse language and self-consciously aggressive tone were signs of poor education and breeding, of temper and emotional haste in expression. These traits became trademarks for his tough-minded disciples, who adopted a deliberately crude style as a gesture of defiance against the established order.

What of the creative writers, the new generation endowed with imagination in a day of militant protest literature? In the tumultuous years between 1855 and 1865, Goncharov had published his greatest novel. Turgenev had reached the height of his popularity. Ostrovsky's plays attracted huge audiences to imperial theatres. The younger men, Tolstoy and Dostoyevsky, had already been heard from. Such writers did not tolerate without remonstrances the literary prescriptions of radical critics; the *Contemporary*'s literary gossip page bristled with reports of internecine feuds. With the instinctive distaste of noblemen for all that was not nobility, Turgenev and Tolstoy derided Chernyshevsky for his humble beginnings which so appealed to hordes of socially insecure young radicals. The critic "smelled of bugs," said Tolstoy; he had no manners, and he preached "that to be worthless, nasty and bitter was very beautiful." Chernyshevsky was a snake, said Turgenev, and Dobrolyubov, a rattlesnake. When the younger critic published an irrelevant, inconsequential review of Turgenev's *On the Eve*, the novelist vowed never again to write for the *Contemporary*.

The objections to literature as a textbook for reality were deep-seated and serious. Dostoyevsky, writing in 1861 for the second issue of his own journal, *Vremya*, questioned the validity of Dobrolyubov's utilitarian aesthetic. Writers must, he agreed, champion social causes, but they must be free in the expression of human needs. Russia must recognize the "independent significance of art, the naturalness of this independence, and, therefore, its complete necessity in the cause of social development and consciousness." Turgenev, too, challenged the fundamental justness of radical criticism:

> Every writer who does not lack talent tries his best to give a vivid and true reproduction of impressions obtained from his own life and that of others, and the reader has the right to judge whether he has succeeded or where he has gone wrong; but who has the right to tell him which impressions are of any use to literature, and which aren't?

As members of the intelligentsia, these writers were committed to social progress, to the exposure of social and political abuses. But utilitarian extremes were only trail blazers to the Revolution; they were not to claim Russian literature until after 1917. While the ideologies of the nineteenth century are to be found in the major works of the age of realism, they are interpreted imaginatively by the prominent literary spokesmen of the era, from Gogol to Chekhov.

7 · Nikolay Gogol 1809-1852

Genius of the Comic-Grotesque

OF ALL major Russian writers, Gogol alone stands apart from the mainstream of political ferment which gives continuity to Russian literature. So individual is his work, it is almost by an accident of time that his writing can be considered—as it traditionally has been—with that of the realists who followed him. His stories, novels, and plays are crammed with the minutia of "life as he saw it"; the world he portrays, however, belongs not to mid-century Russia, but to the most Gothic of romantic imaginations. He owed much to the European romanticists of the early nineteenth century, but it is his own psychology that animated his genius, just as it set his limitations.

Gogol first broke into print successfully in 1832 with *Evenings Near the Village of Dikanka*, tales mingling the natural and supernatural elements common to Ukrainian folklore. Against the colorful landscape of the southern steppe, Cossack peasants and the sly, but rarely successful, Devil spar with the animation of a Punch and Judy show. Pushkin praised the gaiety and freshness of the stories, and suddenly Gogol was read everywhere, while everyone wondered who the young author was.

He was born into a family of small Ukrainian landowners, founded like so many of its kind in superficial piety and sentiment. His father, an amateur musician and playwright, suffered mental disorders, and at his premature death, Nikolay was left completely in the care of his mother, who had borne him when she was just fifteen. Emotionally unstable, and

mentally an adolescent, she pampered the boy abnormally.
When he was eleven, intellectually underdeveloped, and emotionally stunted, he was enrolled in the nearest provincial high
school, eighty miles distant, where for eight years he was
taught little, and learned less. He distinguished himself only
for his love of contemporary Russian literature—he copied and
memorized many Pushkin poems—and school theatricals,
where he excelled in mime. Timid, withdrawn, and undersized,
he was nevertheless feared by his schoolmates, who called him
the "mysterious dwarf"; students and teachers alike were the
butt of his sharp epigrams and jokes.

Gogol's extreme secretiveness was apparent even during
his schooldays. His letters to his mother seem consciously and
melodramatically literary, modelled, no doubt, on the mawkish
Karamzinian prose which filled the high-school manuals of the
time, but painfully unnatural from a schoolboy, who wrote as
though trying to conceal his real thoughts in a profusion of
conventional sentiments. Throughout his adolescence, he was
obsessed by the wish to become a great statesman; with the
idealism that was never to leave him, he yearned to be useful
to his country and to the world at large. More, he feared
obscurity and a life mired in trivialities. Immediately upon
graduation, therefore, he set off for St. Petersburg in great
excitement, convinced that fame awaited him there. His
ambitions came to nothing. Neither in the government office
where he endured three miserable months as a junior clerk,
nor in the casting office of the Imperial theater where he was
rejected as an actor, could he surmount the huge indifference
of the city.

Characteristically, Gogol did not envisage writing as a
career. The Ukrainian stories, while they established his success
as a fledgling author, were written solely for money, in a
businesslike venture to capitalize on the current vogue for
Ukrainian songs and Ukrainian literary motifs. Utilizing
materials forwarded to him by his mother—information about
legends, superstitions, songs, customs, and his father's comedies,
some of which had been inspired by Ukrainian puppet shows—
Gogol plunged into the folk art of his home region with all the
nostalgia of an exile. He fashioned stories around the stock

characters of popular village tradition: the suitor, the young girl, the drunken sexton, the blacksmith, the witch, devil, and river nymph. He humanized nature, intensifying its beauty, and recreated the abundance and carefree ease of his childhood years. Inventing little, he built sequences from conventional comic episodes, allowing his folk materials to dictate the content of his stories, now boisterous and brimming with infectious laughter, now eerie or extravagantly lyrical in scenic descriptions. As he wrote, he forgot the loneliness and drab reality of his life in St. Petersburg.

He distrusted his creative ability; writing seemed hardly the grand fulfillment of his idealistic dreams. After a brilliant entry on the literary scene, he was in 1833 still looking for a suitable profession. His study of Ukrainian songs and an adolescent love for Walter Scott's romances prompted his grandiose plan for a multi-volume history of the Ukraine. With this project in mind, he applied for the post of historian at the University of St. Petersburg, and, astoundingly, through the good offices of influential friends, received an appointment to teach medieval history. For one academic year, Gogol tried obstinately to fulfill the assignment for which he had no qualifications. He turned in a performance ludicrous enough to warrant satiric treatment in one of his own stories. After an introductory lecture made up of brilliant generalizations which the "historian" had prudently prepared and memorized, he gave up all pretense at erudition and teaching, missed two lectures out of three, and when he did appear, muttered unintelligibly through his teeth and displayed small photographs of classic monuments. At the final examination, he sat in utter silence with a black handkerchief wrapped around his head, simulating a toothache, while another professor interrogated the students.

Meanwhile, he continued to write, and by 1835, two more volumes dealing with Ukrainian life had appeared. *Taras Bulba,* based on Cossack ballads, is an historical romance of epic scale. The adventurous, brawling Cossacks of the fifteenth century are its heroes—fugitives, robbers, and runaways banded in a mighty military brotherhood to protect their settlements from marauding Turks and Tartars and to defend Russian

Orthodoxy against Catholic Poland. With little regard for historical accuracy, but with a sharp eye for the telling details of manners, customs, and dress, Gogol exalted the toughness and zest of his bandit ancestors with a rhetoric to match their own savage vitality. For the first time since the *Lay of the Host of Igor*, a Homeric mood touched Russian literature, and with it, to the delight of Gogol's Slavophil readers, came the first literary expression of Russia's messianic role in history that was later to obsess Dostoyevsky. On the eve of a battle (which is ultimately lost), Taras speaks to his men: "Let us first drink to our holy Russian Orthodox faith and to that time when it will spread everywhere and become the only faith."

The novel lacks balance in composition, and battle scenes are needlessly repetitive, but of all its weaknesses, the most glaring occur, as they did in *Evenings on the Farm*, in scenes between young lovers. Gogol, who apparently had never been intimate with a woman, seemed incapable of writing about one. His young heroines all possess the same doll-like beauty—egg-shaped face, black hair, flashing eyes—as though he had learned a formula to apply whenever necessary. Old or aging females appear in his stories, but his only other concept of woman seems based on atavistic fear. In a powerful story called *Viy*, a voluptuous vampire-witch pursues a seminarist from Kiev across a darkening field, and her frightful vengeance is the climax of steadily mounting horror.

The more conventional life of squiredom in Southern Russia fills *Old-World Landowners* and *The Story of How Ivan Ivanovich Quarrelled with Ivan Nikiforovich*. In the first, a kind of idyll on vegetation, an aging couple spend pleasantly indolent, uneventful days in a succession of succulent meals which Gogol describes with indulgent, sentimental affection. The second is a tale of irony. Two bosom friends, feuding over a trifle, spend their lives and fortunes in litigations against each other.

Had he written nothing more, Gogol would have emerged in history as a middling writer of regional interest. Even his St. Petersburg stories, 1831–1835 (*The Portrait, Nevsky Prospect, The Carriage, The Diary of a Madman*), are but trial balloons. Indicating little of his great work to come, they are

interesting largely for their illumination of Gogol's inchoate
tensions and psychological distress, which, in the dismally "wet,
gray, foggy" climate of the capital, he now attempted to ex-
ternalize in fiction. *The Portrait* and *Nevsky Prospect*, the two
most conventionally romantic and humorless of the group,
represent a search, in the one, for a definition of true art, in
the other, for the ideal of happiness in love. *Diary of a Madman*
reads somewhat uncomfortably like a tape recording of gradual
mental collapse, but resurges into the grotesque perspective
which was to be the hallmark of Gogol's mature work. Influenced strongly by the tortuous tales of E. T. A. Hoffmann,
then very popular in Russia, Gogol endows his madman with
the matter-of-fact ability to understand the language of dogs,
hence to read a peculiarly informative canine correspondence.
Uncannily, the madman's last feverish mutterings, with which
the story ends, foreshadow Gogol's own last delirious words.
The muffled ending of *The Carriage*, more ironical and de-
tached than the rest, suggests something of the author's
identification with the main character, a braggart and pretender.

The Nose, of the same period and first published in Pushkin's *Contemporary*, is a gem apart. Absurd, depressing, and
extraordinarily funny, it has been explained as being everything,
from a castration fantasy to a straight dream sequence or a
fanciful extension of any of the hundred "nose" jokes current
in popular Russian humor. It is simply "genuine grotesque,"
Gogolian style, in which a man, waking noseless one morning,
sets out to recover it with all the workaday nonchalance of
any errand runner. The nose is at last returned in ordinary
shape and size, but not before it has descended from a carriage
in the splendid uniform of a state councilor, and snubbed
its owner.

Obviously contrived elements of fantasy in these stories
recall similar devices used by Western writers of the Gothic
school, particularly Victor Hugo and the Englishman Maturin.
Gogol borrowed from the German Romantics Tieck and Hoffmann as well, but it is to Pushkin, with whom he associated
closely during the major period (1830–1837) of his most
productive years, that he is principally indebted. It was Pushkin
who urged the younger man to develop the most conspicuous

feature of his work, a remarkable exploitation of trivia. When Gogol dropped, for once, his posturing and reserve to ask for advice and criticism, Pushkin opened to him the worlds of Shakespeare, Cervantes, and Dante. And Pushkin suggested the basic plots for two of the three works, unsurpassed in Western literature, on which Gogol's reputation as the master of grotesque comedy rests: *The Inspector General, Dead Souls,* and *The Overcoat.*

Not of the self-starting variety, Gogol's genius for story-telling relied upon some external stimulus. Given a ready-made plot—a vignette, an anecdote, a reminiscence—he could, in the fashion of a master puppeteer, build a story, animate a cast of characters. His gift for satire, however, was an integral part of his psyche. His characters develop not from any objective observation of real people living real lives, but, if we are to believe his own words, from his own distorted view of reality. Thus, while they are furnished with the paraphernalia of real life, they never partake of genuinely ordinary experience, and none are truly "normal" human beings. An unusually keen observer and avid collector of minutia, Gogol constructed them out of quantities of apparently irrelevant detail, all of it bizarre, and in cumulative effect, devastatingly revealing. His fund of such "useless" information seems inexhaustible, his use of it as natural to him as his urchinlike view of humanity. Once, waiting for a change of horses at a station master's house, Gogol and his friend Obolensky passed the time by leafing idly through the travellers' book of complaints. When Obolensky read one amusing comment aloud, Gogol asked, "Have you any idea of this man's character, habits, occupation?" "Of course not," replied the other. "Well, let me describe him to you," said Gogol, and within minutes, while Obolensky held his sides with laughter, Gogol brought the unknown stranger to life, his appearance, family, habits, and hobbies limned in a spontaneous sequence of slyly significant detail.

When Gogol begged Pushkin to suggest "something, any-thing, that I can make into a play, and I promise to drench it with laughter," the poet recalled that as he once travelled through Nizhni-Novgorod, he had been mistaken for a govern-ment inspector sent from the capital to check on municipal activities. Gogol exploited the comic possibilities of the incident to their fullest in *The Inspector General* (1836). He envisioned the complacent officials of a small provincial town routed from lethargy by the news that an inspector, travelling incognito, is about to pay them a visit. Khlestakov, an irresponsible young braggart stopping at a local inn, is mistaken for the inspector, a role he fills expansively in order to collect huge bribes before he is unmasked by the arrival of the real *revizor*. The curtain falls on a scene identical to the first, the officials again thrown into panic by a castastrophe about to repeat itself. The play rocks with hilarity as Gogol exposes the disorder of town affairs. The worried mayor advises each of his subordinates to reform his own department, and we thereby learn that the porter breeds geese in the vestibule of the court, and that mental patients wander about their wards looking like chimney sweeps and smelling of vodka, left to die unattended because "those who are meant to get better will survive by themselves." The history teacher breaks up classroom chairs to more realistically illustrate the victories of Alexander the Great; and the postmaster habitually unseals letters for diversion's sake, keeping the ones that have pleased him best. Each thieving bureaucrat is caricatured with an individuality and comic depth which even Gogol was not to surpass. The action is tight and circular; what is said and done derives solely from the anticipated arrival of the inspector. Scenes move exuberantly through thickets of comedy, yet the world of the play is a static one, befitting a satirical exposure in which people and states of affairs must remain basically unchanged.

The harebrained Khlestakov (from the Russian verb, "to lash with a whip") is *The Inspector General*'s most memorable character. All sound without substance, foppish, frivolous, feckless, he is one of the most spontaneous and unconscious liars of all time, and possibly Gogol's greatest creation. "There is something of Khlestakov in me," he once said, and indeed, Khlestakov does display Gogol's self-intoxicating gift for outrageous fabrication. In Russian theater's best known satirical monologue, Khlestakov, in his cups, spellbinds the provincials as he spins image out of image to summon the glories of his life in the capital:

"O, Petersburg! What a life it is, truly!—I can't begin going
out anywhere without the people saying, 'There goes Ivan
Alexandrovich!' I know all the pretty actresses. And literary
chaps. Pushkin and I are buddies. I often say to him, 'Well,
how goes, Push, old boy?' And he answers, 'O, just about as
usual.' Great character.—I contribute to all the magazines.
Besides, I've written many works: *The Marriage of Figaro,
Robert the Devil, Norma.* . . .—And the balls! Beyond description. A watermelon, for example—a seven-hundred-ruble
watermelon. Soup delivered by boat right out of Paris; you
open the tureen cover and such steam comes out as you can't
find anywhere else.—The Minister of Foreign Affairs, the
French Ambassador, the English and German Ambassadors
and I—we've formed a whist club.—My director's post was
vacant. So there was nothing to do, they gave it to me. And
along the streets dashed messengers. They sent me messengers
and messengers; imagine, 35,000 of them!—The Council of
State itself is afraid of me.—I drive to the Palace every day.—
Why, tomorrow, I shall be made field-marsh . . ."
(He slides to the floor, sprawling, but respectful officials hold
him up.)

By some miracle, chiefly the cunning of Gogol's admirer,
the poet Zhukovsky, and other friends at court, *The Inspector
General* was first read not by the censor, but by Nicholas himself. The Tsar not only allowed its appearance on the Imperial
stage, but, laughing heartily at the *première*, declared that
"Everyone got his innings, and I most of all." While the
comedy caused a great stir, and each performance played to
standing room only, it received blistering criticism from St.
Petersburg officialdom and the conservative press. Some called
it an unpatriotic, cynical piece which undermined the bureaucracy. Others were indignant at the lack of positive characters;
still others, incensed by the missing love interest. But among
the liberals, the author was a hero; never before had the corruption of tsarist institutions been exposed so cunningly and
so adroitly.

Gogol himself, who harbored nothing but deep veneration
for the person of the Emperor, and yearned only for greater
prominence among the literary conservatives, could not understand why his little comedy that he had tried to make as funny
as possible had provoked a storm of political dissent. Convinced that he was being persecuted beyond endurance, he

determined to leave the country where his first direct contact
with the Russian people had been so misunderstood. Without
a farewell to even his most influential admirers he embarked for
Western Europe in 1836, and returned to Russia only twice
during his twelve years abroad. It was in Rome that he completed his major work, *Dead Souls*.

Again, it was Pushkin who suggested the plot for this
comic epic, in which a con-man sells not the Brooklyn Bridge,
but the names of those no longer among the living. Because
the Russian population was counted only once a decade, landlords were required to pay poll taxes for any male "souls" (as
serfs were then called) who may have died between visits from
the census taker. A clever swindler could easily purchase such
"dead souls," register their settlement on distant prairies estates,
and then mortgage the estates at the State Landlord's bank.
To conduct this traffic in corpses, Gogol created Chichikov, a
most respectable, if needy, nobleman, whose knowledgeable and
ingratiating ways with tax-burdened landlords are as smoothly
persuasive as any modern huckster's. His partners in fraud are,
likewise, prototypes. Who has not known such a man as Manilov, flaccid and sentimental, a procrastinator who, with a
blondly vacuous look, gives gentle, halting expression to soulful
inanities? Or a massively built Sobakevich, brutish and coarse-
grained, whose opaque, unwinking stare halts the liveliest
chatter? Or a shrewd, wizened widow, Korobochka, her brain
stuffed only with petty husbandry until the chance of a bargain
transforms it into a human computer. Or a Nozdrev, bully and
cheat, shudderingly recognizable as the boisterous "life of the
party." Or a Plyushkin, a half-starved hermit whose door is
locked against the theft of a half-a-million in yellowed bank-
notes beneath the floor, while reports of his death crop up regularly in quarter-column obituaries.

Larger than life, their eccentricities magnified to nightmare proportions, the characters of *Dead Souls* might seem the
more terrifying for their appearance against the background of
an ordinary Russian provincial town of the 1830's. But when
Gogol has done with them, they become huge explosions of his
comic-grotesque imagination, reduced to the ridiculous by his
abrasive malice and the hilarious quality of his satirical genius.

In the usual way of storytelling, inanimate objects are subordinated to people, a normal, "sane" emphasis which disappears in Gogolian composition. Here, the narrative sequence is broken again and again by incongruous catalogues of *things*, a profusion of objects which seem to be endowed with the life of their owners. The latter in turn begin to assume the shape and nature of their possessions. Objects become living symbols of persons, and people become less human.

So persuasive is this rearrangement of the habitual order of reality that we are not sure, for example, whether we remember Sobakevich, a heavy bear of a man, or his "pot-bellied, walnut bureau on four huge legs, a perfect bear of a bureau" which seems to imply that it, too, is Sobakevich. Not Manilov, but his chairs seem more real to us; all but two are upholstered in expensive silk, and they, in plain buckram, wait eternally to be covered. Of Manilov's face, all that remains is the languid kiss he gives his wife, one lasting fully as long as it takes to smoke to the end a small cigar. Nozdrev, with his incessant, scatter-brained chatter, is a personification of his own hurdy-gurdy; as though something had gone wrong inside, it plays a mixture of mazurkas, marches, and waltzes long after it has run down. The process reverses itself when Gogol speaks of a young woman who, wearing a patterned shawl, takes her place self-effacingly at mealtimes: "There are faces that are there not as primary objects, but just to be foreign dots or spots upon objects. They always sit in the same way and on the same seat, and you might consider them as furniture. . . ." Or again, a girl of eleven is distinguished only by the mud on her bare feet, which, from a distance, look as though she had shoes on.

Every moment of Chichikov's skullduggery is enriched with the most virulent of details. No rogue or charlatan, gossip or government clerk, is spared Gogolian embellishment: here, a wheezy breathing, a rash of blackheads, a left eye always winking; there, a pointed paunch, a special odor, a mass of pockmarks. No person or object escapes, not even the restful, two-ruble-a-day bedroom "with cockroaches peeking out of each corner like so many glossy black plums." As though these touches of startlingly unsavory realism were not hypnotizing enough, Gogol treats us to yet another set of peripheral details.

These burst into the narrative with an irrepressible life of their own. Quite independent of Chichikov's adventures, they illuminate in a flash people who never appear, who have no relation to the story, yet who live for an instant in a bright marginal reality.

Such parenthetical characters appear in *The Inspector General* as well. There, for example, we learn from a letter of Sister Anne's brother "who has grown very fat but still plays the violin." Or, while the police sergeant explains why the main street is not patrolled, we hear irrelevantly that Prohorov, just brought in from the suburbs where he was sent to break up a brawl, got drunk himself, was doused with two buckets of water, but has not yet come to. In *Dead Souls*, where there is little dialogue, such "never-again" personalities are not so simply introduced. They appear instead under the guise of similes, taking on momentary life as the subjects of subordinate clauses. Here is a superb instance of this literary tour de force:

> And suddenly, a warm ray glided over the wooden features, a ray that expressed not exactly feeling, but the reflection of feeling somewhat like that of the unexpected sight on the water's surface of a drowning man which evokes a joyous shout from the crowd gathered on the bank; but his brothers and sisters who now throw a rope hoping that the man's back or his arms worn out with the struggle would re-appear, are waiting in vain: he had come up for the last time. It is over, and even more fearful and desolate becomes the sight of the irresponsible elements now that the water is calm again. So did Plyushkin's face, after the momentary glimmer of feeling on it, become more insensible and vulgar than ever.

The eloquence of this passage, although instantly apprehended by educated Russians, is a challenge to the translator. Gogol's prose contains no middle style. His so-called "lyrical" digressions from storytelling are a kind of travesty of romantic rhetoric, declamatory asides borrowed, perhaps, from *Eugene Onegin* or the rambling discourses of *Tristram Shandy*. In contrast, the originality of his narrative language is explosive. Written in the pattern of popular speech, where broken sentences play havoc with syntax, it is pungent with colloquial idiom, diminutives, personalized endings, nicknames, and preposterous family names. The whole effect rests on an intricate system of assonance, words brought together for their auditory appeal, as though Gogol wished to saturate the page with the phonal variations in which the Russian language is so rich. His prose, read aloud, only gains in power and comicality.

When Pushkin heard Gogol read the first chapter of *Dead Souls*, he at first laughed, then exclaimed gloomily, "God, what a sad country Russia is!" Taken aback, Gogol protested that the caricatures were only fancies, outpourings of his own unhealthy imagination. The Symbolist writers and critics of the early twentieth century agreed; they saw Gogol's heroes as "hollow men," automatons whirling in a vacuum, attached neither to time nor place. But in his own day, Gogol was thought to be a passionate social reformer. Prescriptive critics were eager to find that truly great talent which would also be a national conscience, and in Gogol's satires, they detected not only the originality they sought, but the picture of corrupted power they were sworn to defeat. Accordingly, Gogol's works were, in Belinsky's words, acclaimed "to the highest degree, a genuine portrayal of Russian reality," and Gogol himself was hailed "the founder of the Naturalistic school."

It was a tragic overstatement, a reputation made by critics rather than by achievement. Gogol remained mentally and emotionally immature to the end, unaware of the political movements which were changing Western Europe during his years abroad, and indifferent to or uncomprehending of the social unrest in his own country. In Rome, where he knew nothing of Pope Gregory XVI's despotic rule, he plunged into religious experience for relief from the frustrations and insecurity he had tried to exorcise in his writing. In the role of spiritual advisor, he counselled his friends in well-meant platitudes to respect autocracy, orthodoxy, serfdom, publishing in 1847 *Select Passages from a Correspondence with Friends*. He provoked only furious accusations, and when Belinsky branded him "champion of the knout, defender of ignorance and the darkest oppression," Gogol almost broke. Religion became his main support, and he conceived a second part to *Dead Souls*, in which Chichikov would be regenerated and "positive" heroes would convey his message of salvation for Russia. It was to be "leviathan, the biggest work I have ever done," and for the rest of his life, Gogol labored to complete it.

The few extant chapters, found among his papers, testify to the moralist's murder of the satirist. The now virtuous landlords are far from convicing, and Chichikov argues ineffectually for Christian temperance in the face of Russia's political and social needs. In despair, Gogol tried to revive his ebbing creative powers with fasting and prayer, even making a vain pilgrimage to Jerusalem, where "it rained and was as uncomfortable as in Russian stage coaches in the winter." Physically ill, in an anguish of self-doubt, he returned at last to Moscow, burned his new manuscript for *Dead Souls*, and, refusing food and medication, died in a prolonged delirium.

Nowhere have we a better glimpse of Gogol's troubled mind than in his last and most famous short story, *The Overcoat* (1842), subject of many a controversial interpretation. Gogol had heard of a government clerk who, on his first day of hunting, lost the new gun he had purchased with the painfully saved earnings of several years. So ill did the clerk become that his colleagues, fearing for his life, pooled their resources to buy him another. The hero of Gogol's story is just such a government underling, balding and liverish, a poorly paid copyist of documents, who only after long privation is able to buy a new overcoat. On the very first day he wears it, it is stolen from his back, and his frantic search for it yields only the brutal indifference of the high official he begs for help. He dies, finally, of the cold, but his ghost returns to haunt St. Petersburg streets, snatching overcoats from terrified pedestrians, until, finding the offensive official, he snatches his, then disappears forever.

With characteristic mockery, Gogol gives his hero the absurd name of Akaky Akakyevich ("akaky," a child's word for excrement), describing him and his surroundings in the accents of grotesque comedy so familiar in his other work. The focus then changes, however; the external world recedes as the private, solitary world of the copyist takes shape. Completely absorbed in his job, Akaky takes his copy work home to spend happy evenings in the making of capital and lower-case letters. In the morning, he wakes content to know that he will soon be at his desk again, with inkwell and pens. He is at first frightened by the sacrifices a new overcoat will require, but, gradually captivated by the idea, he saves each kopeck with the rapture of a bridegroom approaching his wedding. Every trifle assumes monumental importance in so diminutive a world, a world shining with a pale radiance Akaky is unable to see elsewhere.

The story afforded Gogol rich opportunity for satire, and it is hardly surprising that he should have once more had the role of social critic thrust upon him. Speaking of his own literary generation, Dostoyevsky wrote, "We have all come out of Gogol's overcoat." He saw the story as an indictment of Russian bureaucracy in which a clerk could be less than the uncials he drew with such care, and his interpretation inspired a vogue for humanitarian fiction about downtrodden "little men," of which his own *Poor People* is a magnificent example.

But while *The Overcoat* is justly regarded as one of the world's masterpieces, it does not, any more than Gogol's other work, exemplify the author's concern for humankind. Like Akaky, Gogol could not adapt himself to the exigencies of real life. While he longed to play a great role in the world's affairs, his aspirations were vague, colored by the conventionally romantic fancies of his youth. Meeting disappointment, he understood it only as a thwarting of his "great potentials"; he discounted his genius for grotesque comedy as a hindrance to "real" accomplishment. Mistrusting people, he was wooden in his personal contacts, yet wrote about himself obsessively in high-strung, melodramatic letters to friends. He understood neither himself nor the world, which seemed ever out of sympathy with his innermost desires. In nothing could he find fulfillment—even his enjoyment of the rich dumpling-and-pancake fare of his native Ukraine had to be spoiled by constant and severe indigestion. Like Akaky, he retreated to his own world, and, like Akaky's ghost, took his revenge by stripping the real world of all but its ugliest aspects. The evidence of both his psychological illness and his intellectual limitations is too strong to suppose that he wrote for any purpose of reform. All of his work must be considered as a record of life as he saw it, a grotesque observance of reality, and *The Overcoat* may be taken as an exposé of his own secretive, inner-directed world.

8 · The Realists

With Gogol's departure from the literary scene, the romantic elements that had dominated Russian writing since the beginning of the century began to disappear. It was as though Gogol had wrung Gothic literature dry, so skillful had been his use of its techniques. Horror and fantasy, the melodramatic, the grotesque and the exotic intrigued Russian writers no longer; even the sentimental philanthropy of fiction inspired by *The Overcoat*, and encouraged by the popularity of Dickens and George Sand, withered before a more compelling line of thought. Gogol's successors wished to express the whole man, not merely his misfortunes or his eccentricities, and heart-wringing stories of the "little people" vanished in more sober statements of sympathy for the underprivileged.

Novelists like Goncharov, Turgenev, and Tolstoy are responsible for the unique literary phenomenon which is Russia's major contribution to the international world of letters—the Russian Age of Realism. Direct heirs to Pushkin's lucid, life-loving realism, they owed little to Gogol. In the Russian tradition, they subordinated plot to character in their works, but in their development of introspective character, they predated the analyses of Proust and Joyce. Unlike Gogol, they were very much aware of the vital issues of the day; their stories were deeply serious, filled with the exciting interplay of social and political ideas. Eager to approximate the tone and color of reality, they shunned the exaggerations of Gogolian style and wrote a clear, low-keyed prose in the manner of Pushkin's last period.

Yet Gogol's influence upon the new literature, though narrow and precise, was nonetheless pervasive. Like a botanist who reveals "new" sights in a familiar garden, Gogol taught his successors the art of seeing and using to advantage the trivia of the ordinary world—details of size and shape, manner and dress, gesture and expression. He likewise enlarged the scope of fiction by his use of subjects previously taboo—the unsavory smells, undignified sights and sounds of daily life. Finally, his *Old-World Landowners* was responsible for the semisatirical, semiaffectionate tone which persisted in later descriptions of the indolent, "vegetable" life of rural Russia.

GONCHAROV (1812–1891)

Of all the realists, Ivan Goncharov most resembles Gogol in his treatment of the landed gentry's comfortable somnolence. His native town, Simbirsk, was, in his words, a "complete picture of sleep and stagnation." The son of a prosperous grain merchant, he was not reared in the manor tradition, but had ample opportunity to learn all he needed to know of irresponsible ease on his godfather's country estate. Ilya Oblomov, pampered and overprotected, is the product of this unruffled, patriarchal existence, and the hero of the novel which places Goncharov among the masters of Russian realism.

During thirty-four uneventful years of civil service in St. Petersburg, Goncharov produced three novels, all concerned with the conflict between a young nobleman's temperament and his aspirations for a career. In *An Ordinary Story* (1847), the young man arrives in the capital with the usual romantic baggage of literary ambition and dreams of idealistic love. Under the tutelage of his pragmatic and successful uncle, he is gradually transformed into as self-satisfied and calculating a bureaucrat as his mentor. Raysky, hero of *The Ravine* (1869), is also a spoiled young provincial, who has vowed to become an artist. He struggles in vain, however, to overcome an inherent passivity and lack of self-discipline which finally condemn him to the life of an amateur in the arts.

In *Oblomov* (1859), Goncharov reaches the height of his

talent for character portrayal. Faced with the impersonal regimentation of government service, and the competitive social bustle of the big city, Ilya rejects the easy solutions which would have made his another "ordinary story." Instead of joining the bureaucrats, or fleeing to his beloved village, Oblomovka, Ilya remains staunchly, authentically, and abundantly himself, a character evolving into full realization of what he is. Tranquil to a fault, he is moved neither by the allure of travel nor by his friend Stolz's practical suggestion that he seek constructive work. Neither the love of a charming and intelligent girl, nor his landlord's eviction notice ruffle his calm, and his passive equanimity is secure when an adoring landlady, whom he eventually marries, arrives at a propitious moment to guarantee him living quarters and innumerable creature comforts. Reclining on a comfortable sofa, in a comfortable dressing gown, indulging in rosy reveries when he is not at meals or sleeping, Oblomov is the triumph of inaction over action. His consistent, pillow-like resistance to will dissolves all sense of purpose in him, leaving only indolence in slow motion. The first sixty pages of the book describe solely how he rises from bed in the morning.

When *Oblomov* was published, the radical critic Dobrolyubov turned it into a bestseller overnight by asking, and answering, his famous question, "What is Oblomovism?" With Belinsky's mania for discovering stark realism and social criticism in imaginative writing, Dobrolyubov saw in Goncharov's novel the end of the line of "superfluous men" like Pushkin's Onegin, Lermontov's Pechorin, and Gogol's Manilov. "Oblomovitis," symbolized by Ilya's dressing gown, he diagnosed as an endemically Russian disease. Its symptoms were chronic inertia, intellectual torpor, failing initiative, and lack of know-how, all induced by the evils of serfdom and the decadent manor life, which had, as Karamzin had early foreseen, infected Russia's middle and upper classes.

Within the wider context of universal fiction, "Oblomovism" continues to fascinate modern readers for its Utopian image of endless, languorous hours, free of frustration and trouble. Yet while Goncharov writes only sympathetically of Ilya, so objective is the cumulative effect of his novel that we come to see that too high a price is paid for this "ideal" existence. Likable, intelligent, friendly, and just, Oblomov nevertheless deliberately absents himself from the main current of society's affairs. He is drained of vitality, admits that he has become a "threadbare, old, worn-out coat," a man in whom "light has been imprisoned and has now gone out." He fully earns the meaning of his name, derived from the word "oblomok," a truncated hulk.

Stylistically, Oblomov contains much that was to typify the writing of the realistic school. Plot is secondary to psychological analysis and introspection. Ilya's personality unfolds gradually, his background, habits, and propensities disclosed little by little. A clear, unhurried prose enhances the sense of character evolution, as does Goncharov's clever and frequent use of revealing detail. Finally, for the first time since Pushkin, women are forcefully drawn and become interesting in their own right, not only in juxtaposition to male characters. In this, Goncharov approaches the achievement of his younger contemporary, Ivan Turgenev, by far the more prolific writer, and a very much greater one.

TURGENEV (1818–1883)

It is a nice psychological question whether the matriarchal tyranny that hung over Turgenev's formative years was not at least partially responsible for the gallery of pure, morally courageous, constructive young women known as "Turgenev heroines" who are his most vivid creations.

Ivan's father, a former cavalry officer, handsome, a rake, and a weakling of a man, married an extremely wealthy, unlovely heiress to whom he was consistently unfaithful. Already scarred by an unhappy childhood, Ivan's mother developed into a monster of ill-temper and willfulness, channelling her bitterness into unbridled cruelty and sadism. Her serfs were flogged or sent into forced labor, her children were beaten for the slightest misdemeanor, and her entire household lived in lively fear of her capricious and hysterical rages. She was, at the same time, a most cultured woman, who read widely in three literatures and maintained a private theater and a serf orchestra. She saw to it that her sons received an excellent early education before they were sent to the University of St. Petersburg where, as befitted their ancient and honorable name, they were to train for brilliant careers in public service.

After taking his degree in 1838, Turgenev spent three years at the University of Berlin, the fount of Hegelian philosophy, and there fell in love with the ways of European life. He met Nikolay Stankevich, apostle of German idealism, Michael Bakunin, Timothy Granovsky, and Belinsky, all then mobilizing the progressive liberalism of the forties. Turgenev became their disciple, and an ardent ally of the West.

In 1843, when publication of a long narrative poem, *Parasha,* and several shorter poems had brought him some acclaim, he gave up his job at the Ministry of the Interior for full-time writing, thereby severing his already strained relations with his mother, who punished her "literary Bohemian of a son" by cutting off his allowance. When she died in 1850, Turgenev came into a large fortune and was freed at last from parental persecution. But it was apparently not in his pliable, indecisive nature to crave emotional independence: by the time of his mother's death, he was already inextricably involved with another woman, who was to dominate his personal life for the next forty years. In 1847, the young poet fell in love with the internationally famous Spanish diva, Pauline Garcia, a striking woman whose dark strong face was very much like his mother's. She was married to Louis Viardot, a Frenchman twenty years her senior, who directed the Italian Theatre in Paris, and, incidentally, later translated several of Turgenev's novels. Pauline accepted Turgenev's love and devotion; he became a close family friend, and managed to live near or with the Viardot ménage during his visits abroad. For the first twenty years of this ambiguous relationship, he shuttled regularly between Russia and Western Europe, at first living in Moscow for most of the year, but eventually following his new "family" to Baden and Italy. Finally he settled permanently in France and returned home only on pressing matters of business and with increasing reluctance.

The significant year 1847, when Turgenev first felt "compelled" to accompany Pauline Garcia on her tour to Dresden, brought him great professional promise as well. Under

Nekrasov's direction, the *Contemporary* was publishing Turgenev's brief stories, which, when brought out five years later in a volume called *Sportsman's Sketches*, rocketed the young writer from comparative obscurity to blazing political and literary renown. When they appeared, the stories had passed the censor as the harmless jottings of a bird hunter who happened also to describe scenery and casual meetings with the serfs and squires of the author's native country near Orel. As the hunter searches for game, he may seek shelter from the weather in a peasant's hut, or spend a night at some manor house, but always he records a conversation held or overheard. In the motley confusion of these disconnected episodes, the modern reader is particularly struck by the narrator's extraordinary sensitivity to the landscape of Central Russia. The smells and sounds of its woods and meadows, the changing colors of its vast and moody skies, had never before in Russian prose been painted with such lyrical precision.

Turgenev's contemporaries, however, were stirred by the cumulative persuasion of the sketches. In one after another, peasants, glimpsed in their daily routines, were presented as individual human beings, possessing far greater reserves of dignity, fortitude, compassion, and native intelligence than their brutish masters. In the agitated prereform years, *Sportsman's Sketches* was endorsed as a manifesto against serfdom, and even Alexander II admitted that reading it precipitated his action toward reform.

In this context, Turgenev's name has been linked with that of Harriet Beecher Stowe, but there is very little artistic resemblance between the emotionally charged *Uncle Tom's Cabin* and the quiet realism of the *Sketches*. Matter-of-fact, stripped of pathos, the writing recalls the best of Pushkin's prose, and in at least two of the episodes. *Bezhin Meadow* and *The Singers*, Turgenev intensifies and expands Pushkin's poetic realism. There exists in print no more natural, yet utterly gripping, description than that of the goblin-and-ghost talk of peasant children by a camp fire, heard by the narrator as he pretends to sleep nearby on a dark summer night in Bezhin Meadow. More obviously emotional and crude, but composed in the same easy style and with the same steady naturalness and unerring choice of detail, is the scene at a village pub during a singing match. The grubby customers are at first deeply, tearfully moved by the artistry of the contestants, but later they engage to a man in a wild, drunken brawl which Turgenev describes with relentless realism. Perhaps his greatest single masterpiece, this sketch was rarely discussed in Russia without emphasis on its social implications. Authorities, alarmed by the increasing power of this new literary voice, bided their time, and when Turgenev's 1852 elegy for Gogol was printed in Moscow but censored in St. Petersburg, they seized their opportunity. The young writer was banished to his estate in the provinces, but the eighteen-month exile only enhanced his reputation among progressives.

Between 1856 and 1876, Turgenev wrote seven novels: *Rudin* (1856), *A House of Gentlefolk* (1859), *On the Eve* (1860), *Fathers and Sons* (1862), *Smoke* (1867), *Torrents of Spring* (1872), and *Virgin Soil* (1876). These established his name as one of the three greatest living Russian writers; each novel was eagerly and widely read, and each provoked a storm of critical controversy. In 1860, Turgenev had written an essay, *Hamlet and Don Quixote,* in which he denounced introspective Hamlets like himself in favor of unquestioning, active Don Quixotes, whom he admired. In his novels, he tried to develop a heroic figure who could, with the verve and abandon of a Don Quixote, grapple with the problems of Russian society, who could, once and for all, overcome "poshlost," the complacent mediocrity and moral degeneration of his environment. The intelligentsia grew increasingly hostile; Turgenev's own pessimism deepened, as in novel after novel he failed to construct a positive hero, a true leader. Always, his protagonist is talented, articulate, comparatively free, a man of abundant good will, yet again and again he emerges from the novel's loosely linked scenes (drawing-room conversations, heated arguments, intense self-analysis, and subjective impressions) as a victim of national inertia and his own introspection. Aware of the powerful forces for change gathering around him, he is yet unable to cast his lot with them. Immobile, he stands in passive resistance to authority.

With a skepticism never far from compassion, Turgenev

tests the spiritual capacity and strength of his heroes in their
encounters with love. In these delicately shifting relationships,
framed unfailingly by the gentleness of a Russian summer,
Turgenev is at his best. Now his heroines come into their own,
worthy successors to Pushkin's Tatiana in their depth and
sweetness of character. Aspiring always to a life larger, more
noble than the manorial existence from which they come, they
are far more courageous than the men they love. In *Rudin*,
Turgenev's first and most tautly constructed novel, nineteen-
year-old Natasha falls in love with an eloquent idealist of the
forties whose poetic enthusiasm for active service and individual
freedom has captivated the young people of her mother's
drawing room. But when she offers to run away with him to his
"better" life, Rudin refuses; he loves Natasha with his brain,
not his heart, and his own power of decision, his sincerity and
self-confidence, have been destroyed by his eternal philos-
ophizing. Lavretsky, of *A House of Gentlefolk*—perhaps Turgenev's most poetic prose work—is of somewhat sturdier stuff,
though he lacks the will to escape an unfaithful, calculating
wife. In his yearning to return to his estate and live among the
peasants, there is something of the Slavophil, as there is in Liza,
the deeply religious girl with whom he is momentarily happy.
Lavretsky, unable to make a decision, loses Liza to a convent,
and, in the characteristically muffled ending of a Turgenev
novel, settles to a lonely, disconsolate life.

Yielding to pressure from Russian critics, to whom he was
abnormally sensitive, Turgenev attempted to give his third
novel, *On the Eve*, more "patriotic" significance. Insarov, a
Bulgarian dedicated to the liberation of his country from the
Turks, was to be the activist hero the critics demanded, but,
almost comically, he dies of a lung illness before he can take
part in the struggle. Too woodenly portrayed for belief, Insarov
might have made *On the Eve* Turgenev's least successful novel.
But his Russian sweetheart, Elena, to whom he has bequeathed
his cause, is probably Turgenev's best-realized heroine. Less
naive than Natasha, bolder than Liza, she is passionately idealistic, committed to proving her worth in some wider sphere of
action. She radiates the selfless heroism which countless young
Russian women were to show in the Populist and revolutionary

movements toward the end of the century. Elena is, nevertheless, a shy, romantic young girl. At the moment she learns of
Insarov's love for her and permits her own heart to rise for the
first time, Turgenev gives her one of his great poetic passages:

> "Elena!" cried Insarov . . .
> He held her close and said nothing. There was no need for
> him to tell her that he loved her. From that cry alone, from
> his immediate transformation, from his heaving chest against
> which she pressed herself in utter trust, from the touch of his
> fingertips on her hair, Elena knew that she was loved. He re-
> mained silent and she did not need any words. "He is here, he
> loves me . . . there is nothing more for me to want."

The controversial hero of *Fathers and Sons*, Turgenev's
masterpiece, is the last "strong" man the author attempted.
Written on the eve of the emancipation, the novel was meant
to reflect the conflict between old-generation Russians, content
with traditional institutions, and their progressive sons, clamor-
ing for reform. Eugene Bazarov, a young doctor just out of
medical school, is one of the "new" men, eager to forsake
concepts not in sympathy with the credo of the sixties, scientific
materialism. Calling himself a "nihilist," he submits to no
authority, however venerable, accepts no principle unless proven.
Contemptuous of sentimentalism, he interrupts his genial, old-
fashioned host's quotation from Pushkin to ask for a match.
His wit is dry, his language crude, often obscene, his behavior,
uncouth—the perennial Angry Young Man defying the Establishment. It seemed that Turgenev had at last succeeded in
producing a forceful extrovert rivaling his most stalwart heroines
in integrity and independence. But Bazarov lacks the idealism
which motivated his predecessors and made them, however
precariously or pretentiously, human beings. Free of self-pity
or even temporary despair, drained of the impulse for romantic
love, Bazarov is somewhat less than human, and is conse-
quently incapable of persuading others to adopt his views. He
is incomprehensible to his parents, who adore but fear him. He
startles and shocks an indulgent, idealistic old squire who is
prepared to welcome him as his son's friend. When he offers
his heart to a beautiful, enlightened society woman, he shatters
their relationship by the intransigence of his opinions and the

angularity of his manners. For all his energy, intelligence, and talent, he cannot succeed; like the others before him, he is doomed to inaction by the contradictions of his personality. Turgenev clearly did not know what to do with him. Unable to demonstrate Bazarov's value in some socially significant endeavor, he brings him, like Insarov, to an early, inglorious death, which is accepted with stoicism and dignity.

By the time Turgenev had published *Smoke* and *Torrents of Spring*, it was obvious that he had lost touch with the trends of change in Russia. Radical critics justifiably damned the political discussions in both novels as spasmodic, often irrelevant bits of caricatural journalism. In *Virgin Soil*, his last novel, he attempted to reconstruct the fiasco of the Populist movement, and again misconstrued many actual events. He envisioned clearly, however, the clash between the untrained intelligentsia and the uneducated masses they hoped to help. Nezhdanov, inspired to "go to the people" by the dedicated young woman he loves, suffers bitter despair when efforts to serve meet only cold hostility. He commits suicide, thereby terminating the line of ineffectual progressives whose fate, like Russia's at that time, was to move, grow, gesticulate, and promise—then withdraw, futilely, inward. As in the earlier novels, a subordinate character succeeds on a less ambitious level where the hero has died trying. In *Virgin Soil*, it is Solomin, representative of the dawning industrial age, who elucidates the cause of Nezhdanov's failure. A successful factory manager who speaks little and accomplishes much, Solomin, like Stolz in *Oblomov*, echoes Turgenev's own moderate belief that political reconstruction and economic reform would be achieved through persistence, clear-headedness, and hard work.

Their political burden aside, both *Smoke* and *Torrents of Spring* explore a young man's fatal attraction to a beautiful and cruel older woman. In intensity of emotional experience, they recall Turgenev's great novellas of an earlier period, *Asya* (1858) and *First Love* (1860). The lovers, locked in a baffling and destructive affair, move in the rarified world of pure passion where renunciation and return are compulsive. Drawn with tenderness and irony, the relationships end in tragedy, the heroes victimized by less reputable beauties than those who aroused not the sexual desires but the idealistic aspirations of the Rudins and Lavretskys. Nonfulfillment is the leitmotif of all Turgenev's work, and even in *First Love*—supposedly based on his father's affair with a lovely neighbor—sexual gratification is only implied; it is the suggestion of a jealous sixteen-year-old through whose eyes the episode is reported.

This "evasion" of direct narration lends further detachment to Turgenev's already objective style. His writing is quiet, as lacking in vigor as the pastoral Russian landscape and listless manor life which fill his pages. His themes are repetitious, and his characters enter and exit with monotonous similarity, introduced with brief but exhaustive biographies, and are then disposed of neatly, no questions about their futures left unanswered. His language, as highly polished as Pushkin's, reads easily and naturally as the educated idiom of his class, but is, in fact, highly stylized. As he lay dying of a spinal cancer, Turgenev dictated a story to Madame Viardot in one or another of the three languages she knew best, now in French, now in German, now in Italian. When she suggested that he dictate in Russian to someone who knew that language, he replied that he was too ill to choose every word and expression in his own tongue.

Leisurely and flaccid, his prose evokes faultlessly both a period and a people. Indeed, it was from his works that Western Europe first learned about Russian life. Handsome, witty, professionally generous, Turgenev was one of the most popular members of the French literary circle, a friend of the Brothers Goncourt, Prosper Mérimée, and Gustave Flaubert. He introduced Emile Zola's works to Russia, and under his sponsorship, Tolstoy's *War and Peace* first appeared in French. His own books were translated into several European languages during his lifetime, and he was well received by European critics. Whatever the ideological impact of his novels upon his compatriots, Europeans praised the lyrical eloquence of his writing, the nobility of his young heroines, and the complexity of his ever articulate heroes, beset by problems Europe found more "morally" interesting than the materialistic questions raised by Balzac and Flaubert. Western critics were particularly im-

pressed by Turgenev's ability to command the reader's unflagging attention without resorting to the sensation and violence
so common in romantic novels of the time. It was his astute
scrutiny of the heart and mind under emotional stress that
made his work compelling, and for that achievement he was
called by many a "romantic realist."

As a fledgling writer, Turgenev composed between 1843
and 1852 ten plays in which the irresolute heroes and resolute
heroines of his novels were already taking shape. Influenced
by the vaudeville comedies, "dramatic proverbs," and sentimental melodramas popular in France and Germany, these were
but the experiments of a writer searching for his medium. *A
Month in the Country* (1855), however, based on Balzac's
sensational play, *The Stepmother*, deserves mention. A psychological drama, it anticipated Chekhov's manner with mood and
setting in the story of a restless lady-of-the-manor's efforts to
lighten country boredom by encouraging the advances of several
men. It is a forceful play, and still a part of Russian repertory,
but Turgenev's other ventures in the theater were soon dated.
The public, as well as the author, lost interest in them when a
vigorously realistic playwright, Alexander Ostrovsky, took the
Russian stage by storm.

OSTROVSKY (1823–1886)

The only outstanding Russian literary figure to write plays
exclusively, Alexander Ostrovsky turned out forty-eight of them
during the forty years of his career. Forty in prose, eight in
verse, all were inspired by purely native sources, and all continued and enlarged upon the "romantic" realism of Fonvizin,
Griboyedov, and Gogol. For a few dramatic chronicles, one
poetic fairy tale, *The Snow Maiden*—woven from folklore
and destined to serve as libretto for Rimsky-Korsakov's opera—
and several dramas depicting life in the provinces, Ostrovsky
would be remembered only dimly in the history of Russian literature. But nineteen of his plays are distinguished for their revelation of a segment of Russian life hitherto untouched in
literature—the lower middle-class mercantile world of Moscow.

Thanks to his father's job as a legal clerk for shop owners,
and his own eight-year employment by the Moscow Commercial

Court, Ostrovsky gained rare entrée to the self-contained, self-absorbed society of the Russian merchant. Originally a rural class, these people had settled in the cities to develop their two interests: money, and the acquisition of more money. Unfazed by two centuries of intellectual, social, and political advances in Russia, they had retained the patriarchal customs and *Domostroy* mentality of the seventeenth century. Outwardly decorous, they pursued the ruble with savage competitiveness, skilled in every form of speculation, embezzlement, extortion, and graft.

It was fertile territory for a playmaker. The moneyed merchant who has made his pile and survived the chicaneries of the market place is inevitably a despot at home, and in Ostrovsky's plays he struts and postures, belches and bellows with all the vividness of the original. His cowering wife, richly dressed as the "mistress" of her household, is but his slave; he has, after all, purchased her from her father on terms agreeable to both men. His daughter, too, will someday go to the highest bidder, for "whatever his little toe tells her to do, she will do." At times, this petty tyrant (*samodur*), falls prey to his own victims, as in one of Ostrovsky's earliest and most famous comedies, *It's a Family Affair* (1850). Here, a chief clerk turns his master's cupidity to his own advantage; by helping him feign bankruptcy, he obtains all of the *samodur*'s tangible assets as well as his daughter's hand. For the most part, however, the *samodur* is invincible, and Ostrovsky never portrayed him better than in *Your Drink—My Hangover* (1856). This play is also typical of Ostrovsky's style: scenes are loosely bound and set in careless sequence, conversations appear to be irrelevant, minor walk-on roles serve to strengthen the impression of the main character. In *Poverty Is No Crime* (1854), plot follows a pattern common to many of the other plays: the *samodur*'s daughter loves the lowly clerk, while her father has chosen for her an old, perverted, but very wealthy merchant. In this case, the plan is frustrated by the girl's drunkard uncle, who manages to avert the wedding.

Most of the characters who wage the unceasing battle between strength and weakness in Ostrovsky's theater are, like Gogol's people, decidedly unappealing. With one exception, the blustering, bellied, bearlike bullies of the plays are by their very robustness more interesting than their ignorant, cowardly, or resigned victims. In *The Thunderstorm* (1860), however, his most structured and unified work and the best known to Western repertory, Ostrovsky clearly pleads the cause of his pure-hearted, idealistically religious young heroine, Katherine. Forced to marry the dull-witted, spineless son of a sadistic merchant's widow, she is persecuted beyond endurance in her new home. Driven to adultery, she finally commits suicide. This once, Ostrovsky approaches tragedy, the elements of comedy diminished by the implications of the familiar story. Like Pushkin's Tatiana, but without her education, Katherine embodies the dreamy, intuitive, deeply religious temperament of rural Russia. She is Ostrovsky's most luminous and enduring creation, and the role of Katherine is one of the Russian theater's most cherished.

What gives Ostrovsky's plays their greatest color and authenticity is language. The dialogue abounds in the slangy semiliterate distortions and turns of speech common to local idiom. For their colloquial vigor and variety, the plays were as much a delight to Russian audiences as they are a despair to translators, one reason why Ostrovsky is so little played abroad. In addition, Ostrovsky never developed the strong dramatic sequence to which Western theater is accustomed. His plots are hackneyed, his endings inconclusive, and nowhere does he pretend to universal or even national significance. Though his plays were immensely popular in Russia during his lifetime, neither reactionary nor liberal camps could rightly claim him as their own. Dobrolyubov called *The Thunderstorm* a "protest from the kingdom of darkness" on behalf of all the underprivileged, and other progressive critics pointed to the narrowing dramas in which the landowners' mistreatment of their human chattel was represented as perfectly normal in the pre-emancipation epoch. The Slavophils, on the other hand, were pleased best by Ostrovsky's use of traditional customs, native songs, mummery acts, and old-fashioned holiday rituals.

Ostrovsky himself refused to acknowledge that his plays served any ideological purpose. He wrote only to recreate as objectively as possible, with the greatest fidelity he could muster, the appearance of a sordidly mediocre social group. In 1869, he wrote to Nikolay Nekrasov, "Don't you know that you and I are the only real national poets? We alone know the people, know how to love them and with all our hearts feel their wants and needs without the trivial theories of the Westerners and the infantile Slavophil ideology."

NEKRASOV (1821–1878)

Ostrovsky could not have been more mistaken in supposing that Nikolay Nekrasov shared his indifference to politics. With Ivan Panayev, a wealthy man of letters and a liberal, Nekrasov acquired the conservative *Contemporary* in 1846, and, with Belinsky's help, transformed it into the most prominent and dynamically progressive journal in Russia. During the darkest days of Nicholas' regime, the magazine was a rallying ground for the insurgent intelligentsia, attracting reformer writers and critics alike. Even when bestsellers like Turgenev withdrew their work, angered by the harshly positivistic critiques of Chernyshevsky and Dobrolyubov, Nekrasov maintained the *Contemporary's* radical tone until an official order banned publication. With characteristic resiliency, he took over the failing *Notes from the Fatherland* in 1868, and gave it new life as the official organ of the nascent Populist movement.

A hard bargainer, a shrewd and grasping businessman who had achieved financial and social success by perseverance and hard work, Nekrasov was a dynamo of energy. He edited personally over a million words each month, corresponded with hundreds of contributors, wrote numerous poems and satires for his own columns, and waged incessant war against censorship. He was a publisher of genius, who recognized talent intuitively: Dostoyevsky's *Poor People* first appeared in his review, and, having seen one chapter of *Childhood*, by a then unknown Leo Tolstoy, he contracted for the entire work. By the late fifties, he was publishing all the important literary men, and they were regulars in the salon of his clever and pretty mistress, Avdotia Panayeva, wife of his former *Contemporary* partner. It was said with justification that "if the ceiling of

Madame Panayev's drawing room had collapsed on any one of her Monday evenings, most of Russian literature would have perished."

A vain, cynical, dissolute man who loved gambling, good wines, fast horses, and pretty women, Nekrasov in his writing was a fervent spokesman for the illiterate masses of Russian people. Tortured by a vision of the millions who were wretched and exploited even after the emancipation, he called his muse one of "vengeance and mourning." He wrote that he had been "chosen to sing of your suffering, O, my people," and indeed, no poet before him came so close to capturing the Russian multitudes. His best poems are impassioned lyrics which record, each in a single emotional experience, the enduring misery of the underprivileged. He writes of the indignities they suffered, the bleakness of their daily lives, their patience and fortitude in the face of famine, disease, and death. In some of the most powerful verse in the language, he extols the moral strength of the Russian peasant woman, her youth, beauty, and pride demeaned by rough labor and the brutality of the men who rule her life. These are tensile, vigorous poems, harsh with a homespun quality well suited to their content. But his most memorable work is a great satirical poem, *For Whom Is Life Good in Russia?* In popular epic style, it relates the adventures of seven peasants who encounter all manner of men in their search for those who live in peace and happiness in their vast country. This and several of his short poems, to be found in all representative anthologies, achieve the flavor and texture of folk songs. All of his poetry, in keeping with the realism of the period, is deliberately unaesthetic, avoiding conventional "poetic" rules and academic standards of taste. Here he is a bold innovator. His rhymes and rhythms are irregular, and his strong use of the vernacular lends emotional force to his imagery, as in these lines which tell of a peasant woman's despair as she speaks to her neighbor of the death of her son:

> The wind shakes my poor little house,
> The barn is falling to pieces,
> I walked down the road, out of my mind,
> Maybe my son will come up to me there.
> He'd pick up the axe and he'd put it all straight

And make his mother happy.
He died, Kas'yanovna, he died, my dear,
What's an axe to me? I'll sell it.

Nekrasov's work turned poetry into another literary weapon against oppression, and it is not surprising that some of his more militant verse inspired not only the radical youth of the sixties and seventies, but also numberless populists who were dedicating themselves to the people. Yet, while he understood the current need for his "nonpoetry," and proudly called himself a citizen first and a poet afterward, Nekrasov was too astute a critic not to recognize and encourage the high talent of two contemporaries, the poets Afanasy Fet and Feodor Tyutchev. Both men were artists for art's sake, and managed to remain aloof from political matters.

FET (1820–1892)AND TYUTCHEV (1803–1873):
ART FOR ART'S SAKE

Of the two, Fet is the more lyrical and "pure" poet, intent upon evoking meaning through sound rather than words alone. His shorter poems on nature, perhaps the loveliest and most melodious in Russian, were first published in 1842 in the Slavophil review, *Moskvityanin*. They were mercilessly panned, of course, by vigorously antiaesthetic critics, who maligned the poet as a useless, effete reactionary. Fet was cowed into a long silence; not until 1883 did he publish again, this time several slender volumes under the title, *Evening Lights*. A number of these poems are metaphysical in mood, expressing in extremely taut verse the secret, halting communion of man with nature, during the fall of the day or in the spaciousness and glitter of a starry night.

Tyutchev is one of the major Russian poets of the nineteenth century. Tolstoy's favorite, he was, like Fet, eclipsed by Nekrasov's huge popularity, and not until the nineties was he rediscovered by the Symbolists, who claimed him as their own. A convinced Slavophil, he believed in the messianic role of "Mother Russia," and devoted several early poems to this lofty theme, poems already distinguished by the melodious richness of his rhyme and a great range of poetic vocabulary. His later work is far more interesting. In Germany with the diplomatic service for many years, he read deeply in the works of Schelling and Schopenhauer, and managed to survive a long, unhappy love affair. His mature poetry reflects a consequent grave and cosmic quality, probing the mysteries of the universe, likening the intangible mobility of the human soul to the changes in nature. Several unusually poignant, yet classically restrained poems, reminiscent of Pushkin, move the reader to apprehensive awareness of an eternal cosmic chaos over which man's reason may not always triumph. Curiously enough, Tyutchev's mastery of a rich and beautiful Russian idiom was confined solely to his poetry. His memoirs and correspondence were written in French, the language he used exclusively in his public and private life.

ALEXEY TOLSTOY (1817–1875)

Among those pure poets who were affected by Populism, Alexey Tolstoy, a distant relative of the novelist, was the best liked by the common reader, and is still read today. In contrast to Fet or Tyutchev, he wrote for a less discriminating public, composing lyrics and folksy ballads which were no more than skillfully condensed, sophisticated versions of the original *byliny*. But he was an eclectic and facile writer. He displayed a wide knowledge of sixteenth- and seventeenth-century Russian history in a dramatic trilogy, *The Death of Ivan the Terrible* (1866); *Tsar Theodore* (1868); and *Tzar Boris* (1870). These recreated the period with imagination and verve; the royal protagonists, drawn with intelligence and skill, come wonderfully alive, and give added impact to the tumultuous events of the plays. Tolstoy's historical novel, *Prince Serebryany* (1862), written in the manner of Walter Scott, is no less successful in its plausibility, color and action.

S. AKSAKOV (1791–1859) AND
SALTYKOV-SHCHEDRIN (1826–1889)

A polarity similar to that which existed between Nekrasov and the pure poets of his time brings together two other men of letters, opposites in temperament, convictions, and way of life. Sergey Aksakov, whose sons Ivan and Konstantin were the brilliant advocates of Slavophilism, and Michael Saltykov-

Shchedrin, satirical journalist and Nekrasov's coeditor on *Notes from the Fatherland*. As the most persistent radical leader of the postreform era, Saltykov was worshipped by the progressives. His attacks on corrupt officialdom were couched in literary circumlocutions to confound the censor and delight his leftist audience, but while they were immensely popular in the heated climate of the mid-nineteenth century, they were too immediately topical to survive. Saltykov-Shchedrin owes his enduring reputation to one masterpiece: *The Golovlevs* (1872), a largely autobiographical novel for which his family never forgave him. It is a study of the rural gentry's decline and fall in the era of the Great Reform; the creeping sickness of all Russian manor life is epitomized in the total debilitation of one family.

The much older Sergey Aksakov entered literature diffidently and very late. He had belonged in his youth to the Shishkov circle and was known as a fervent nationalist whose great house in Moscow was a headquarters for leading Slavophils. There, Gogol, that lonely wanderer, received Aksakov's unstinting hospitality, praise, and patronage, and it was Gogol who encouraged his friend to write down what he remembered of his ancestors and youth. Aksakov thus began his *Family Chronicle*, which, published in 1856, was an instant success. Written in the meticulously clear, unhurried, and objective prose which distinguishes most late nineteenth-century fiction, it is the unusually interesting story of how Aksakov's grandfather resettled his family and serfs in the beautiful, fertile lands of the Orenburg country. In the provincial city of Ufa, Aksakov's parents pursue a long courtship, and the author's own years in high school and the University of Kazan are detailed. Above it all looms the Homeric figure of the patriarch serf-owner, Stepan Bagrov, whose will and mercurial temperament knew no controls except his own sense of moral integrity, his distant obeissance to Catherine II in the remote capital, and his fidelity to Russian Orthodoxy. The chronicle is rich with incident and as tangy with excitement as the pioneering tales of the American Far West. Aksakov depicts the full, active, enduring life of the eighteenth- and early nineteenth-century borderland manor—its steady cycle of seasons and holidays, family joys, births and deaths—with such wealth of detail that these memoirs might well have served Tolstoy as voluminous notes for *War and Peace*.

The history of the Golovlevs is so contrapositive a look at manor life that it would not be too far amiss to consider Saltykov's novel a superbly engineered parody of the Bagrov saga. Where Aksakov's family revel in the goodness and plenty of life, Saltykov's matriarch landowner and her three sons are viciously rapacious and finally destroy each other in a climate of moral disorder and virulent hatreds. Money-grubbing saps the energies of each of the four in turn, and as each yields to the stronger miser, he succumbs to an unseemly and unmourned death. The story is threaded with sociological questions. Saltykov's landowners cannot cope with the new status of their "freed" serfs, nor can they face an agricultural economy modernized on a large scale. Even more appallingly evident is the stagnation of mind and spirit common among the lower gentry. Bored, literally, to death, these people stare out from their isolated manor windows onto a flat, monotonous landscape, and lull their endless hours with sleep, drink, and petty-abusive talk until their minds are as dulled as their servants'. It is a rare neighbor or relative who crosses the great and often impassable distance from another country estate or small town to break the routine of apathy and inertia.

Porfiry Golovlev, nicknamed "Little Judas," dominates this portrait of gloom and gives the novel a universal dimension. There are few heroes in modern fiction to equal him in brutishness and petty meanness of spirit. Saltykov-Shchedrin builds him with biographical care and rare restraint, assigning him a singularly effective colloquial language with which to display his hypocrisy. To obtain his shabby ends, Little Judas placates, wheedles, flatters, and begs, as necessity demands, in an abundant flow of diminutives and augmentatives characteristic of common Russian speech. Even when he is alone, he cajoles the saints in unctuously whispered prayers and justifications. He is a tireless babbler, and those whom he fails to destroy by financial trickery he drives away or reduces to numbness with his compulsive gossiping. At times, his hypocrisy verges on the surrealistic, as when, fearing additional expense, he refuses to acknowledge as his son the child born in his house to his mistress with whom he has been living for several years. But Porfiry has neither the vitality and stubbornness of a Polonius, nor the hidden sensuality of a Tartuffe. Like all the rest of the Golovlevs, whom he has survived, he dies at last of the vacuum he has created around himself, so overcome by the senseless, lonely boredom of his life that he ends it in a drunken delirium. Understandably, this savagely satirical novel has been widely acclaimed by Soviet critics as a true exposure of moral rottenness among the gentry.

9 · The Great Truth-Tellers

AMONG THE ARCHITECTS of modern literature, Tolstoy and Dostoyevsky are titans. Because of their acumen in portraying modern man, their vision of his future, they are the greatest novelists of our time. Their influence on twentieth-century letters is so profound that four generations of critics have not yet exhausted the implications of their work.

Ironically, the literature surrounding these two very similar men reflects not so much the enduring power of their genius as the literary tastes and moral temperaments of changing times. Like Shakespeare, both Tolstoy and Dostoyevsky were to provoke the most passionate of partisan criticisms. When the French critic de Vogüé introduced the Russian novel to his countrymen in 1886, he gave many eloquent pages to analysis of Tolstoy's superbly impassive realism, apologizing for including in his study at all the "morbid barbarisms" of Dostoyevsky. But by 1922, Dostoyevsky was ascendant. André Gide made him the subject of an entire book, declaring that although Tolstoy still loomed large on the European horizon, the figure of his great compatriot was emerging triumphant. Georg Brandes, Meier-Graefe, Maurice Baring, and others wrote of Dostoyevsky at length, judging him to be the more talented, original, and clairvoyant of the two.

In Russia, both writers, published in serial form, were read avidly. But it was Tolstoy who, during the last thirty years of his life, was acclaimed as a great social and moral force, not only by an adoring Russian public, but by millions abroad who had not read a single line of his works. After the revolution, his stock soared again among Russian emigré writers and scholars, and prominent Soviet novelists like Mikhail Sholokhov, Alexander Fadeyev, and Boris Pasternak were identified, for their sweep and realism, as Tolstoy's direct heirs. In the Soviet Union itself, Tolstoy's novels and stories have been steady best sellers, grist for thousands of commentaries published by the Tolstoy Museum in the monumental ninety-volume jubilee edition of his complete works. Dostoyevsky's "diseased talent," on the other hand, has been deliberately de-emphasized by Soviet critics. Considered harmful reading for Soviet citizens, he has at times been written off as the "super pathologist" of a disintegrating, Westernized faction of prerevolutionary Russia.

In 1959, George Steiner, a young American critic, breathed new life into the debate with his long essay, *Tolstoy or Dostoyevsky?* Re-examining their accomplishments by stressing their differences, Mr. Steiner found himself agreeing with the judgment of the twentieth-century Russian philosopher, Nicholas Berdyayev: "It would be possible to determine two patterns, two types among men's souls, the one inclined toward the spirit of Tolstoy, and the other toward that of Dostoyevsky. . . . They exemplify an insoluble controversy."

Yet viewed within the tradition of nineteenth-century literature, as products of a developing stream of Russian thought, the two men are strikingly similar. Through an accident of genius, each became, in his own day, the highest representative of Russian literature. Writers of high seriousness, they were deeply affected by the conditions of life around them. Each, in his own way, tried to discover how to live and what to live by, probing beyond immediate social and political issues to wrestle with moral and religious questions and define the nature of man. Both repudiated the utopias of science and materialism, placing the burden of perfecting humanity on the individual, the solitary man who must struggle inwardly for answers. They foresaw a crisis in human endeavor, a crisis that could be averted only if men behaved in the spirit of redemption. Supreme realists, they were nevertheless, in the Russian tradition, of a didactic and reforming bent. Between them, they restored to the strictly secular European works of imagination a world of belief; they envisaged for their heroes a total experience of life, political, social, and metaphysical. In this mania for totality, and in their sense of a gathering storm, Tolstoy and Dostoyevsky haunt the modern consciousness; their message is of immediate relevance to our own moment in history. Here their divergence is complete, for they were men of opposite views. But in their basic urges, their ideas, their moral and psychological involvements, the worlds of *War and Peace* and of *The Brothers Karamazov* amplify and complete each other.

Both men were writers first, and early. By a curious coincidence, each was twenty-four when he first published successfully. In 1842, Dostoyevsky had written *Poor People*, and when, ten years later, *The Russian Messenger* ran Tolstoy's *Childhood*, he inquired from his Siberian prison about the talented young man who had signed his work with the initials "L. N." (Tolstoy's *nom de plume* at that time).

LEO TOLSTOY (1828–1910)

Only from the distance of a century can the clarity and consistency of Tolstoy's genius be fully appreciated. Ranging from great works of the imagination to the most didactic of religious tracts, his writings touch upon every live issue of his day. Very much a man of his class, he suffered the guilt of every other enlightened nobleman confronted by the brutal squalor and semislavery in which ninety per cent of his countrymen wasted. Education, agrarian economy, literary theories, moral and religious ideas consumed his thought, becoming his personal problems, which he explicated in print. The ninety volumes of his *oeuvre* may be looked upon as an immense autobiography, a personal confession and an affirmation of self, written from such convictions of conscience and such extremes of independent thought that he remained all his long life the most controversial and "public" figure of the nineteenth century. The very bulk and breadth of his reputation tended to obscure the fundamental unity of his accomplishments. He was artist, social reformer, evangelist, and from 1880 to his death, the most powerful single moral force in the Western world.

Although, like most serious writers, Tolstoy shared the social concerns of the intelligentsia, he differed drastically from most progressives in his concept of Russian problems and in his manner of grappling with them. To liberals under the banner of Nekrasov and Chernyshevsky, the liberation of the masses had become a kind of mystique, inspired by their own underprivileged status. Spurred by personal dedication, they were consolidating a united, articulate front to oppose the tsarist regime. From this militant union, Tolstoy remained aloof. With something of the peasant's suspicion of organized effort, as well as the aristocrat's disdain for *raznochintsy* (educated men of mixed social standing), he looked to his own conscience, his own intellect, for guidance, preferring from the first to form his opinions freely, arbitrarily, and alone.

His ancestors had played prominent roles in Russian history since the fifteenth century, and both he and his brothers were reared in the cultivated wealth of rural nobility, at Yasnaya Polyana, in the Tula province, some 130 miles south of Moscow. Proud of his heritage and financially secure, the young Tolstoy could, like Pushkin, choose the pleasures and dissipations of St. Petersburg before he settled into the indolent comfort of a landowner's life. But he was soon to realize that this conventional pattern of living did not suit him. He was restless, inquisitive, incapable of passive acceptance. He had to forever reject the formula answers; had to examine, test, recast traditional ideas until his skeptical nature was satisfied.

He was, on the one hand, an extremely sensuous, and sensual, man; in him, the senses were heightened nearly to exaggeration. Anyone who reads the thirty-one pages of the hunting scene in *War and Peace* does not forget the wild, boisterous joy of the chase, the sounds, smells, and movements evoked in a fierce mingling of primitive urges, man's and beast's. But avid as he was for spontaneous and purely physical sensation, Tolstoy was yet a man of coldly analytical intelligence, determined to discover a permanent meaning to life that would insure positive and enduring happiness be-

yond the voluptuous pleasures of the moment. At once pagan
and moralist, he struggled unsuccessfully to strike a balance
between the two. His diaries, letters, treatises, and especially
his creative works are filled with his quest for that fundamental, inviolable truth which would motivate man's highest
moral behavior. He found only pat answers. Rejecting these
and disdaining compromise, he remained to the end an uninhibited, intransigent, and somewhat terrifying iconoclast, the
reverberations of his splendidly incorruptible war ringing in
all his imaginative writing, even the greatest novels that were
composed at the lowest ebb of his discontent.

Tolstoy's early fictional narratives, *Childhood, Boyhood
and Youth* (1852–1856), diverge from the story of his own
upbringing only in minor details. Appearing as a serial, they
recreated "Nikolay's" daily round of tutors, outings, and games
with an impressionistic and wholly relevant wealth of detail
that was new to realistic writing. As he grows up, Nikolay's
mindlessly happy moments are shadowed by introspection; he
wonders whether his happiness will last, whether he is worthy
of it. Imperceptibly, his spontaneity and exuberance are curbed
into the more decorous behavior expected of him; wise beyond his years, he believes that what joy he experiences must
be paid for by obedience to his elders, wiser and "better"
than he. Schooled to conventional sentiments, he is, for example, at the age of nine, too absorbed in his role as a grief-
stricken orphan to feel any grief at all at his mother's death.
With that ruthless attention to analytical detail which has
been called his "eavesdropping" technique, Tolstoy takes the
boy through painful adolescence, exposing his vanity, his in-
ordinate fear of ridicule, and his pitiful yearnings to be admired, to be handsome and considered "comme il faut."

He was still writing about himself in *A Landowner's
Morning* (1852). Here, it is "Prince Nekhlyudov" who stands
in his stead, abandoning excruciatingly dull courses in law
and oriental languages at the University of Kazan to manage
his inherited estate personally, in hopes of improving life for
his 350 serfs. And like his creator, the humanitarian Prince is
frustrated by the stubborn apathy of the peasants. Tolstoy
joined a regiment in the Caucasus (1851), and, at his own

request, was transferred to serious fighting in the Crimea. *The Sebastopol Stories* (1855) record his impressions of that war, its valorous and venal deeds detailed with equal terseness and impassiveness. The reader was not to be allowed a conventional response, for Tolstoy debunked the vaunted heroism of war, pondering the power of mass indoctrination which compelled men into premeditated murder.

The stories were an immediate success. In St. Petersburg, Tolstoy was courted by the literary liberals, and Chernyshevsky attempted to convert the twenty-seven-year-old officer to his brand of socialism. In this first and only personal contact with the writing intelligentsia, Tolstoy proved characteristically intractable, deeply suspicious of *raznochintsy* panaceas, and, according to Nekrasov, "socially insensible" to the fervor of the Populists. He preferred the company and amusements of his social peers, and with Turgenev, a country neighbor, discussed the destructive influence of radical criticism on pure art. Although his tactlessness, temper, and contempt for what he saw as Turgenev's "spiritual spinelessness" eventually created a permanent rift between the two writers, their talks helped Tolstoy to formulate his own aesthetic theories. He believed that the writer must remain independent, write about what he knew best, and write the truth as he saw it, obligated only to write it clearly. Forty years later, he was to expand his ideas in the controversial essay, *What is Art?* but in the meantime, he set about testing them in the field of primary education.

Like many others in the heady prereform years of the late fifties, Tolstoy believed education could transform Russia into a thriving agricultural economy, run by a literate peasant class. In 1857, and again in 1860, he made extended trips abroad to observe teaching methods in the lower schools of France, Germany, and England. He noted a direct ratio between the material prosperity of these countries and the lack of enrichment in their classrooms, where children learned by rote and the rod. Workers and the children of workers, he wrote in his diary, acquired more knowledge from the press and their unconscious assimilation of popular novels and songs than had ever been drummed into them on school benches.

Whatever they did learn in school, Tolstoy argued (an ardent reader of Rousseau, he had at sixteen worn around his neck a miniature portrait of the French philosopher), forced the untutored young minds into an unnatural mold, encouraging discontent by tempting lower-class children with power and status symbols beyond their reach. To illustrate his views, Tolstoy returned to Yasnaya Polyana and organized elementary classes for the children of his serfs, an experiment that could have served as a blueprint for our own principles of progressive education. The curriculum, built around the child's needs, was taught with spontaneous improvisation, exploiting the child's natural curiosity and relating subject matter to his environment. Intellectual achievement was balanced with manual skill, and the entire program was braced with visual aids, field trips, dramatics, and music.

Professional educators, outraged at Tolstoy's sweeping attacks on all formal subject matter at preuniversity level, and his claim that strict discipline in the lower grades stunted the mind instead of developing it, failed to understand that Tolstoy was fundamentally opposed to authority in any form. Inner harmony, natural to any child, was to him the one element necessary for human happiness, and he believed that civilization as it existed tended to destroy that harmony. He developed the thought in *The Cossacks* (1863), a masterful story in which Olenin, a highly educated, inhibited, and self-conscious young officer, comes to envy the robust, careless life of the Cossack village where he is quartered. There, people eat, drink, feud, and plunder as unthinkingly as plants or trees. "You die and the grass grows; that's all there is to it," says Uncle Yeroshka, an old Cossack hunter, summing up the substance of primitive living. But Olenin's moral qualms and intellectual ponderings remove him from these self-assured men to whom all is one, God, death, and the laws of nature. As late as 1896, Tolstoy was still finding the "pagan" life attractive. The Caucasian warrior chief of *Hadji Murad*, as savage and treacherous as he is boldly courageous, is eventually killed by his Russian enemies, after one of Russian literature's most harrowing descriptions of pursuit. But as a prisoner, Hadji displays all the calm, dignity, and singleness of purpose his high-ranking military captors lack.

With his marriage to eighteen-year-old Sophia Behrs in 1862, Tolstoy seemed to achieve a balance between tension and intention, his overcharged energies and compulsive moral quest brought into harmony by a full life on his estate. Yasnaya Polyana prospered under his management; he made wine, gathered honey, built roads, increased his family. "I have lived to the age of 34 and did not realize that one could live so, and be so happy," he wrote to the poet Fet. In the deep contentment of the first fifteen years of his marriage, he produced his two greatest novels.

From 1863 to 1869 he wrote *War and Peace*. One of the world's greatest literary monuments and the longest of the nineteenth-century novels, it develops 559 characters and runs, in a standard English translation, to some 1,650 pages. It explores historical, social, ethical, and religious issues on a scale never before attempted in fiction, but its most remarkable feature is its ability to engross the reader throughout, so persuasive are Tolstoy's arguments, so vivid his descriptions and powerful his unfolding of events. A family chronicle and an antihistorical novel, it is first and foremost a prose epic. Vast in concept, it scrutinizes every level of Russian society during the tumultuous years between 1805 and 1815, just before and after the Napoleonic invasion. It commemorates great military victories and defeats, and the historical figures who made them, but more significant, it celebrates the spaciousness of spirit reflected in individual relationships: man to man, man to woman, citizen to nation. Small wonder that *War and Peace* is still a best seller in the Soviet Union, or that it was read by hundreds of thousands during the Nazi invasion of the USSR.

It is the first work of fiction to strip war of its glory, to reject the historian's view of war as strategy planned by military and diplomatic experts. Tolstoy saw history not as a catalogue of conscious deeds done by a few valorous men, but as events shaped by the anonymous motives and largely unconscious actions of masses of men. From this iconoclastic concept of war, he arrived at his concept of peace. It existed everywhere, even in the greatest stress of battle, because it lived unalterably, serenely in the private deeds and thoughts of real but forgotten people whose private lives were their inspiration. Napoleon and Alexander, therefore, appear only incidentally in *War and Peace*. The real heroes are the members of the Moscow family Rostov, the St. Petersburg Bezukhovs and Bolkonskys, the landed gentry and urban aristocrats Tolstoy knew best. Three generations of them move through scenes of kaleidoscopic variety—bear hunts, balls, receptions, prayers, parades, domestic quarrels and military staff sessions at the front—linked by three main characters: Prince Andrey, Pierre Bezukhov, and Natasha.

The two men are a composite of the author, each in his own way seeking self-justification and a satisfactory meaning to life. Andrey, handsome, egotistical, intellectual, lives a carefully rational life, absorbed in himself until, nearing death, he becomes at last indifferent to life and, ironically, almost happy in it. Pierre, lumbering, emotional, and immensely rich, is no less intelligent than his friend, and equally intent upon the search for truth. He experiments in vain with marriage, Freemasonry, science, and social reform, even an impulsive attempt to kill Napoleon. But because he is receptive to others, spontaneous, naive, and eager to learn, he eventually achieves a measure of peace, influenced by the simple faith of Platon Karatayev, a peasant whom he meets in prison.

The women of *War and Peace* are individualized for the first time in Tolstoy's work. Conversations, letters, and confidences catch all the more subtle shades of feminine psychology, counterbalancing the predominantly masculine, forthright world of the novel with grace and delicacy. Natasha Rostova, with whom nearly every male reader falls in love, is the most enchanting, alive heroine in all fiction. Tolstoy modelled her on his wife's pretty, affectionate younger sister, Tania Kuzminskaya, but endowed her with even greater spontaneity, animal-like vigor, gaiety, and naturalness. In all her roles, from that of a fourteen-year-old treasuring a first, furtive kiss, to her final appearance as a solid, bustling, henpecking matron, she remains abundantly herself, a supremely ordinary and satisfactory female who wants only to love, marry, and have children.

In style, *War and Peace* brings to its apex the realism begun in *Childhood* and *The Cossacks*. Objective, equable, humane, the writing recalls Pushkin's, but where the poet defined his characters in a few indelible strokes, Tolstoy's characterizations are blocked solidly and with prodigious care. Moods and attitudes, shifting under inner tensions, circumstance, or age, are analyzed exhaustively in a clear, spare, and unhurried prose. His major characters are endowed with physical traits or gestures which instantly identify and reveal. Princess Maria's heavy walk and mottled blushes betray her awkwardness and timidity; voluptuous Helene Bezukhov, absorbed in her own beauty, dresses to reveal her marble-like white shoulders; the small, plump hand of Napoleon, whom Tolstoy detested, bespeaks the complacent and vulgar parvenu. Such details are marshalled to evoke an array of sensations. Outside a hospital tent, a surgeon in bloodstained apron holds a cigar between carefully spread fingers, and the hideous aftermath of battle is instantly summoned. While Natasha flings old dresses from a trunk, carts filled with returning wounded push slowly along the cobbled street; three lines catch all the confusion and dismay of Moscow fleeing before the French army.

A more daring and forceful indictment of war than Stendhal's *Charterhouse of Parma*, which Tolstoy claimed to have emulated, *War and Peace* emanates a profoundly optimistic philosophy. While the carefully laid plans of the military remain in blueprint form or are abandoned in the heat of battle, the more irrational forces of nature rise to achieve victory. Guerilla bands, untrained and undirected, assault the retreating French with vigor and joy, and the inarticulate peasant resists the invader more successfully than a regiment of generals. In Platon Karatayev, Tolstoy creates the soldier of all nations and of all time; suffering, the eternal victim, he wears the halo of victory modestly and unconsciously, unaware of his heroism. It is the commonplace that is heroic in

War and Peace. Tolstoy assures us that in the dynamics of ordinary living there is enough goodness and meaning to live by.

Comparing *Anna Karenina* (1878) to *War and Peace* is like comparing a single painting to a frieze. Tolstoy's second major work of fiction is much shorter (there are only 150 characters) and less ambitious in scope than the first. Although it contains many illuminating references to social issues of the postreform period, it is concerned primarily with the closed world of Tolstoy's peers, the privileged members of high bureaucracy, the military and the landed gentry. It is Tolstoy's crowning achievement in realistic writing, and the world's greatest modern novel.

The famous opening lines sound its major theme, introduce its protagonists, and plunge the reader into a story of many strands: "Happy families resemble one another; every unhappy family is unhappy in its own way. Everything was in confusion in the Oblonsky household . . ." By the end of the first part, the parallel lines of action have been established. In 108 chapters of the total 239, Anna's illicit love affair with the young officer, Vronsky, is developed against the background of upper-class St. Petersburg society, while Kitty and Levin live in lawful union on their country estate in Central Russia. Shifting from one locale to the other, short, dramatic scenes propel the story forward, each scene moving independently and at the pace of "real life." The novel seems scarcely fiction. Anna and her lover, her brother Stiva, and his wife Dolly, Kitty and Levin become as familiar to us as our closest friends, and we can bear to leave one scene only because we must know what the next will bring.

Tolstoy's "eavesdropping" technique, which is what T. S. Eliot has called the "objective correlative" in art, reaches perfection in *Anna Karenina*. We know, for example, what must happen in the great ballroom scene by the gowns the women wear. Vronsky turns from flirting with Kitty, artlessly pretty in a rosetted gown of pink tulle and lace, to fall deeply in love with Anna, dazzling and worldly in her simply cut, decolleté black velvet. Anna's unruly black curls bespeak a passionate nature; Vronsky's large, even, white teeth are evidence not only of sound health but of a certain mental obtuseness; Levin's nervous, awkward manners with strangers betoken his impatience with social decorum and his urgent need to speak, like Tolstoy, of whatever is on his mind.

Levin is, in fact, the novel's most autobiographical character. A country gentleman, he reflects not only Tolstoy's patriarchal heritage but his agrarian views. He dislikes urban sophistication and distrusts systematic philosophies, respects agricultural labor and loves his own land. He suffers the dilemma of all enlightened gentry in the sixties, being torn between sympathy for his freed peasants who resist innovation and the desire to develop his estate according to modern scientific methods. Searching for a pragmatic solution to the problem, he reads, works with his serfs, and consults the local municipal officials, affording Tolstoy many a jab at the pretensions of pseudoreformers, intellectuals, and philanthropists. As a guilty landowner, Levin is historically authentic. As a seeker of truth, he is timeless and universal. Born in an age of disbelief, he is, literally, god-haunted. Marriage, a child, physical and intellectual labor assuage his spiritual need only temporarily; he lives primarily to discover a religious meaning in life.

Anna's quest for happiness is no less relentless, and though she and Levin meet only once, and casually, their pursuit of the absolute provides the basic unity of this polyphonic novel. Levin approaches joy when the simple faith of a peasant discloses a divine presence which is probably God. Paganlike, Anna grasps the only joy she has ever known, her passion for Vronsky. Equally idealistic and pure in heart, neither achieves fulfillment, for the society to which they belong cannot long tolerate the heat and intransigence of their behavior. If they are to live successfully, they must return to the proprieties of normalcy, compromising, adjusting, prevaricating to maintain the status quo. For Anna, the price of life is too high. Vronsky's faithlessness shows her that in the mundane, normal, real world, she cannot live fully, generously, or honestly. Before she flings herself under a moving train, she cries that it is "all lies, all humbug, all cruelty."

Where *War and Peace* dealt with the externals of reality, *Anna Karenina* turns inward, laying bare the myriad subtleties by which a human being preserves his individuality. It is in this sense that the novel is most modern, for it prophesies the retreat of the individual before the will of the group, the most significant social phenomenon of our century. The greatness of the novel is in Tolstoy's refusal to deny or condemn the mores of the group. *Anna Karenina* contains no extraordinary humans, neither villains nor saints. These are the ordinary people, frivolous and ethical, loving and hypocritical, who are responsible for perpetuating human existence by adhering to a pattern of conformity. That Anna should be destroyed because she disrupts the pattern is only just. The epigraph to the novel, from Rom 12:19, reads, "Vengeance is mine; I will repay, saith the Lord."

But while Tolstoy, the writer, understood the necessity and indestructibility of the pattern, Tolstoy, the moralist, could not tolerate it. Though he had appraised human nature with compassion and lucidity, he abhorred what he discovered of its meanness. While he was completing *Anna Karenina*, his perplexity and depression grew, deepened by deaths in the family, quarrels with his wife, and his own illness. The crisis came in 1878. In a vigorous, candid *Confession*, he denounced the softness and self-seeking cynicism of his own class and castigated himself as its literary spokesman. Like Levin, realizing the emptiness of his life, he had begun to fear the tempting sight of a rope or a revolver. What followed was both ennobling and shattering. Protesting against the shallowness and vanity of aristocratic ideals, he withdrew from his peers entirely, cloistered himself in one plain room of his rich mansion, adopted peasant dress, ate simply and frugally, and, by a great effort of will, contained his pride and temper sufficiently to dissociate himself from the laws of society which *Anna Karenina* had ratified. Subjected to the sullen opposition of his sons and the bitter disapproval of his wife, neither a courageous man nor an ascetic, he nevertheless lived thirty years in this manner as the "prophet" of Yasnaya Polyana, urging the world to live more simply, more individualistically, and by a purer ethic.

As a writer, his first concern after his "conversion" was,

not surprisingly, a literature for the people. Drawing from legends and fables, he created a series of fine tales centered on village life, each teaching an obvious moral. Pungent with everyday language, as clear as water with their short, simple sentences, they set a new standard in fiction writing. But Tolstoy's principal energies went into his quest for religious meaning. He plunged into a study of comparative religions—at his death, his library contained 24,000 volumes, of which over 14,000 were annotated—but his pragmatic mind refused to accept the strictures of mystery, miracle, and revelation. Searching for a more concrete way in which to justify his life, he settled at last upon the primitive Christian commandments to love one's neighbor and resist evil passively. With the logic of extremism, characteristic of all his thinking, he then ventured to measure the success or failure of society by these yardsticks. Tract after eloquent tract accused the State, the army, the judiciary of coercing human conscience and destroying individuality. Again and again he implored men to return to the principles of simple equality and kindness. Impatient for Russia's well-being, he openly attacked high-ranking members of the Establishment, among them the powerful Pobedonostsev, archconservative head of the Russian Church. When the inevitable excommunication came, it only insured his popularity among the persecuted and underprivileged, and, ironically, among the progressive radicals whose revolutionary views he despised.

Tolstoy's championship of the common people and his hatred of bureaucracy were not the only reasons for his reputation as a "progressive." His widely criticized essay, *What Is Art?* (1897), reiterated the credo of Belinsky and Chernyshevsky that art must serve mankind, and added some iconoclastic views of his own. The main function of art, he wrote, "is to transmit the highest feelings which humanity has attained"; art is, therefore, "religious" in nature, and must be of universal value, accessible and comprehensible to all. French critics were stung by his contemptuous review of leading French Symbolists, whose hermetic poetry he compared to the "decadent and useless" operas of Wagner, then at the height of popularity in Paris.

Clearly, this man who had forsworn art, even spoken disparagingly of Anna Karenina and "her white shoulders, which could be of no possible consequence to any serious-minded peasant," could not deny his keen interest in literary matters. It was with the educated foreigners who paid their respects at Yasnaya Polyana that he felt most at ease, discussing European men of letters with astonishing insight in idiomatic French, German, or English. Nor was Tolstoy able to permanently suppress his creative bent. The numerous stories of his postconversion period, his plays, and the third and last novel, *Resurrection*, reflect, of necessity, his evangelical point of view, but all attest to the unflagging power of his genius.

Resurrection (1899), artistically his most disappointing novel, was written sporadically over ten years, and was completed only to finance the mass emigration to Canada of the Dukhobors, a religious sect persecuted for their refusal to enter military service. As penance for having long ago seduced a kitchen maid who then became a prostitute, the novel's hero, Prince Nekhlyudov, follows the girl to exile in Siberia, where she is bound as a prisoner of the State. The Prince is little more than the puppet of Tolstoy's didactic intent, but in its satirical passages on court procedures, its wonderfully vivid account of the journey to Siberia, and its vignettes of prison life, *Resurrection* recalls the best pages of the two great novels which precede it.

The Power of Darkness (1886), a morality play in spirit, is a rousing drama of peasant life, built on the contrast between the "Cheat, or Reason" of self-interest, and the "Heart" that strives to live by God's commandments. Macbethian in tone, it treats of the evil which evil breeds, and is all the more gripping for the placidly realistic village setting of its scenes. As successful, but in a satiric vein, is Tolstoy's second venture into theater, *The Fruits of Enlightenment* (1899). A sprightly, sly exposé of charlatan spiritualists, it permitted Tolstoy another jab at the credulity and pseudointellectualism of the upper classes.

Easily the most masterful works of the postconversion period are *The Death of Ivan Ilyich* (1886) and *The Kreutzer Sonata* (1889), both treating of the death and sex themes which pervade all Tolstoy's writing, and which held for him an unconquerable terror. The first is a slow and painfully realistic account of physical disintegration by disease. Having written of many forms of death more poignantly than any other modern writer, Tolstoy nevertheless could not resign himself to his own. He had to discover a permanent meaning to existence in the world, that it might promise life in the next. Ivan Ilyich is thus granted perception of purpose and immortality; in his last moments he finds hope in the simple words of his servant, who believes in God.

The Kreutzer Sonata, a monologue heard in the darkness of a moving train, as delivered by a man just acquitted for the murder of his wife in a fit of jealousy, is the harshest and most direct indictment of loveless marriage in all literature. The first piece of serious fiction in Russia to deal exclusively with the question of sex, it created a sensation in Europe and was for a long time banned in the United States. The fruitful family love which gave color and warmth to *War and Peace* is here replaced by the horrors of a marriage consummated only physically, the partners ultimately destroyed by the viciousness of their passion. The father of thirteen legitimate children, a man intensely virile even in old age (when he considered sexual desire degrading and a torment), Tolstoy understandably gave *The Kreutzer Sonata* a savage tone, ending by exorcizing his own demon with the preachment that a successful and happy marriage must rest on chastity.

The *Sonata* also reflects the growing conflict between Tolstoy and his family. He was, on the one hand, a world figure to whom disciples flocked for advice and sympathy. Not constituted for public adulation, he became the victim of his admirers, though he withstood the glare of publicity with all the independence he could muster. Conversely, to his relatives, closest friends, and particularly to his wife, he was no great religious reformer, but a petulant eccentric who squandered his talent on "idealistic nonsense" while his family and estate were neglected for the whims of strangers and curiosity seekers.

Between the two images of himself, Tolstoy suffered alone. While many of his followers were exiled or imprisoned for preaching his doctrines, he, as an internationally famous figure, remained unmolested by the government. By 1892, he had put his holdings in his wife's name, wishing to live his last years in the simplicity and obscurity of a peasant. Ironically, his writings brought him only greater wealth and prestige, provoking, finally, bitter disagreement among his closest disciples concerning the literary merit of his work. His wife, jealous of his following, fell more and more frequently into fits of nervous hysteria, and at last, on the night of October 28, 1910, Tolstoy determined to flee Yasnaya Polyana altogether. Accompanied by his physician, he left hastily, but catching cold, was forced to stop at the small railroad station of Astapovo. There, two days later, he died in the station master's hut, mourned by the entire civilized world.

DOSTOYEVSKY (1821–1881)

For sixty turbulent years, Feodor Dostoyevsky endured all the poverty, physical hardship, and mental anguish coveted by Tolstoy as a test of moral strength. The gloom and confinement of his childhood were to taint his entire life.

With his elder brother Michael, five younger children, and his parents, he lived in a dark, three-room flat adjoining a public hospital in Moscow. His father, a physician there, was a petty tyrant, requiring his sons to stand at attention when they spoke, forbidding them to leave the house unaccompanied or to consort with young people of their own age. When he was seventeen, Feodor was placed in the Military Engineering Academy at St. Petersburg. His tiny allowance barely provided for a uniform and food, but he was free at last to indulge in long, solitary walks across the city. In the bleakness of his room, literature satisfied his craving for adventure and melodrama. He devoured the works of Goethe and Shakespeare, the romances of England and Germany, and the popular novels of Hugo, Sand, Balzac, and Eugène Sue. He even began a translation of Schiller's poems, which he knew by heart. Within a year his mother died, and his father, retiring to drunken eccentricity on his small estate, was murdered soon after by his own brutally treated serfs. Feodor squandered his inheritance recklessly, catering to the whims of a mercurial temperament. He had no sooner graduated from the Academy than he decided against the mechanical precision of a draughtsman's board, resigned from the army, and began to write.

The instantaneous success of his first prose piece, *Poor People* (1846), seemed the more dazzling to him for the penury in which the last chapters were written; he had lived for days on barley and water. It was a short epistolary novel, submitted to Nekrasov by Dostoyevsky's friend, the budding novelist, Grigorovich. Both read it through the night and at 4 A.M. burst in on Dostoyevsky to congratulate him on his masterpiece. Nekrasov gave the manuscript to the all-powerful Belinsky who, enraptured, compared the work to *The Overcoat*. Makar Devushkin, Dostoyevsky's elderly government clerk, does indeed, like Gogol's copyist, live out a dream, writing long, anxious, tender letters to a destitute young seamstress across the hall. Though he deprives himself of the barest necessities to send her small gifts, he loses her, just as Akaky loses his overcoat, to a wealthier, if cruder, suitor. But where Gogol had grafted a structure of fantasy to the externals of his story, Dostoyevsky wrote a compassionate analysis of Makar's emotions, building his story in a movement from the heart outward with a vitality and intensity already peculiarly his own.

Belinsky's enthusiasm for *Poor People* thrust this morbidly self-conscious young man into the small but influential literary set of the city. Introduced to the famous and near-famous —Turgenev, Panayev, Paul Annenkov, and others—Dostoyevsky boasted in letters to his brother that he had reached the apogee of his fame, that all St. Petersburg lay at his feet. He was to be rudely awakened, but not before he had written *The Double* (1846) and *The Landlady* (1847). Hoffmannesque in approach and painful to read, *The Double* seems but the cruel fantasy of yet another pitiful civil servant, his efforts to assert himself confounded by a maddeningly superior "alter ego" whose frightful jeers persecute him in dream and reality. The story is remarkable, however, for its vision of that submerged nightmare world which distinguishes Dostoyevsky's best work, the intuitively accurate summation of the inferiority complex and its attendant hallucinations. In style and content, *The Landlady* is surprisingly romantic, borrowing from Gogol's inflated rhetoric for its effects and from Hoffmann and Balzac for its plot. The heroine is an interesting adumbration of the proud, "demoniac" woman of the great novels. She appears again in *Netochka Nezhdanova*, a work Dostoyevsky had planned on a larger scale and that remained uncompleted up to his arrest in 1849.

The Petrashevsky circle, a gathering of young rebels who at secret meetings read and discussed the socialist theories of Fourier and Saint-Simon, remains a persistent footnote to literary history because Dostoyevsky's membership in the group led to his Siberian exile. That he was a leading and active member is doubtful, but, given to ready enthusiasms, he would certainly have been drawn temperamentally and intellectually to the heady talk of would-be conspirators over endless cups of tea. When the secret police, more canny and cautious after the Paris revolt of 1848, slipped an informer into the circle, it was learned that one Feodor Dostoyevsky had read aloud Belinsky's famous letter to Gogol, and he, with the others, was sent to the dreaded Fortress of St. Peter and St. Paul.

During the last three months of his solitary confinement, when he was permitted paper and pen, he wrote *The Little Hero*, a delicate, joyously realistic story of an eleven-year-old boy's emotional awakening. Then, in December, 1849, all members of the group were taken to the execution square to be shot. The death sentence was read, the priest delivered last rites, the first few prisoners (Dostoyevsky was the fourth) were tied to stakes. The firing squad had taken aim when in a show of clemency staged by the Tsar himself, Nicholas' messenger galloped forward, waving a white handkerchief. One prisoner's hair turned white, another went mad, and it is difficult to exaggerate the effect of so shattering an experience on the highstrung writer. Under the true sentence, Dostoyevsky was condemned to four years' hard labor and then to service as a common soldier. On Christmas Eve, he took leave of Michael, the person ever closest to him, and as guards stood by, ten pounds of chain were riveted to his ankles. He was driven in a sleigh to Siberia, and after twenty-five days of almost continual travel, reached the convict prison of Omsk.

House of the Dead (1861), written three years after his release, is the thinly disguised account of the four-year inferno where prisoners lived in swinish proximity and were beaten senseless for the slightest infraction of rules—even to sleeping on the left rather than the right side. Never once alone, Dostoyevsky suffered perhaps more intensely than most. Thrown among common criminals from the lower classes, he endured the hostility invariably accorded a "gentleman." He was permitted only the Bible to read, and here began the epileptic seizures which were to persist with varying frequency until his death. When the fetters were at last struck from his feet, he was sent as a common soldier to a distant Siberian outpost of some five thousand inhabitants at the edge of the Kirghiz steppe. As though making up for lost time, he now gulped life, begging from Michael the books on philosophy, history, economics, and physics he had craved in prison, and falling in love with the same frenzy he brought to his reading. Marya Isayeva, slight, somewhat hysterical, and given to intellectual pretensions, was a recent widow with a young son and no means of support. After a long and passionate courtship, she and the "strange," persistent Feodor were married in 1857.

Two years later, Dostoyevsky was pardoned by Alexander II and returned to St. Petersburg. As an ex-convict, he was forbidden to direct a publication under his own name, but with Michael's help, the first issue of *Time* (*Vremya*) appeared in 1861. It boasted several loyal and interesting contributors, among them, the rising young philosopher, Nikolay Strakhov. *House of the Dead* was serialized, as was *The Insulted and Injured*, a novel written in exile and acclaimed for its mystery and suspense, if not for the promiscuity of its heroine. Middle-of-the-road politically, *Time* dramatized the need for a unified national spirit in the critical days of the Great Reform and soon began to compete with the established weeklies. Too quickly, the tide of good fortune ebbed. A Polish insurrection, violently put down by tsarist troops, made headlines in 1863; Strakhov's article, essentially progovernment, was misread by the censor; *Time* was suppressed. In an unhappy marriage, the torment increased: Marya was dying of consumption; quarrels followed stormy reconciliations; Dostoyevsky's attacks of epilepsy came more frequently. He was just beginning to outline a new work, *Notes from the Underground* (1864), when doctors advised prolonged rest, and a new chapter in his own life opened.

Apollinaria Suslova, twenty, beautiful, and a fanatic feminist, was the antidote to despair. Jaded by experience and overburdened by debts when he met her, Dostoyevsky resisted for four months, then yielded to his desire for a tempestuous romance and a new life. Apollinaria had supposed that the writer would dominate her intellectually; instead, he was dominated by her body. She fled to Paris, and Dostoyevsky, borrowing 1,000 rubles from the Fund to Assist Needy Men of Letters, followed, stopping on the way to lose all but 5,000 francs at the Wiesbaden casino. By the time he reached Paris, Apollinaria had deserted him for a handsome young Spaniard who soon tired of her, leaving Dostoyevsky in the humiliating position of a "brother." At Baden-Baden, he tried to recoup his losses at roulette, and though he lost more than he won, found relief from Apollinaria's jeering cruelty in the excitement of the gambling. Exhausted at last by the wretched adventure, they returned to Russia, Dostoyevsky pawning his watch, and she, her rings.

With the help of a small legacy, the Dostoyevsky brothers hopefully launched a new magazine, *Epokha* (*Epoch*). It was doomed from the start. Having taken his wife to the drier climate of Moscow where after protracted suffering she died in a state bordering madness Feodor produced very little for the publication. Michael assumed complete responsibility, amassed large debts, and within four months of the first issue, died. Grieving deeply over his loss, Dostoyevsky accepted with characteristic willingness the staggering financial burden not only of *Epokha*, but of his brother's family, mistress, and bastard child. It was the opportune moment for an offer from the notorious publisher-swindler Stellovsky. He would pay 3,000 rubles for rights to all previously published works, if Dostoyevsky would deliver a new novel by November 1, 1866. Should the novel be but one day late, the advance would have to be repaid, and all rights to past, present, and future works surrendered. Dostoyevsky agreed, settled his most urgent debts, and hurried to Wiesbaden, hoping to meet Apollinaria once more and make the grand coup at roulette. Instead, their few days together exhausted his funds, and Apollinaria left him to subsist on bread and tea while he waited for loans from friends to whom he sent despairing letters.

One "black day," as he pawned his last bit of jewelry, a ring, for a third of its value, the plot for *Crime and Punishment* flashed into his mind. Hastily, he drafted an outline for Michael Katkov, editor of the *Russian Messenger*, promising to write the novel in six weeks for an advance of 300 rubles. It was his first crucial race with time; even as he wrote the second part of the novel, Katkov was serializing the first chapters. He returned to Russia, struggling to finish the book at his sister's country house; November 1 was only two months away, and not a line of the four-hundred-page novel for Stellovsky had been written. The latest writer's aid, stenography, saved him from financial—and personal—ruin. With the steady assistance of Anna Snitkina, the calm-eyed young ash-blonde who took his dictation, Dostoyevsky completed *The Gambler* (1867) on time and then made Anna his second wife. Though her unswerving love and respect for his talent afforded him the only emotional security and contentment he had ever known, their marriage was not without tribulation. To escape debtor's prison, they left Russia soon after their wedding and for four years lived in extreme poverty while Dostoyevsky gambled in the casinos of Germany, Italy, and Switzerland. Despite illness and near despair after the death of their child, it was a productive period. *The Idiot* and *The Eternal Husband* were completed by 1869; *The Possessed*, by 1873. In that year, they returned to Russia and a national reputation.

Again Dostoyevsky plunged into journalism, writing of current events and literature in *The Diary of a Writer* (1876–1878), which became a heavily subscribed monthly. Anna,

managing his affairs, saw to it that his novels were reprinted
in volume form, and in relative tranquillity, he set about
writing *The Brothers Karamazov* (1879–1880), his head
crowded with writing projects for ten years to come. In June,
1880, he spoke to delirious applause at the unveiling of Pushkin's monument in Moscow, then responded excitedly to
nationwide demands for readings from his own as well as
the poet's work. The hectic pace destroyed his health, and
in February, 1881, he died, the first Russian writer to receive
a state funeral. Two days before his death, he addressed a
final plea to Katkov for the 4,000 rubles the publisher owed
him: "At the present moment, I am in great need of money.
You do not know how much you will oblige me by paying
it to me at once; it is extremely urgent for me to obtain this
sum."

The ordeals that might have broken less resilient men
seemed but transfusions to Dostoyevsky, who admitted to the
vitality of a cat. He wrote best under tension, and the disorder, instability, and feverish sense of pressure in his own
life are reflected in the dishevelment of his prose. His dis-
organized, headlong narratives, too often written at breakneck
speed, brim with ideas and counterideas, but nowhere had
he the time (or the talent) for the subtleties which flesh and
sustain some of the best of Russian literature—the delicacy
of Turgenev's nostalgic landscapes, the steady accumulation
of Goncharov's external detail, the unhurried sweep of Tolstoy's epics.

His work falls into two parts: the shorter novels and
stories produced before his Siberian exile, and the major novels,
together with the formidable monologue of *Notes from the
Underground*, written after his return to St. Petersburg. For
their preoccupation with the underprivileged, the works in
the first group have been compared to the stories of Gogol,
but Dostoyevsky's treatment of his "injured and insulted"
heroes is rooted in a compassion alien to Gogol. While the
theme of *The Double* is superficially akin to that of *The
Overcoat*, its psychological depth is far removed from the
ambiguity of Gogol's laughter. Nevertheless, had Dostoyevsky died before the firing squad in 1849, his early work would

not have survived, nor would *The Gambler* (1866), a semi-autobiographical study of his own weakness for roulette, nor even *The Eternal Husband* (1870), one of his most cogent and psychologically astute variations on the "double" theme. His genius must be judged by the four massive novels on which his fame now rests.

Their most salient feature is their overabundance—of ideas, philosophical dialogues, emotional scenes, and melodramatic turns of plot calculated to sustain the serial reader's mystification and sense of alarm. In *Crime and Punishment* (1866), men and women swoon seventeen times, and two able-bodied ghosts, five apparitions, four prophetic dreams, and six highly contrived coincidences further contribute to the suspense. *The Idiot* (1868) contains two apparitions, seven fainting spells, and a wake during which the suitor and murderer are closeted with the ripening corpse of the lovely victim. *The Possessed* (1871–1872) boasts a secret wedding, an elopement, six deliriums, and two brutal assassinations. Nor is *The Brothers Karamazov* (1879–1880) innocent of such sensations: its brutalities are appropriately bloody, its ghost as lively and cocky as the hero of Eugène Sue's *Mémoires du Diable*, a favorite serial of the youthful Dostoyevsky. Saturated with the supernatural and fantastic elements of his boyhood reading, he drew freely from the stock-in-trade devices of such writers as Balzac, George Sand, Victor Hugo, and a host of more minor novelists like Ann Radcliffe, Lewis, and Maturin of the English Gothic school. It is hardly surprising that his contemporaries should have appreciated his greatest work not for its psychological depth, of which they were unaware, but for its value as sheer entertainment. The barest of plot summaries leaves no doubt that his novels are melodramas par excellence.

In *Crime and Punishment*, Rodion Raskolnikov determines in the solitude of his attic room to kill an old pawnbroker. With her money, he will complete his studies and rescue his sister from ignominious marriage to a wealthy older man. The murder itself will rid the world of a human parasite, "a louse" thriving on the misfortune of others. Then he meets the impoverished Marmeladov family, headed by

a drunkard who drives his daughter, Sonia, to prostitution.
Their misery strengthens Raskolnikov's resolve, and with an
ax he fells not only the old moneylender but also her sister
who arrives at the moment of the killing. He flees in horror,
leaving the money behind. Pursued by guilt, he seeks courage
from Svidrigaylov, a mysterious and powerful stranger who
attempts to seduce his sister and then, having apparently
raped a child, commits suicide. Distraught, Raskolnikov con-
fesses the murder to Sonia and at last surrenders to the suspicious police inspector he has taunted. The novel ends with
a sequence of his agonizing dissimulations, hallucinations,
fainting spells, and nervous attacks. He is condemned to seven
years in Siberia, where Sonia, who is in love with him, will
attempt his regeneration.

Released from a Swiss sanitarium, the saintly hero of
The Idiot returns to Russia to claim a large inheritance.
There he meets two young women, a general's daughter and
the cast-off mistress of a wealthy merchant, both of whom
fall in love with him. Unable to reciprocate in either case,
the "idiot" offers to marry the second woman out of pity.
She refuses, runs away with another, younger merchant, who
kills her in a jealous rage, and in literature's most gruesome
wake scene, both men guard the corpse. Deranged by the
events, the "idiot" returns to Switzerland. The murderer is
exiled to Siberia, and the general's daughter is consigned to
the mercies of a rake who later deserts her.

The action of *The Possessed* takes place in a small town
where Peter Verkhovensky, megalomaniac and amoralist, directs a nihilist conspiracy. He, as well as his group, is under
the influence of the ruthless Stavrogin, lately cashiered from
the army, perpetrator of allegedly terrifying deeds, and husband of a feeble-minded cripple. Prompted by Stavrogin, one
young nihilist vows to commit suicide to prove his power
over God, then agrees to confess to the murder of Shatov,
a member who wishes to leave the conspiracy. In a play for
power, Verkhovensky implicates the entire group in Shatov's
murder. Meanwhile, with Stavrogin's consent, the group sets
fire to a slum where the cripple and her brother have been
murdered—to free Stavrogin for marriage with a suitably well-

born girl who loves him. A postal clerk denounces the nihilists and is driven mad by the events. Stavrogin hurries to the capital to avoid arrest for murder, then returns to put a noose around his own neck, realizing the futility of his life.

The more concentrated plot of *The Brothers Karamazov* brings an entire family into focus as three brothers are confronted with the murder of their father. Feodor Karamazov, lecher and drunkard, has abandoned his sons and appropriated for his own use the property bequeathed to the eldest, Dmitri. Wayward, passionate, lovable despite his shortcomings, Dmitri harbors a deep hatred for his father. Ivan, a skeptic and the most intellectual of the three, is a materialist. Alyosha, a saintly boy, is a monk who devotes his boundless energy to the service of God and man. Smerdyakov, Feodor's bastard and an epileptic, is Ivan's sycophantic disciple.

Dmitri is in love with Katerina Ivanovna, whose father, a superior officer, has embezzled funds and threatens suicide. Dmitri offers to pay the debt if Katerina will visit him secretly, but when she submits, his generosity triumphs and he humiliates her with dismissal. The Karamazov violence and sensuality now assert themselves. Infatuated with the beautiful Grushenka, former mistress of a wealthy merchant, he buys her favors with a considerable sum of money entrusted him by Katerina for a relative in Moscow. Feodor also covets Grushenka and offers her 3,000 rubles for her attentions. Dmitri threatens to kill his father if he finds them together.

Smerdyakov, Feodor's confidant and lackey, advises Ivan to leave the village, predicting his father's death and estimating the Karamazov fortune at 4,000 rubles for each son. He suggests that should Ivan be absent at a time when he himself suffers an epileptic attack, none could protect Feodor from Dmitri. Against his better judgment, Ivan leaves, aware that his departure may facilitate murder.

Searching for Grushenka, who is occupied elsewhere with passions of her own, Dmitri proceeds to his father's bedroom, pistol in hand. He is restrained by the old servant-watchman of the estate. Meanwhile, Smerdyakov strikes the mortal blow, then simulates an epileptic seizure near Feodor's body. Dmitri is convicted by circumstantial evidence; Ivan, brooding over his role in the murder, develops brain fever; and Smerdyakov, disenchanted by his mentor's moral anguish, hangs himself. Dmitri, exiled to Siberia, is joined by the spiritually renewed Grushenka.

At first glance, it seems preposterous that Dostoyevsky could have claimed to inaugurate a new kind of realism. The worn conventions of the Romantics—the Byronic villain, the "pure" prostitute, the ragged Dickensian children, and the urban poor—are like spare parts selected at random from a common shed to set outlandish plots in motion. Yet like all Russian writers of his time, Dostoyevsky was committed to the portrayal of contemporary life. What was exceptional or fantastic in his plots he justified on grounds that his basic material came from press reports of actual crimes. These he devoured; what history had been to Tolstoy, journalism was to Dostoyevsky. The murder central to *The Brothers Karamazov* he based on a parricide attributed to a fellow prisoner but actually committed by the convict's brother. When Ivan condemns God, he offers as evidence of divine perfidy a catalogue of bestialities to children, gathered by Dostoyevsky from current tabloids and judicial dossiers. The reports of brutality and aberration seemed to him not merely facts, but expressions of a larger truth; he believed he only dramatized reality when he turned newspaper stories into fiction. Certainly it was in them that his invention began, but the dynamic stresses and strains of his novels flow also from the agony of private experience. For his transposition of that experience into universal terms, he ranks foremost among the great writers.

He had written of the underprivileged in his early stories, but he appears to have actually experienced their degradation during his four years in prison. Omsk altered his total spiritual and psychological outlook. His reading, limited to the Bible, filled him with the love and teachings of Jesus, and the brutality he saw on all sides turned his hatred of human pain into an obsession. When he returned to the world of free men, his new convictions set him apart from his former associations among the intelligentsia of Moscow and St. Petersburg. Like the radicals he had come to despise and distrust, he championed the oppressed but protested that the monarchy and the Church, rather than any political instrument, particularly one of terror, must cure Russian ills. He no longer believed that Western-inspired socialism could lighten the long suffering of the people. What he had witnessed in Siberia persuaded him that evil existed ineradicably in the soul of man, to be dislodged neither by science, nor enlightenment, nor reason. Caprice alone shaped private lives; the strong dominated the weak. Although the laws of nature and manmade laws might be understood, freedom came only if both were spurned.

Notes from the Underground expounds this philosophy of the irrational. Written to refute Chernyshevsky's *What Is to be Done?* it is cast as a confession in which the original antihero, Dostoyevsky's major contribution to modern literature, disgorges his state of mind. For twenty years, he has lived in willful isolation and permanent rebellion against all things. He tramples his early ideals, curses established values, and denies all intellectual achievement—he cannot submit to the "tyranny" of twice two making four; given the choice of saving the world or drinking a cup of tea, he must settle unhesitatingly for his tea. His pleasure is in planning pain for others as revenge for imagined slights. Exulting, he lists the humiliations he has both suffered and inflicted. He emerges as the prototype of extreme alienation, odious even to himself, an unbalanced individualist with great potential for destruction. But his fury is impotent. Essentially rabbit-hearted, he never takes action.

Raskolnikov, whose name in Russian means "schismatic," is another Underground Man. It is left to him to forge his grievances into a willfully destructive act, a crime that will liberate him from man-made laws into freedom. Despising society, he must transgress it (in Russian, the word "crime" means, literally, "transgression"), thereby proving that he, like his idol, Napoleon, is of a superior race of men. A victim of abject poverty, he must perform the extraordinary to find a place in the sun. He therefore sets out in a sultry St. Petersburg July to commit murder. Far from liberating him from the world he detests, Raskolnikov's deed only binds him to

it more closely. Distracted by the sense of guilt he had not
expected to experience, he is in agony lest he be suspected,
yet longs for discovery so that he might assert himself, if only
by identification with so monstrous and pointless an act. He
therefore dogs the steps of the police inspector and at last
finds relief of sorts by confessing to Sonia.

  Crime and Punishment is probably Dostoyevsky's most
tautly constructed and dynamic work, recording as on a seismo-
graph the semidelirious thoughts and raging emotions of an
amateur criminal both before and after the crime is committed. But Raskolnikov's approach to salvation through
Sonia's love and piety is not only an implausible ending to
the story, it is no ending at all. The novel culminates at
mid-point with the appearance of its real hero, the sinister
Svidrigaylov. In his notes and letters, Dostoyevsky returned
again and again to the definition of literary genius as the
power which should bring "a new word" into literature.
Svidrigaylov is his "new word," a character created to express
his own doubts and despairs in terms of flesh and blood.
He is both less and more than human, all that Raskolnikov
aspires and fails to be. Seeking proof of God, Svidrigaylov
discovers only pain. Seeing pain, he denies God. Denying
God, he must declare his own divinity. With that premise,
he emerges beyond concepts of good and evil, crime and
punishment. He is committed only to the naked working of
his own will, performing whatever deeds are required to free
his individuality from the checkreins of convention. Should
he instinctively recoil from an act of evil, he must perform
the act to crush the instinct. If he performs good, it is because no law of man or nature commands him. Finally, no
challenges remain. Emptied of all living desire, he must choose
suicide in a final attempt to give his existence meaning.

  Weak of will, Raskolnikov commits his crime and then
cowers before his own audacity. Svidrigaylov, a monolith of
will, is his other self, his double. Long before modern psy-
chiatry revealed the amazing shapes of schizophrenia, Dostoyevsky was engrossed by the contradictions he detected in
personality. He had observed in prison and noted time and
again in *House of the Dead* that hardened criminals could

show spontaneous delight in the most naive of diversions and in the next moment attack a man brutally, without qualms. This "otherness" of men, one of his most persistent themes, Dostoyevsky generalized as the suave, aggressive alter ego of the protagonist in revolt against his deepest humiliations. The duality takes many forms as the idea of the "double" develops. At times as mystifying to the reader as the Raskolnikov-Svidrigaylov composite, it reaches its greatest complexity in Ivan Karamazov, who creates in Smerdyakov a debased version of himself and yet is tormented by a discarded code of morality.

Each of the "doubles" is an alter ego for the author himself, a kind of personal champion dispatched to tilt for answers to the unanswerable. Svidrigaylov fails; the ruthless assertion of individual will accomplishes only destruction and emptiness. Perhaps, then, a will dedicated to absolute good can succeed. Laboring on the eighth plan for *The Idiot*, Dostoyevsky wrote his niece that "the chief idea of the novel is to portray a positively good man. There is nothing more difficult to do, and especially now. All writers who have tried it have always failed. . . . There is only one positively good man in the world—Christ." If he had hoped in *The Idiot* to turn Sonia's passive humility into an actively healing force for a deranged world, he failed utterly. Prince Myshkin, the "idiot," manages only to complicate the lives into which he stumbles, entangling good and evil with an intricacy even Dostoyevsky was not to surpass. Myshkin is a selfless man. His judgments are pure, and he therefore earns the trust as well as the skeptical laughter of his companions. Compassionate, generous, and guileless, he absorbs their guilt and passion, suffering vicariously all that they suffer until he is left a gibbering madman. Ironically, his humility works no reforms in return. It becomes, rather, a corrosive influence, particularly on the sensuous, hot-tempered Rogozhin, Myshkin's "brother in Christ" (they have exchanged crosses) and his complementary double. The saintliness of the one urges the other toward homicidal madness, a climax reached with the violent death of Nastasya Filipovna. One of the most compelling women in all of Dostoyevsky's portraiture, Nastasya

inspires in her admirers the same ambivalence Dostoyevsky
had experienced with Apollinaria Suslova. She is a proud,
passionate creature whose "demoniac beauty" exerts great
power while her tempestuous nature confounds understanding. Rogozhin is driven to murder when Nastasya, scorning
his "respectable" offer of marriage, tosses his gift of 100,000
rubles into the fire and departs with the aging merchant who
had seduced her at sixteen. Her gentle silences flare into
wildness, her tears dry into laughter, her hysterics vanish
beneath icy dignity in transformations of mood so swift that
the pace of the novel quickens each time Nastasya appears.
Like all of his successful characters, Nastasya comes tumultu-
ously alive not by virtue of a descriptive tour de force, but
because Dostoyevsky achieves realism by illuminating ideas.
Moods and emotions, not details of the physical world, animate his people, and his creation of mood is as deft and lucid
as his plots are murky.

The Nechayev affair of 1870 inspired Dostoyevsky's third
novel, *The Possessed*, as involuted of plot as *The Idiot*. When
a young revolutionist claimed that his cell of five students
was but one of thousands dedicated to the government's
destruction, Russian authorities were thoroughly aroused. What
captured Dostoyevsky's imagination was Nechayev's cold-
blooded treachery. There had been no other cells; he had
forced his group to murder one of their number suspected
of deserting the cause; had executed a sardonic hoax singlehandedly. While more than a thousand of the intelligentsia
were being exiled to Siberia each month on suspicion alone,
Dostoyevsky serialized a satirical recreation of the incident into
which he poured all his hatred of the radical movement, its
terrorism and its nihilism.

The novel appears to be a poorly conceived farce written
for the general purpose of creating indiscriminate confusion.
The chaos was intentional, meant to argue Dostoyevsky's re-
buttal to *Fathers and Sons* and his contempt for Turgenev,
that symbol of the detested West. Stepan Verkhovensky, a
caricature of the historian Granovsky who had influenced Herzen and Belinsky, is the comfortable idealist of *The Possessed*, an old-fashioned liberal of the forties who drinks,

gambles, and talks to excess, expounding for the elite of the provinces his ideas of utopia, impractical and purposeless. His son, a far more dangerous breed, is a nihilist of the seventies. Unlike Eugene Bazarov, Turgenev's scientific materialist who sees his purpose but dimly, Peter Verkhovensky is wholly committed to political action. That the group he leads is isolated without political status in a small, apathetic town does not diminish its menacing power. It commits arbitrary murder; it reasons that "starting from unlimited freedom, I arrive at unlimited despotism." With that axiom, the concept of totalitarianism is already a commonplace.

Halfway through the chaotic action of *The Possessed*, the narrator suddenly breaks off, apparently routed by the confusion, and the novel becomes a metaphysical drama wherein the saturnine Stavrogin dominates the scene. Direct heir to Svidrigaylov, Stavrogin (whose name means "cross" in Greek) precipitates danger, death, and darkness. Indifferent to the effect of his actions, he not only inspires Peter's political fraud but encourages Shatov's belief in God and urges Kirilov, a half-mad epileptic, toward a vision of man as God, exalting the Christian mysteries while he raises tormenting doubts about God's existence. The more wantonly Stavrogin asserts his will, the more empty he becomes, until, paralyzed by the futility of existence, he hangs himself by slipping a strong silken cord thickly smeared with soap around his neck.

Just as Dostoyevsky's novels illustrate his steady development as a writer, so do they mark the successive stages of his inquiry into the existence of God. Alyosha Karamazov tells Ivan that "for real Russians, the question of God's existence and of immortality, or, as you say, the same questions turned inside out, come first and foremost, of course." *The Brothers Karamazov*, Dostoyevsky's final work, offers not only an amalgam of all that is profound and astute in his knowledge of human nature, but his most definitive argument for Christianity as interpreted by the Russian Orthodox Church. Father Zosima, Alyosha's mentor, is the representative of an unquestioning faith which prescribes universal love at the same time that it shares in the burden of guilt carried by all men. Set against this power for good is the murder of

Feodor Karamazov, an act of evil which is, as in the preceding three novels, the center of the action. The contest ends in theodicy with Dostoyevsky's acknowledgement that natural or moral evil exists only for the purpose of defining the greatest moral good.

A gripping murder mystery as well as a proclamation of faith, *The Brothers Karamazov* explores on another level the mysteries of heredity in an extraordinary family. The vitality and the baseness of the Karamazov strain (in the Tartar language, *karam* means "black") originates in Feodor, "all will to live and will to power." He sires not only the servility of Smerdyakov, but the emotional intensity of Dmitri, the passionate intellectualism of Ivan, and the religious fervor of Alyosha. Discordant by nature, the Karamazovs experience nothing that is not turbulent, and all the terrifying energies of Dostoyevsky's imagination are released to create their world. It is Dmitri who emerges to dominate the major part of the novel. At the mercy of his unruly emotions, he is as raw and reckless as the primitive forces shaping Russia herself. And like Russia, guilty of much but capable of long endurance, he believes that suffering will hasten his redemption. Accused wrongly of his father's murder, he therefore accepts his prison sentence gladly, choosing trust in God as the only authentic form of freedom.

Freedom and the idea of freedom are, in fact, the ideological center of *The Brothers Karamazov.* Ivan, a brilliant student of the natural sciences, is, like Raskolnikov, an atheist, ranging himself with those few who are able to surmount the perplexities of life. His "Euclidian mind" cannot grasp the meaning of, nor understand, the need for a God who permits the innocent to suffer. He "respectfully returns his ticket" and gives Alyosha his own views in the *Legend of the Grand Inquisitor*. Perhaps the best known prose poem in Russian literature, this "legend" tells of Christ's return to earth in the Spain of the sixteenth century. The Grand Inquisitor accuses Christ of destroying the happiness of humanity by demanding from man not forced obedience, but the allegiance of his free spirit. The power of free choice is too great a burden for ordinary men, the Inquisitor insists. The human conscience must be held captive if men are to be happy, and three powers alone can lead it into captivity: the miracle, the mystery, and the authority of the Church.

Ivan's doctrine is put almost immediately to the test when Smerdyakov, taught by his half-brother that all things to an intelligent man are lawful, commits the murder which is Ivan's unspoken wish. Although atheism eventually fails him—he disintegrates under the realization that he is morally responsible for the murder—the power of his argument cannot be denied. Deeply troubled by it, Alyosha perceives that his brothers are destroying themselves. "And they are destroying others. It's the primitive force of the Karamazovs—a crude, unbridled, earthy force. Does the spirit of God move above it? Even I do not know. I only know that I am a Karamazov." Summing up the case, the prosecutor at Dmitri's trial sees the spiritual perplexity of the Karamazovs as a symptom of degenerating society. Russia is, he says, like "a swift troika galloping toward an unknown goal," not, as in Gogol's image, a proud leader of nations, but a frightening specter unleashed into the civilized world. Like so many Slavophils, Dostoyevsky believed Russia could liberate herself and Europe as well, but only if she renounced the dehumanizing materialism of the West and reclaimed the power inherent in her devoutly Christian heritage. But like Alyosha, he could not ignore the profound truths of Ivan's heresy. While *The Brothers Karamazov* arrives at only tentative, fragmentary answers to Dostoyevsky's most compelling questions, it states the whole of his—and our—metaphysical dilemma with such poignance and lucidity that it remains not only his most inconclusive and controversial work, but his greatest.

It is only artistic justice that Dostoyevsky's literary achievements rather than his political and religious convictions earned him the status of prophet. In exploring the reaches of human reason, he anticipated psychoanalysis by exposing what is irrational and hidden in the motives of men. To the development of the modern novel he contributed a technique whereby fiction could more dramatically illuminate reality: recreating the physical world only as it impinged upon the consciousness of his characters, he prepared realistic writing for the uses of expressionism, surrealism, and fantasy. But Dostoyevsky's readability is perhaps his most striking accomplishment. His plots, beginning and ending in extremes, generate enough excitement to carry even so bulky a work as *The Brothers Karamazov* (939 pages). Crisis after crisis intensifies the already excessive emotional impact of his stories. Dmitri, for example, has motive enough for murder when his father robs him of his inheritance. But then Feodor uses the purloined wealth to bid publicly for his son's mistress! Grushenka, in turn, inflames Dmitri's jealousy by seeking out her long-lost ex-lover, and Dmitri himself compounds his anguish with remorse and guilt over Katerina.

These complexities of plot are mortised by great blocks of metaphysical debate, interesting enough for their endless abstractions on love, death, and religion. But what enhances their interest is their form, the key to Dostoyevsky's genius. They are cast as dialogues, not mere appendages to plot wherein the author pursues his private thoughts, but living conversations which shed light on the events of the story because they illuminate the characters who precipitate those events. The dialogues are more truly the substance of "what happens" in Dostoyevsky than all the sensational acts of love, lust, cruelty, and hate. Protagonist after protagonist, male and female alike, bares himself in talk, stripping his mind to its most secret core with an abandonment shocking to the Western sensibility. Feverish, frequently incoherent, and always uninhibited, he is possessed by one idea: to communicate the essence of his being so that he will be understood and clarified by another. Invariably, he fails. Although he never lacks a willing listener, the dialogue breaks off abruptly before any common ground of understanding can be reached. Dmitri is thus condemned by a peasant jury unable to grasp his moral agony, just as the Populists were routed by the very people they hoped to serve, just as, in our own day, the individual protest is lost in conformity and indifference. Communicating without understanding, each Dostoyevsky hero moves in an atmosphere of unresolved tensions, his quest for metaphysical absolutes attended by violence in the real world, and delirium in the world of dreams.

To read Dostoyevsky, then, is to be left with an overwhelming sense of energy in a void, one reason for his appeal to youth. His novels are like reports of a devastating flood, accounts of individual courage and mass heroism alternating with statistics of destruction and death. Writing hastily, nervously, creating his "supreme reality" in terms of ecstasy and excess, Dostoyevsky offers no consolation to the twentieth-century reader in search of stability. For that we must turn to the loving portrayal of all that is normal in life, the imperceptibly changing, always healing commonplaces of which Tolstoy wrote with such confidence and restraint. He could not be orphaned in the world, Gorky said, as long as Tolstoy lived.

10 · The Twilight Age

LESKOV (1831–1895)

The worlds of Tolstoy and Dostoyevsky encompass so much of Russian life, it must seem to the foreign reader that no other writer of the age could contribute significantly to literary history. A large number of Russians, however, savor the short stories and novellas of Nikolay Leskov for the diversity and authenticity of the Russian experience they recreate.

A secondary figure in an epoch of giants, Nikolay Leskov is not easy to classify. He was born into the mixed class of priests, merchants, and gentry, and for seven years travelled widely through remote sections of Central Russia in the employ of a nonconformist Englishman, owner of a far-flung Russian estate. He was thirty before his literary career began with an easy, flowing narrative into which he poured the exuberant dialogue, humorous anecdotes, and picaresque adventures encountered in his travels. Too practical to participate in politics, he disgraced himself with the intelligentsia by mocking the radical movement in his early novels, *No Way Out* (1864) and *At Daggers Drawn* (1870). While they are deservedly forgotten, they earned him so poor a press that his bad reputation still lingers unjustly in Russian criticism.

His worth lies elsewhere. Leskov was the first Russian writer to exploit little known aspects of life in provincial areas obscure enough to be unaffected by great national events. Many of his stories are of village priests, portraying the daily life

of the parsonage and the trials of the lower clergy with
warmth, generosity, and a wealth of sharply observant detail.
Cathedral Folk (1872), the second and most popular "chronicle" of an ecclesiastical trilogy (1869–1874), introduces the
unforgettable Deacon Akhila, innately and obstinately good,
exuberantly alive, and somewhat absurd in his handling of
parish affairs. He is an excellent foil for the scrupulous archpriest, Tuberozov, who chides Akhila regularly for his un-
clerical escapades. The archpriest, on the other hand, is Leskov's
most consistent and serious attempt to create a *pravednik*,
or righteous man, unworldly, just, and incorruptible. Like
Dostoyevsky, he researched Russia's ancient roots in religion
for the attributes of a positive hero. He steeped himself in
popular religious lore, even learning the techniques of icon
painting, persuaded that the vitality of medieval Russia could
be revived if her religiosity were but restored. Several of his
stories celebrate the tenacious faith of the Old Believers in
Avvakum's austere tenets, and Tuberozov, created as his personal spokesman for Russia's religious past, is equally stern
and strong of ethic. Leskov later moved away from traditional
orthodoxy to come under Tolstoy's influence and assert that
it was not dogma that identified faith, but the humility and
charity of human kinship. A Siberian snowstorm is the setting
in *Edge of the World* (1876) for a poignant encounter between a Russian missionary and a pagan. The more primitive
man responds intuitively to the truths of the missionary's
message, but only when the encumbrances of dogma have
been stripped away.

Leskov's ideas, however, are less potent than his ability
as a teller of stories. His material comes from a bewildering
array of sources: oral legend, folklore, the historical past, current tabloids, his encyclopedic readings, and his wide travels.
His moods are just as diverse, ranging from the bizarre, the
mystifying, and the grotesque, to crude or malicious humor,
hair-raising adventure, and even the starkly macabre. The famous *Lady Macbeth of the Mtsensk District* (1865) tells of
a merchant's wife who murders three members of her family
for the sake of her lover, then drowns herself and the girl
who usurps his affections. Equally well known, *The Enchanted*

Wanderer (1873) is as merry a tale as the capers of a former serf can make it. Roaming northern Russia as a jack-of-all-trades, this picaresque hero ends, in the fashion of popular folk tales, as a novice in a monastery. Yet again, pure farce and good-natured slyness blend in a story over which generations have roared with delight, *The Tale of the Squint-Eyed, Left-Handed Smith from Tula and the Steel Flea* (1881). Having presented a mechanical dancing flea to Alexander I, British craftsmen are bested by a Russian smith who attaches horseshoes to the microscopic feet. The admiring British lure the illiterate hero to London, but he runs from the foggy climate, the skinny wenches, and the weak whisky to drink himself sodden and die in a charity hospital at home.

Leskov's language, as full-blooded as the content of his stories, has served as a model for Gorky and several contemporary Soviet writers. Like Gogol's, it is best read aloud; its racy colloquialisms and folksy tang are a precious record of the now forgotten provincial vernacular. He excelled in reproducing the lower-class garbled renditions of scientific terms and words of foreign origin, a kind of "popular etymology" which is responsible for much of the enormously comic effect of his dialogues. Bold, inventive, and sonorous, it is now a linguistic curiosity and, unfortunately, almost untranslatable.

For sheer entertainment value, Leskov has no serious rival. He would have remained on record as Russia's foremost writer of short stories, had he not been eclipsed, in his own lifetime, by a more universal and altogether greater talent.

CHEKHOV (1860–1904)

The last of the great makers of Russian classics, Anton Chekhov did for the short story what Tolstoy and Dostoyevsky had done for the novel: he gave it modern form, and he made it reflect modern times. Like Dostoyevsky, he was influenced early by Western writers, chiefly Guy de Maupassant, first among the moderns to make drama of the commonplace. And, just as Dostoyevsky set the course for the development of the Western novel, so Chekhov dominated the history of the short story. He so perfected the form that his name is linked with every one of his successors, regardless of nationality or place in time.

The short story in Russia evolved from the folk adventures of traditional lore through Pushkin's *Belkin Tales,* Gogol's *St. Petersburg Stories,* Turgenev's *Sportsman's Sketches,* and the short fiction of Tolstoy and Dostoyevsky. With Chekhov, it came fully of age. It shed the last vestiges of the tall tale and dropped the self-conscious introductions which pad the stories of Turgenev and Leskov. Explanatory footnotes and superfluous details of biography and dress vanished. Conclusions were no longer explicit and pat. It has been said that Chekhov's story is like a tortoise—all middle. The ending, never stated, is implicit in the frustration, nostalgia, loneliness, pretension, or despair of the story's one brief moment selected from a life to illuminate it in its entirety.

That Chekhov wrote with pessimism and only of Russia's "submerged" society must be attributed to his personal circumstances and the period in which he lived. The assassination of Alexander II brought the "heroic revolution" of the nineteenth century to an end. By 1881, Siberian prisons were overflowing with political subversives, and all magazines or newspapers directed by radicals were being closed down. Apathy, boredom, and bureaucracy seized control of the country. The intelligentsia, hopeless for their cause, retired into humdrum private concerns. It was an era of conformity and opportunism, which intensified as industry expanded and the railroads lengthened. In this period of stagnation, Chekhov was becoming a writer. He had been born in the miserable little port of Taganrog, on the Azov Sea. His grandfather, a serf, had purchased freedom for himself and his sons at 700 rubles a head, and until he was sixteen, Anton spent all his leisure time learning to shortweight and shortchange the customers in his father's scruffy grocery shop. When his family moved to Moscow, he was left behind to give lessons, run errands, and curry financial favors until he graduated from high school. With a small stipend, he then enrolled as a medical student at the University of Moscow and assumed the permanent support of his destitute parents, sister, and younger brother.

He began his career as a hack writer of humor. In order
to buy a pie for his mother's birthday, he sent a twenty-line
anecdote to a third-rate comic weekly soon after his arrival
in Moscow. It was promptly accepted, and Chekhov discovered that at five kopecks a line (to a mandatory length
of 80–120 lines), he could scribble one joke, farcical episode,
literary parody, dramatic sketch, or comical anecdote a day,
thus providing for his family while he continued his medical
studies. Fun-loving and gregarious, he was insatiably curious
about people. He prowled for material in courtrooms, markets,
race tracks, railroad stations, and workmen's taverns, and with
the cartoonist's gift of caricature, caught the gestures and
speech of clerks, peasants, factory hands, priests and vagrants,
chorus girls and servants, in some six hundred pieces. Written
for the crude taste of the weekly's semiliterate readers, most of
them focus on the perennial drunks, in-laws, and cuckolds
of street humor, their themes carefully edited of any notes
of sadness or social satire. But here and there among the
"trash, and what trash!" as Chekhov called it, a glimpse of
character or a fleeting mood promised great stories to come.
As early as 1883, he had caught in the three pages of *Fat
and Thin* as candid a close-up of officialdom as he was ever
to write. The satire has two former schoolmates meeting on
a railroad platform, pleased to see each other again, until the
thinner of the two learns that his friend is nine grades higher
in rank than he. To the confusion and disgust of "Fat,"
"Thin," his wife, and adolescent son shrink suddenly into
timorous flattery. Three years later, Chekhov composed what
is surely one of modern literature's most moving studies of
loneliness. In *Misery*, a cabdriver tries in vain on a wet winter
night to tell his indifferent passengers of the death of his
son. He returns at last to the stable and unburdens his grief
to his mare.

Established in his medical practice, Chekhov continued
to write for the steady income his patients from the Moscow
slums could not provide. He published two collections of his
longer comic pieces, both instantly popular, and when the second elicited respectful press notices, he scraped enough money
together for a visit to the literary Mecca of St. Petersburg.

There, Dmitri Grigorovich, eminent in 1886 as a novelist but better known today for his discovery of Chekhov, persuaded him to abandon comic writing for serious literature, and his stories, longer and more carefully worked out than the sketches, began appearing regularly in Suvorin's powerful *New Time,* largest of the Russian dailies. In 1887, his third collection, *In the Twilight,* won the 500-ruble Pushkin Prize, and *Messenger of the Month,* an influential Moscow journal, published *The Steppe* (1888), his long, lyrical story of a boy's journey across the great southern plain. His reputation was made.

Yet Chekhov was restless and dispirited, affected no doubt by criticism of his work for its failure to provide social and moral guidance. Child of a disillusioned age, he seemed unable to formulate a consistent philosophy of life, and he was inclined to agree with his critics that the lack of it vitiated his art. In a much-quoted letter to Suvorin, he compared his own writing to that of Tolstoy, whom he greatly admired:

> The best of them are realists and paint life as it is, but because every line is steeped in the consciousness of a goal, you feel, besides life as it is, the life that ought to be, and that captivates you. And we? We! We paint life as it is but beyond that, nothing at all. Flog us and we can do no more! We have neither immediate nor remote aims and in our souls there is a great empty space. We do not believe in politics, we do not believe in revolution, we have no God. . . .

When one of his brothers died in 1890, Chekhov undertook a long journey by horse cart across Siberia to the penal island of Sakhalin, returning home by sea, from Ceylon to Odessa. His objective, partly to ease his sorrow and partly to make a purposeful contribution to society, was to expose the barbaric conditions in which convicts lived; his report, detailed and trenchant, played a part in the prison reforms of 1892. When it was finished, he settled with his family at Melikhovo, 50 miles south of Moscow, where for the next six years he gave free medical care to the peasants of the district, built a hospital, directed a sanitary station during the cholera epidemic of 1892–1893, and continued his writing.

His seven or eight hundred stories are remarkable first

for the variety of their characters, whether in the earliest sketches (to 1886) not included in final editions, in those of the transitional period (1887–1892), or in the most mature *povesti*, or novellas, of the last period (1892–1897). Justly called the chronicler of nineteenth-century Russia's last two decades, Chekhov wrote of those people who formed the middle strata of every social class—nobility, clergy and bureaucracy, rural and urban intelligentsia, merchants and peasants. As interesting, varied, and authentic as this sociological aspect of his work is, his writings could not have survived for that alone. What carries them beyond the confines of history is his unique ability to display the whole of an ordinary life in one commonplace moment from it, reflecting as he does so the emotions shared by all men of all times and all places.

Nothing of consequence happens during these momentary illuminations of reality. The stories receive their color and texture from impressionistic details of a landscape, a time of day, a season, or a turn in weather. Even Chekhov's language, which loses very little in translation, is carefully unemphatic, unmarked by idiomatic refinements, somewhat colorless in the manner of everyday living. It was exactly the drab continuity of existence that fascinated Chekhov. The only action in *Vanka* (1886), for example, is the writing and mailing of a letter: nine-year-old Vanka, apprenticed to a shoemaker who treats him roughly, writes on Christmas Eve to his grandfather in the country, recalling his happy days there and begging to be taken back. He drops the letter into the mailbox, addressed simply to "grandfather in the village." In *Enemies* (1887), a country doctor whose small daughter has just died receives a wealthy man's imperious summons to attend his wife, who appears to have suffered a heart attack at their distant estate. When the two men arrive, they discover a note from the woman: she has feigned the attack to allow her time to elope. Half-crazed with his own grief, the doctor insults the husband for subjecting him to such frivolity, and the two part, enemies. Or again, in *The Witch* (1886), an ugly, superstitious old parish clerk convinces himself that his young wife, bestowed upon him with his job, is a witch who lures strangers to their single-room shack in bad weather. When a young postman takes shelter on a stormy winter night, a momentary attraction flares between him and the lonely girl, and in the violent quarrel that follows, the old man accuses her of practicing the "black arts."

So "plotless" are the stories and so easily are they read that the presence of a double theme is frequently missed. Chekhov's narrative travels on what has been interestingly called "straight and curved" lines. Vanka, for instance, wants, straightforwardly, to go home. But in his nostalgia for the "trees silvery with hoarfrost, the snow drifts and the star-studded sky" of his native village, lies the story's curve: he hankers for and is happiest in a beauty too fragile to compete with the tough practicalities of real life. The doctor, offended by what proves to be a farcical intrusion on his grief, is righteously angry. But the husband has received a severe blow as well. Impatient with each other's plight, the men are unable to communicate as human beings, a persistent Chekhovian theme.

Although Chekhov's civic conscience was clearly subordinate to his passionate interest in the individual self, he was not unaware of the social injustice of his day, nor indifferent to the stark misery of the peasants. The grandson of a serf, he could not share Count Tolstoy's illusions about the sanctity and joy of rural life. His own stories reflect the penury and semislavery inflicted by the Great Reform: *Peasants* (1897) is a somber picture of bestial life in a village hut; *In the Cart* (1897) describes a village teacher's losing battle against provincial ignorance and her own chronic poverty; in *Nightmare* (1886) a conscientious village priest, wretchedly underpaid like all low-ranking officials, demeans his office and destroys his health as he makes parish rounds on foot, in rags and near starvation. Such catalogues of social abuse are in the best tradition of Russian writing, as are Chekhov's satires on bureaucratic *poshlost* (*The Privy Councillor*, 1886) or the sterile idealism of superfluous men (*On the Road*, 1886). Countless other stories are of the trivia poisoning Russian

happiness and ambition, matter treated again and again in
the works of Gogol, Turgenev, and Goncharov, and in the
early fiction of Dostoyevsky.

In approach and style, however, Chekhov most resembles
Pushkin; for all the apparent simplicity of his story, it is as
intricately constructed as an Onegin stanza. Both men, the one
launching the century and the other bringing it to a close,
display the restraint and economy of the classicist, and both are
extremely thorough technicians. Pushkin learned incisiveness
from his eighteenth-century predecessors; Chekhov's gift for
brevity came of long apprenticeship in pulp writing. Pushkin
naturally maintained aesthetic distance from his work; Chekhov's objectivity derived from his medical training. Medicine
was his lawful wife, he said wryly, and literature, his mistress.
As is frequently the case, intimacy with the one greatly affected
relations with the other. A man of science, Chekhov was inclined to despise rhetoric. A respecter of facts, he saw in technology the guarantee of a better future for mankind. Like
many of his generation, he had been attracted to Tolstoy's
primitive Christianity, but then he read Darwin and wrote,
"A sense of the practical and of justice tells me that in elec-
tricity and steam there is more love of humanity than in chastity
and abstinence from meat." Thus, the most positive characters
of stories and the spokesmen of his plays are doctors, whose
service is unstinting and practical. There is something of the
physician's pragmatic attitude in the very structure of his
writing: a figure is isolated for examination, the diagnosis is
succinct, remedy is neither sure-fire nor quick.

The prognosis, however, is always clear. "We live so badly!"
one of the stories ends. It seemed to Chekhov that one could
not but live badly in a society so rife with venial sins. Wasted
talent, thoughtlessness, vulgarity, pettiness, complacency, and
sham make up the general air of pessimism in his work. The
Russians who crowd his stories are submerged in the listlessness
and futility of living; mentally sluggish, spiritually bereft, and
socially underprivileged, they remain on the threshold of
decisions, defeated by a sense of their own inadequacy to cope
with the problems of their day. Chekhov himself believed
firmly in the potential of the individual civilized man and

loved to see "life affirm itself" in obstinately growing things. An ardent gardener, he cared for large plots of flowers on his estate, and when a camellia he had planted in Yalta bloomed for the first time, he sent a rejoicing telegram to his wife. Sacred to him was "the human body, health, intelligence, talent, inspiration, love and absolute freedom from violence and falsehood in any form." Wherever these attributes are lacking is where the Chekhovian dilemma begins.

With the logic of his profession, Chekhov asserted that mental distress arose from physical disorder, a theme that carries the first great story of his maturity, *The Namesday* (1888). Through three harrowing days, crisis builds between a man and his wife; though they are deeply in love, the woman's painful pregnancy turns her spiteful and suspicious. Tightly corseted to conceal her condition, she moves among her namesday party guests, struggling against pain and searching her past for some insight that will order her chaotic thoughts. In the famous *Boring Story* (1889), an eminent scholar, nearing retirement, looks in vain among the fragmented achievements of his career for the antidote to failure in his twilight years: he cannot understand or communicate with those closest to him. In *Ward Number 6* (1892), it is again a matter of wasted life, rich resources of intelligence and talent dissipated by apathy and carelessness. Architecturally, it is one of Chekhov's most unified pieces, a starkly realistic story and a controversial one. When his efforts to improve ward conditions are thwarted by the hostility and indolence of his staff, Dr. Ragin, the deeply sensitive director of a *zemstvo* hospital, withdraws into the private consolations of philosophy and literature. He is stirred from his intellectual seclusion by a mental patient, and the ensuing friendship ends with the shattering violence of a detonated bomb. So affected was Lenin by the story that he was compelled to leave his room for the out-of-doors, feeling that he, too, had been imprisoned in a ward. For him and many Soviet critics, the abuse showered on helpless patients by their sadistic attendants symbolized the political oppression of Alexander II. Another interpretation gives the story far more universal significance. Dr. Ragin's weak retreat from adversity is a virus of character which results in his willful evasion of responsibility. He alone is to blame for the deterioration of his hospital and staff.

Like all Chekhov's characters, the protagonists of *The Lady with a Dog* (1899) are motivated from within. A favorite of critics and readers alike, the story treats of the intimacy between man and woman, a theme predominant in Chekhov fiction. What begins as a banal, summer-resort affair between two married people ends as far more than either had bargained for. He is a middle-aged ladies' man, bored and at loose ends; she too is restless, out of love with her husband. Their vacation over, they part with little sorrow to resume their separate lives in distant cities. Thus far, they seem as transparent as drops of water on a slide before the microscope is lowered. But now the Chekhovian curve, the revelation of what lies beneath the surface: neither can forget the other, and realizing that their relationship is the one ingredient vital to the happiness of each, they meet secretly to "spend many hours advising each other, and speak of ways to avoid all the necessary deceit. . . . And it seemed that a solution might be found, and then a new and magnificent life would start for them; but they also knew that this was still very far away and what was difficult and extremely complicated for them was only just beginning."

By 1897, Chekhov's active life had changed radically. The tuberculosis he had refused to acknowledge for a decade grew worse, and he was forced to live his last seven years a semi-invalid at Yalta and foreign health resorts. Their atmosphere of artificial good spirits was redeemed for him in part by the friendships he formed with other writers in search of the sun: Ivan Bunin, Alexander Kuprin, and particularly Maxim Gorky and the aging Tolstoy. In 1901, marriage brightened his exile. It was a strange match at best. Olga Knipper was a rising young actress with the Stanislavsky troupe; high-spirited and beautiful, she revelled in applause and the gregarious life of the theater. Restricted by his illness to solitude and rest, Chekhov was with her rarely. While he was hospitalized in the warm south, she was bound by contract to repertory performances eight months of the year in Moscow. "Yes, I am married," Chekhov wrote to Bunin, "but at my age it can make very little difference." To Gorky he complained that he felt "worn out, like an old shoe, ill and lonely." But even as he begged his wife for details of her busy, exciting days in the city, he was hard at work on one of his greatest plays, *Three Sisters*, envisioning Olga's triumph in the role of restless, passionate Masha.

He had been drawn to the theater early. An excellent mimic, he and his brothers had staged amateur theatricals for the family, and during his comic-weekly days, he had written several one-act farces (*The Bear, The Wedding, The Anniversary, The Proposal*) boisterous enough in plot and lively enough in language to be instant successes. Technically flawless, they are still popular in the repertories of provincial theaters. His first serious play, *Ivanov* (1887), was well received but imitative of the currently popular style of melodrama. Not until 1898, when the Moscow Art Theatre gave *The Sea Gull* its first performance, did Chekhov come into his own as a playwright. The association he formed with the company's founders—Nemirovich-Danchenko and Stanislavsky—carried Russian theater to its zenith and influenced the entire course of twentieth-century drama.

Uncle Vanya followed *The Sea Gull* in 1900, *Three Sisters* in 1901, and *The Cherry Orchard* in 1904. Between them Chekhov and his producers, the Moscow Art Theatre, sounded the death knell of melodrama. Gone from intimate theater were the traditional concepts of comedy and tragedy; what has become known as the Stanislavsky Method introduced to the stage a new realism in naturalistic settings. Actors created roles by submerging their own personalities in the parts they performed, rehearsing endlessly to perfect the play's most delicate nuances of character. Every piece of stage business, every setting, prop, and costume contributed to the projection of the playwright's intent. It was precisely the instrument required to effectively display the subtle progression of a Chekhov drama, a play in which there existed no intense dramatic conflict between principals, in which dialogue and gesture were remarkably undramatic, in which there was no dramatic climax.

Like his short stories, Chekhov's plays are rooted in commonplace events which take on dramatic meaning as each act discloses new details of time, place, and personality. As unhampered by traditional methods as his brilliant predecessors, Ostrovsky, Gogol, and Griboyedov—iconoclasts who impressed upon Russian drama their own individualism—Chekhov gave his plays movement by denying them strong action. What happens is muffled and ambiguous; each scene and each act is deliberately inconclusive in the manner of his short fiction. The sense of life in his plays, however, is larger than in his stories. Chekhov the story-writer is a lapidary, engraving and polishing his statement, with a mania for brevity. Chekhov the dramatist suggests the whole flowing process of life in a structure far less taut, achieving his effect in the accumulation of the unemphatic but telling details which give his plays their greatest originality. Long silences are broken by desultory conversations, humdrum activities, or sounds familiar yet oddly unexpected—the hooting of an owl, strains of band music from a neighboring street, the rattle of a watchman making nightly rounds. People eat and smoke and drink, light lamps against the growing darkness, take a breath of outdoor air—and gradually the haunting, poetic mood of Chekhov theater takes shape, filling the spectator with the knowledge that time is relentlessly passing.

Mood permeates each of the plays to underscore Chekhov's fundamental theme, the tragedy of attrition. An atmosphere of disintegration seems to cling to the very walls of the country houses from which his protagonists struggle to escape, almost always in vain. Each character exists wholly within himself, isolated by failure from the others, who are as deaf as he to musings on wasted talent and ambition. Here and there, flashes of optimism throw the melancholy landscape of their world into sharp relief. In *The Sea Gull*, ardent, impetuous Nina, abandoned by the egotistical, second-rate novelist she loves, gives her life meaning by becoming a hardworking actress. But Treplev, a young playwright who dreams of creating a new dramatic form, suffocates in the mediocrity and indifference of his environment and ends his despair with a pistol. Uncle Vanya, in the play of that name, sacrifices his own career to his brother, a reputedly important academic figure who proves to be a pompous nonentity, and realizes that his vitality has been sapped by a life spent in useless service. The intelligent, energetic, well-educated women of *The Three Sisters* are equally frustrated in the confines of a tiny provincial town, petty, vulgar, and dull. In this almost plotless play, the shrivelling of the spirit has the major role. Over a period of four years, monotony and apathy infect the lives of the three women and their brother until all but a fraction of hope is blighted. The brother, his ambitions for an active academic life in Moscow destroyed by a selfish and ignorant wife, becomes a petty bureaucrat; the sisters relinquish their deepest desire of escaping to "Moscow, to freedom, to fulfillment." They aspire, nevertheless, to a better life. "We must live!" Masha cries, and Vershinin, in love with her, hopelessly since both are married, admits that "life is hard to bear" but believes profoundly that in "two or three hundred years, life will be extraordinarily beautiful."

The optimism expressed sparsely in these earlier plays is sounded more vibrantly and strongly in *The Cherry Orchard*, Chekhov's last and deservedly best-known work for the stage. Written during 1903–1904, it brought all of his favorite themes into focus and was instantly recognized as his masterpiece. In the forty-six consecutive years of the Moscow Art Repertory, it has received more than twelve hundred performances and remains abroad the most frequently played and discussed of all Russian dramas. A comedy of manners and a study of character, it is also a powerful social document which records the collapse of the old aristocratic order while prophetic voices, just thirteen years before the October Revolution, speak of a new society "in which everyone shall work."

Better than any historian, Chekhov dramatizes in *The Cherry Orchard* the reasons for the violent change that was sweeping toward Russia at the close of the nineteenth century. After five profligate years in Paris, Madame Ranevskaya returns with her charming and ineffectual brother to save their family estate from bankruptcy. The sympathetic Lopakhin, a wealthy merchant whose grandfather had been a serf of the estate, urges his former employer to cut down her celebrated cherry orchard and divide the land into building lots, valuable for the proximity of a new railroad. But the trees are her dearest memory of the past. Refusing to destroy them, she retreats from disaster into impractical planning, abetted in her sentiment by her brother, who eulogizes the very furnishings of their childhood home. Incapable of a decisive move, they see the estate sold at auction to Lopakhin, representative of a New Russia, and even before they leave, hear the sound of axes as the land is cleared for economic progress.

For all its implied heartache, *The Cherry Orchard*, more than any of its predecessors, expresses a serene faith in Russia's future, although its protagonists still fail to communicate as human beings. Madame Ranevskaya cannot comprehend Lopakhin's genuine distress at her plight, nor can Lopakhin appreciate her sentimental attachment to the past. The social gulf between them intensifies their lack of understanding. Trofimov, a young student, tells eighteen-year-old Anya that she cannot know what it is to work, because she comes of a class that has lived by the labor of others. Reiterating the optimistic notes of *The Sea Gull* and *The Three Sisters*, he prophesies that only in work will social barriers disappear for the good of all. In the last act, he and Anya run from the house "toward a new life" to come. As for the others, Chekhov broods over them with a tenderness and compassion alien to the deliberately objective short stories. While the cherry branches press a profusion of delicate pink blossoms against the panes of the ancestral house, he shows again the tragic weakness of those inside who are unable to realize that so fragile a loveliness cannot resist the encroachments of practical life. Yet he insists upon the charm and grace of their outmoded values. By contrast, Lopakhin is as crude and heavily direct as the new mercantilism he represents, but he, too, receives Chekhov's sympathy. All his insecurity and humanity come warmly to the surface when he announces, without triumph, his purchase of gentry land. For all its tough social and political implications, the play is intensely poetic in effect, and in every aspect, the culmination of Chekhov's understated theater.

The premiere of *The Cherry Orchard* was set in Moscow for January 17, 1904, Chekhov's forty-fourth birthday. Stanislavsky recalls that "after the third act, he stood deathly pale and grim and could not control his coughing while gifts were showered upon him." This was in 1904, when for the first time the axes were heard felling the cherry trees, and it was in that very year that Chekhov died as if upon their stroke.

PB indicates paperback edition

HISTORICAL BACKGROUND

Charques, R. D. A *Short History of Russia*. New York: E. P. Dutton & Co., 1956. (PB)

Kochan, Lionel. *The Making of Modern Russia*. Baltimore: Penguin Books, 1962. (PB)

Lawrence, John. *A History of Russia*. New York: New American Library (Mentor Book), 1962. (PB)

Spector, Ivar. *An Introduction to Russian History and Culture*, 4th ed. New York: D. Van Nostrand Co., 1964.

Vernadsky, George. *The Mongols and Russia*. New Haven: Yale University Press, 1953.

Weidle, Wladimir. *Russia: Absent and Present*. New York: John Day Co., 1952.

Wren, Marvin. *The Course of Russian History*. New York: Macmillan Co., 1958.

CRITICISM

Bowman, H. *Vissarion Belinski*. Cambridge, Mass.: Harvard University Press, 1954.

Bruford, W. *Anton Chekhov*. New Haven: Yale University Press, 1957.

Cizevskij, D. *History of Russian Literature from the Eleventh Century to the End of the Baroque*. The Hague: Mouton Co., 1960.

Gifford H. *The Novel in Russia.* London: Hutchinson University Library, 1964.

Lampert, E. *Studies in Rebellion: Belinsky, Bakunin, Herzen.* New York: Frederick A. Praeger, 1957.

Magarshack, David. *Chekhov, the Dramatist.* New York: Hill and Wang, 1960. (PB)

Malia, M. *Alexander Herzen and the Birth of Russian Socialism.* Cambridge, Mass.: Harvard University Press, 1961.

Mirsky, D. S. *Pushkin.* New York: E. P. Dutton & Co., 1963. (PB)

Setchkarev, Vsevolod. *Gogol*, tr. Robert Kramer. New York: New York University Press (Gotham Library), 1965. (PB)

Simmons, Ernest J. *Leo Tolstoy.* Boston: Little, Brown & Co., 1946.

———. *Introduction to Russian Realism.* Bloomington: Indiana University Press, 1965.

Slonim, Marc. *Russian Theatre.* Cleveland: World Publishing Co., 1961.

Steiner, George. *Tolstoy or Dostoevsky.* New York: Alfred A. Knopf, 1959.

Wasiolek, E. *Dostoyevsky: The Major Fiction.* M. I. T. Press, 1964.

Yarmolinsky, Avrahm. *Turgenev: His Life.* New York: F. P. Collier & Son, 1961. (PB)

ANTHOLOGIES

An Anthology of Russian Verse, 1812–1960. New York: Anchor Books, 1962. (PB)

Includes, among others, poems by Derzhavin, Zhukovsky, Pushkin (46 selections), Tyutchev, Koltsov, Lermontov, Nekrasov, Alexey Tolstoy, and Fet.

Bowra, C. M., ed. and tr. (with some poems translated by F. Cornford and E. Polianowsky-Salaman). *A Book of Russian Verse.* London, Faber and Faber, 1943.

Includes poems by Fet, Tyutchev, Alexey Tolstoy, and others.

Deutsch, Babette, and Yarmolinsky, Avrahm, ed. and tr. *Modern Russian Poetry*. New York: Harcourt, Brace & Co., 1923; London: John Lane, 1923.

Great Russian Short Novels. Dial Press, 1951.

Includes Leo Tolstoy's *Hadji Murad*, tr. Aylmer Maude.

Gudzy, H. K. *History of Early Russian Literature*. New York: Macmillan, 1949.

Guerney, Bernard Guilbert, ed. and tr. *The Portable Russian Reader*. New York: Viking Press, 1947.

Includes folk satire, short works by Fonvizin, Krylov, Pushkin, Gogol, Turgenev, Dostoyevsky, Leskov, Saltykov-Shchedrin, Leo Tolstoy, Chekhov, and others.

MacAndrew, Andrew, tr. *Nineteenth Century Russian Drama*. New York: Bantam Books, 1963.

Includes Pushkin's *The Stone Guest*, Ostrovsky's *Thunderstorm*, and Leo Tolstoy's *The Power of Darkness*.

Manning, Clarence A., ed. and tr. *An Anthology of Eighteenth Century Russian Literature*. 2 vols. New York: Columbia University Press, 1953.

Noyes, George R. *Masterpieces of the Russian Drama*. New York: Dover Publications, 1960.

Includes Fonvizin's *Young Hopeful* (called *Junior* in present book), Griboyedov's *Wit Works Woe* (called *The Misfortune of Being Clever* in present book), Gogol's *Inspector General*, Turgenev's *A Month in the Country*, and Ostrovsky's *Poor Bride*.

Riha, Thomas, ed. *Readings in Russian Civilization*. Vol. I: *Russia before Peter the Great* (900–1700); Vol. II: *Imperial Russia* (1700–1917).

Yarmolinsky, Avrahm. *A Treasury of Russian Short Stories*. New York: Macmillan, 1944.

Zenkovsky, Serge, tr. *Medieval Russia's Epics, Chronicles and Tales*. New York: E. P. Dutton & Co., 1963. (PB)

RECOMMENDED TRANSLATIONS OF INDIVIDUAL WORKS

The Song of Igor's Campaign (called *Lay of the Host of Igor*, in present book), tr. Vladimir Nabokov. New York: Vintage Books, 1960. (PB)

Aksakov, A. *Chronicle of a Russian Family,* tr. M. Beverley. London: Routledge, 1924.

——. *Years of Childhood,* tr. A. Brown. New York: Vintage Books, 1960. (PB)

Belinsky, Chernyshevsky, and Dobrolyubov. *Selected Criticism.* New York: E. P. Dutton & Co., 1962. (PB)

Chekhov, A. *The Portable Chekhov,* tr. Avrahm Yarmolinsky. New York: Vintage Books, 1961.

> Includes 28 short stories, 2 plays, and a selection of Chekhov's letters.

——. *Plays,* tr. Elizabeth Fen. Baltimore: Penguin Books, 1951. (PB)

Chernyshevsky, N. *What Is to Be Done?,* tr. B. Tucker; rev. and abridged by L. Turkevich. New York: Vintage Books, 1960. (PB)

Dostoyevsky, F. *Poor Folk* and *The Gambler,* tr. C. J. Hogarth. New York: E. P. Dutton & Co., 1960. (PB)

——. *The Double, Notes from the Underground,* and *The Eternal Husband,* tr. Constance Garnett. New York: Doubleday & Company, 1960. (PB)

——. *The Insulted and Injured,* tr. Constance Garnett. New York: Grove Press, 1962. (PB)

——. *The House of the Dead,* tr. Constance Garnett. New York: Dell Publishing Co., 1959. (PB)

——. *White Nights and Other Stories* (including *A Little Hero*), tr. Constance Garnett. New York: Grove Press, 1961. (PB)

——. *Crime and Punishment,* tr. David Magarshack. Baltimore: Penguin Books, 1962. (PB)

——. *The Idiot,* tr. Constance Garnett. New York: Bantam Books, 1962. (PB)

——. *The Possessed,* tr. Andrew MacAndrew. New York: New American Library (Signet Book), 1962. (PB)

——. *The Brothers Karamazov,* tr. Constance Garnett. New York: Modern Library (Random House), 1950. (PB)

Gogol, N. *Evenings Near the Village of Dikanka,* tr. Ovid Gorchakov. New York: Frederick Ungar Publishing Co., 1962. (PB)

* *(Poor People)*

——. *Tales of Good and Evil,* tr. David Magarshack. Anchor Books, 1962. (PB)

Includes *The Terrible Vengeance, Shponka and His Aunt, The Portrait, Nevsky Avenue, The Nose,* and *The Overcoat.*

——. *The Diary of a Madman and Other Stories,* tr. Andrew MacAndrew. New York: New American Library (Signet Book), 1961. (PB)

Includes *The Nose, The Carriage, The Overcoat,* and *Taras Bulba.*

——. *Dead Souls,* tr. Bernard Guilbert Guerney. New York: Holt, Rinehart and Winston, 1961. (PB)

Goncharov, I. *A Common Story,* tr. Constance Garnett. London: Heinemann, 1890.

——. *The Precipice* (called *The Ravine* in present book), tr. M. Bryan. New York: Alfred A. Knopf, 1916.

——. *Oblomov,* tr. Natalie Duddington. New York: E. P. Dutton & Co., 1962. (PB)

Herzen, A. *My Past and Thoughts,* tr. Constance Garnett. 6 vols. London: Chatto and Windus, 1924–27.

Karamzin, N. *Travels from Moscow through Prussia, Germany, France and England,* tr. from the German. 3 vols. London: Babcock, 1803.

Krylov, I. *Fables,* tr. Bernard Pares. London: Jonathan Cape, 1926.

Lermontov, M. *A Sheaf from Lermontov,* tr. J. Robbins. Lieber and Lewis, 1923.

——. *The Demon,* tr. G. Shelley. London: Richards Press, 1930.

——. *The Prophet and Other Poems,* tr. E. Kayden. Sewanee, Tenn.: 1944.

——. *A Hero of Our Time,* tr. Vladimir Nabokov. New York: Anchor Books, 1944. (PB)

Leskov, N. *Cathedral Folk,* tr. Isabel Hapgood. New York: Alfred A. Knopf, 1924.

——. *The Tales of Leskov.* London: Routledge, 1944.

——. *Selected Tales,* tr. David Magarshack. New York: Noonday Press, 1962. (PB)

Includes *Lady Macbeth of the Mtsensk District, The Enchanted Wanderer, The Left-Handed Craftsman, The Sentry,* and *The White Flag.*

――――. *The Enchanted Pilgrim,* tr. David Magarshack. London: Hutchinson, 1946.

Ostrovsky, A. *Poor Bride,* tr. George R. Noyes. In *Masterpieces of the Russian Drama.* New York: Dover Publications, 1960.

――――. *Thunderstorm,* tr. Andrew MacAndrew. In *Nineteenth Century Russian Drama.* New York: Bantam Books, 1963.

――――. *Easy Money and Other Plays,* tr. David Magarshack. London: Allen and Unwin, 1944.

Pushkin, A. *Selections from the Prose and Poetry of Pushkin,* Laurel, 1962.

Includes, among other selections, the first chapter of *Evgeny Onegin, The Bronze Horseman, The Tale of the Golden Cockerel, The Stone Guest, The Queen of Spades, The Captain's Daughter, The Snowstorm, The Station Master, The History of Goryohino Manor,* 46 lyrics and ballads, and letters.

――――. *Poems, Prose and Plays of Alexander Pushkin,* tr. Avrahm Yarmolinsky. New York: Random House, 1936.

――――. *Eugene Onegin,* tr. W. Arndt. New York: E. P. Dutton & Co., 1963. (PB)

――――. *The Captain's Daughter and Other Great Stories,* tr. Natalie Duddington and T. Keane. New York: Vintage Books, 1962. (PB)

Also contains *The Tales of Belkin, The Queen of Spades, Kirdjali,* and *The Negro of Peter the Great.*

Radishchev, A. *A Journey from St. Petersburg to Moscow,* tr. Leo Wiener. Princeton: Princeton University Press, 1952.

Saltykov-Shchedrin, M. *The Golovlovs,* tr. Andrew MacAndrew. New York: New American Library (Signet Book), 1961. (PB)

Tolstoy, Leo. *Childhood, Boyhood and Youth,* tr. Michael Scammel. New York: McGraw-Hill, 1966. (PB)

――――. *Landowner's Morning,* tr. Aylmer Maude. Vol. V of Tolstoy's Centenary Edition. New York and London: Oxford University Press, 1928–37.

——. *Sebastopol,* tr. F. Millet. Ann Arbor: 1961. (PB)

——. *The Cossacks* and *The Raid,* tr. Andrew MacAndrew. New York: New American Library (Signet Book), 1961. (PB)

——. *Hadji Murad,* tr. Aylmer Maude. In *Great Russian Short Novels.* New York: Dial Press, 1951.

——. *Anna Karenina,* tr. Constance Garnett. New York: Modern Library (Random House), 1965. (PB)

——. *War and Peace,* tr. R. Edmonds. 2 vols. Baltimore: Penguin Books, 1962. (PB)

——. *A Confession,* tr. Aylmer Maude. Vol. XI of Tolstoy's Centenary Edition. New York and London: Oxford University Press, 1928–1937.

——. *Resurrection,* tr. V. Traill. New York: New American Library (Signet Book), 1961. (PB)

——. *The Power of Darkness,* tr. Andrew MacAndrew. In *Nineteenth Century Russian Drama.* New York: Bantam Books, 1963.

——. *Fruits of Enlightenment.* tr. Leo Wiener. Vol. XVII of Tolstoy's Centenary Edition. New York and London: Oxford University Press, 1928–1937.

——. *Six Short Masterpieces by Tolstoy,* tr. M. Wettlin. New York: Dell Publishing Co., 1963. (PB)

   Includes *Two Hussars, A Happy Married Life, Yardstick, The Death of Ivan Ilyich, The Kreutzer Sonata,* and *After the Ball.*

Turgenev, I. *A Sportsman's Notebook,* tr. C. and N. Hepburn. New York: Viking Press, 1950. (PB)

——. *Five Short Novels,* tr. F. Reeve. New York: Bantam Books, 1962.

   Includes *The Diary of a Superfluous Man, Rudin, First Love, A King Lear of the Steppe,* and *Spring Torrents.*

——. *The Vintage Turgency,* tr. H. Stevens, 2 vols. New York: Vintage Books, 1961–62. (PB)

   Vol. I contains *Smoke, Fathers and Sons,* and *First Love.* Vol. II contains *On the Eve, Rudin, A Quiet Spot,* and *The Diary of a Superfluous Man.*

————. *Fathers and Sons*, tr. George Reavey. New York: Noonday Press, 1961. (PB)

————. *A Nobleman's Nest*, Isabel F. Hapgood. New York: Charles Scribner's Sons, 1907.

————. *Selected Tales of Ivan Turgenev*, tr. David Magarshack. New York: Anchor Books, 1962. (PB)

Includes *The Singers, Bezhin Meadow, Mumu, Assya, First Love, Knock . . . Knock . . . Knock . . . , Living Relics*, and *Clara Milich*.

A *son Esprit*, 48
Academy of Sciences, 33, 45, 47, 52
Adam's Address to Lazarus in Hell,
4
Addison, Joseph (1672–1719), 61
*Adventures of Alexander the Great,
The*, 5
Aesop's Fables, 34, 65
*Aesthetic Relations of Art and Re-
ality, The*, 125
Aksakov, Ivan (1823–86), 113, 115,
160
Aksakov, Konstantin (1817–60),
113, 160
Aksakov, Sergey (1791–1859), 160–
62
Alexander I (1801–25), 59, 68, 77–
80, 82, 83, 86, 89, 93, 94, 98, 172
Alexander II (1855–81), 87, 120,
123, 124, 148, 183, 203, 209
Alexander III (1881–94), 124
Alexis, Tsar (1645–76), 50
All Kinds of Things, 61
Angel, 107
Anna, Empress (1730–40), 45, 51
Anna Karenina, 174–76
Anna, Princess, 9
Annenkov, Paul (1812–87), 181
Anniversary, The, 211
Anthes, George d', 104
Apollon of Tyre, 30
Arab of Peter the Great, The, 99
Araia, Francesco, 51
Arakcheyev, Count Alexis, 79, 93

Aristophanes, 63
Art poétique, 48
artel, 120
Arzamas Club, 84, 85, 86, 100
Asya, 125, 152
At Daggers Drawn, 200
Attila, 1
Avvakum, 29
Avvakum, Life of, 29

Bakunin, Michael (1814–76), 118,
124, 147
Balzac, Honoré de (1799–1850),
153, 154, 180, 182, 187
Baratynsky, E. A. (1800–44), 105
Basil the Golden-Haired, 30
Batu, 15, 16, 20
Batyushkov, K. N. (1787–1855),
84, 87–88, 92, 104
Bear, The, 211
Behrs, Sophia, 171
Belinsky, V. G. (1811–48), 107,
108, 114–17, 118, 125, 126, 127,
145, 147, 157, 177, 181, 182, 194
Belkin Tales, The, 102, 109, 203
Bell, The (Kolokol), 120
Bentham, Jeremy (1748–1832), 125
Berdyaev, Nicholas (1874–1948),
165
Bezhin Meadow, 148
Bible, The, 3, 183
Blanc, Louis (1811–82), 124

Bludov, Count, 84
Boccaccio, Giovanni (1313–75), 31
bogatyri (warrior knights), 40, 42
Boileau, Nicolas (1636–1711), 46
Book of Degrees of the Imperial Genealogy, The, 28
Boring Story, 209
Boris Godunov, 97, 99
Bova Korolevich, 30
Boyar's Daughter, The, 70
Brandes, Georg (1842–1927), 164
Bridegroom, The, 98
Brigadier, 63
Bronze Horseman, The, 103, 104
Brothers Karamazov, The, 166, 186, 187, 188, 189, 190, 195–98
Bueves d'Anston, 30
Bunin, Ivan (1870–1953), 101, 210
Bürger, Gottfried (1747–94), 85
Burgomistress Marfa, 70
Burns, Robert (1759–96), 110
byliny (oral epic poems), 39–44, 74, 109, 160
Byron, Lord George Gordon (1788–1824), 85, 95, 100, 107
Byronism, 95, 105, 107, 108, 190
Byzantine faith, 2
Byzantine influence, 2, 3, 4, 6, 9, 10, 32
Byzantine prose, 3, 6
Byzantium (Constantinople), 2, 19, 23, 38

Captain's Daughter, The, 103
Carlyle, Thomas (1795–1881), 118
Carriage, The, 132, 133
Cathedral Folk, 201
Catherine I (1725–27), 45
Catherine II (the Great), (1762–96), 47, 55–59, 61, 62, 67, 68, 70, 73, 76, 84
Catholicism, 4
Catullus, 92
Caucasian Prisoner, The, 95
Cervantes, Miguel de (1547–1616), 134
Chaadayev, P. (1794–1856), 93, 94, 112, 113, 115
Charterhouse of Parma, 173

Chateaubriand, François-René de (1768–1848), 109
Chekhov, Anton (1860–1904), 101, 128, 154, 202–215
Chernyshevsky, Nikolay (1828–99), 123, 124–27, 128, 157, 167, 169, 177, 191
Cherry Orchard, The, 211, 213–14
Chetyi-Minei, 3
Chicanery, 64
Childe Harold, 95
Childhood, Boyhood and Youth, 157, 166, 168, 173
Children's Magazine, 69
Chronicles (letopisi), 7
Church Slavonic, 3, 10, 27, 30, 32, 34, 38, 48, 53, 71, 75, 83, 84
Clarissa Harlowe, 109
Colloquy of the Three Prelates, The, 4
Comedy of the Parable of the Prodigal Son, The, 50
Confession, A, 176
Confessions, 70
Constantinople (see Byzantium)
Contemporary, The, 103, 115, 116, 125, 128, 133, 148, 157
Corneille, Pierre (1606–84), 49
Corsair, The, 95
Cossacks, The, 170, 173
Crime and Punishment, 185, 187
Cyrillic alphabet, 3

Danilov, Kirsha, 43, 109
Dante (1265–1321), 4, 91, 134
Darwin, Charles R. (1809–82), 208
Dashkova, Princess, 58, 59
Dead Souls, 134, 137–141
Death of Ivan Ilyich, 178
Death of Ivan the Terrible, The, 160
Death of a Poet, 105
Decameron, The, 31
Decembrists, 80, 81, 82, 85, 86, 88, 89, 105, 111, 112, 119
Deeds Beyond the Don (Zadonshchina), 25, 37
Deeds of Troy, 5
Demon, The, 106

Derzhavin, Gavrila (1743–1816), 58–60, 61, 84
Destruction of Aesthetics, 127
Diary of a Madman, The, 132, 133
Diary of a Writer, The, 185
Dickens, Charles (1812–70), 143; influence of, 190
Diderot, Denis (1713–84), 57
Dmitri (pretender during Time of Troubles), 28, 41
Dmitri, Grand Prince of Moscow, 19
Dmitri of the Don, 88
Dobrolyubov, Nikolay (1836–61), 123, 124–27, 145, 156, 157
Domostroy (Manual of Household Management), 27, 28, 31, 73, 155
Don Juan, 100
Dostoyevsky, Feodor (1821–81), 90, 102, 112, 116, 119, 127, 128, 132, 142, 157, 164, 166, 180–99, 200, 201, 202, 203, 208
Double, The, 181, 186
Drone, The, 61, 74

East Slavs, 1
Edge of the World, 201
Elegy, 85
Eliot, T. S. (1888–1965), 174
Elizabeth, Empress (1741–62), 45, 49, 51
Enchanted Wanderer, The, 202
Enemies, 206
Epokha (Epoch), 184
Eternal Husband, The, 185, 187
Eugene Onegin, 74, 96, 98, 99, 102, 105, 139
Evening Lights, 159
Evenings Near the Village of Dikanka, 129, 132
Exploits of Digenes Akritas, 5

Fadeyev, Alexander (1901–1956), 165
Family Chronicle, 161
Fat and Thin, 204

Fathers and Sons, 149, 151, 194
Feast During the Plague, The, 102
Felitsa, 59
Fénélon, François (1651–1715), 63
Feodor (son of Ivan IV), 20
Fet, Afanasy (1820–92), 159–60
Fichte, Johann G. (1762–1814), 113, 114, 116, 123
Filofey, 19
Fingal, 88
Finnikov, Ivanets, 31
Finnish tribes, 2
First love, 152, 153
Flaubert, Gustave (1821–80), 101, 153
Fonvizin, Denis (1744–92), 47, 59, 63–64, 65, 69, 90, 154
For Whom is Life Good in Russia? 158
Fountain of Bakhchisaray, The, 95
Four Small Tragedies, 102
Fourier, Charles (1772–1837), 182
Franklin, Benjamin (1706–90), 68
Frederick II, 76
Free Russian Press, 119, 123
Fruits of Enlightenment, The, 178

Gambler, The, 185, 187
Garcia, Pauline (see Viardot), 147, 153
Garibaldi, Giuseppe, 118
Genghis Khan (1162?–1227), 15
Genius of Christianity, The, 109
Gide, André (1869–1951), 164
Goethe, Johann Wolfgang von (1749–1832), 68, 85, 180
Gogol, Nikolay (1809–52), 9, 44, 47, 64, 83, 102, 105, 115, 125, 128, 129–44, 145, 149, 154, 155, 161, 181, 182, 186, 202, 203, 208, 212
Golden Horde, 16, 19, 24
Golitsyn, Prince A., 79, 93
Golovlevs, The, 161–63
Goncharov, I. A. (1812–91), 116, 126, 127, 143, 144–46, 186, 208
Goncharova, Nathalie, 99, 104
Goncourt, Edmond (1822–96), 153
Goncourt, Jules (1830–70), 153

Gorky, Maxim (1868–1936), 199, 202, 210, 211
Granovsky, T. N. (1813–55), 118, 147, 194
Gray, Thomas (1716–71), 85
Great Reform Bill, 120, 121
Gregory XVI, Pope, 140
Gregory, Johann, 50
Gresset, Jean Baptiste Louis (1709–77), 92
Griboyedov, Alexander (1795–1829), 88–90, 101, 154, 212
Grigorovich, D. V. (1822–99), 101, 181, 205
Grimm, Frederic-Melchior (1723–1807), 57
Gypsies, The, 95, 96, 100

Hadji Murad, 170
Hamlet and Don Quixote, 149
Hannibal, Abram, 91, 99
Haxthausen, Baron von, 121
Hegel, Georg Wilhelm Friedrich (1770–1831), 113, 114, 116
Helvetius (1715–71), 66
Henry I of France, 9
Herder, Johann Gottfried (1744–1803), 68, 69, 113, 114
Hero of Our Time, A, 108, 109
Herzen, Alexander (1812–70), 68, 101, 107, 112, 117–23, 124, 194
Hilarion, 6
Histoire des deux Indes, 67
Historical Lexicon About Russian Writers, 58
History of the Russian Empire, The, 72
Hoffmann, E. T. A. (1776–1822), 132, 182; influence of, 102, 181
Holberg, Ludvig (1684–1754), 63
House of Gentlefolk, A, 149, 150
House of the Dead, 183, 192
Hugo, Victor (1802–85), 118, 133, 180, 186

I Go Out on the Road, 107
Idiot, The, 185, 187, 193, 194

Igor, Prince, 11
In the Cart, 207
In the Twilight, 205
Industrious Bee, The, 61
Inferno, The, 4
Inspector-General, The (Revizor), 64, 134, 136, 139
Instruction, 5
Instructions, 57
Insulted and Injured, The, 183
It's a Family Affair, 155
Ivan I (Kalita) (1325–41), 18, 19
Ivan III (1462–1505), 19
Ivan IV, known as Ivan the Terrible (1533–84), 20, 22, 26, 27, 28, 29, 35, 39
Ivanov, 211

Jewish War, The, 4
Josephus, Flavius, 4
Journey Beyond Three Seas, 26
Journey from St. Petersburg to Moscow, A, 66, 67, 68, 72
Joyce, James (1882–1941), 143
Julius Caesar, 69
Junior, 63, 64, 65

Kaleki (wandering beggars), 38, 42, 97
Kantemir, Prince Antioch (1708–44), 46–47, 58
Kapnist, Vasily (1757–1823), 64
Karamzin, Nikolay (1766–1826), 68–72, 74, 75, 83, 85, 86, 92, 94, 105, 145
Katenin, P. A. (1792–1853), 88
Katkov, Michael (1818–87), 184, 186
Kheraskov, Mikhail, 62
Khomiakov, A. S. (1804–60), 113
Khorev, 49
Khrushchev, Nikita, 119
Kiev, 1, 9, 15, 23, 28
Kiev Academy, The, 28
Kiev Crypt Monastery, 6, 7
Kiev, Grand Prince of, 2
Kireyevsky, Ivan (1806–56), 113

Knipper, Olga, 210, 211
Kolokol *(The Bell)*, 120, 122, 123
Koltsov, Alexey (1809–42), 110
Kremlin, 17, 19, 20, 21
Kreutzer Sonata, The, 178, 179
Krudener, Julie de, 79
Krylov, Ivan (1769–1844), 47, 64–66, 90
Kulikovo (battle of), 25
Kunst, Johann, 50, 51
Kurbsky, Prince Andrey (c. 1528–83), 26, 27
Kuprin, Alexander (1870–1938), 210

La Fontaine, Jean de (1621–95), 65, 90
La Harpe, 77
Lady Macbeth of the Mtsensk District, 201
Lady With a Dog, The, 210
Lament of Daniel the Exile, The, 10
"Land and Liberty", 124
Landlady, The, 181, 182
Landowner's Morning, A, 168
Lavrov, P. L. (1823–1900), 124
Lay of the Host of Igor (Slovo o Polku Igoreve), 11–14, 25, 37, 74, 132
Legend of the Grand Inquisitor, 196
Lenin, V. I., 115, 125, 209
Lermontov, Michael (1814–41), 71, 101, 105–109, 116, 126, 145
Leskov, N. S. (1813–95), 9, 44, 200–202, 203
letopisi (Chronicles), 7
Letter to a Nobleman from a Nobleman, 31
Letters from France, 64
Letters of a Russian Traveler, 69, 70, 74
Lewis, Matthew Gregory (1775–1818), 187
Life of Saints Boris and Gleb, 6
Literary Magazine, 59
Literary Musings, 115
Little Hero, The, 182
Lomonosov, Michael (1711–65), 47, 52–54, 60, 71, 75

Macpherson, James (1736–96), 68
Maid of Orleans, 93
Manual of Household Management (Domostroy), 27, 28, 31, 73, 155
Martynov, Major N. S., 108
Maturin, Charles R. (1780–1824), 133, 187
Maupassant, Guy de (1850–93), 202
Mazzini, Giuseppe, 118, 121
Mémoires du Diable, 187
Merchant of Kalashnikov, The, 109
Mérimée, Prosper (1803–70), 153
Messenger of Europe, The, 72, 85, 86
Messenger of the Month, 205
Metternich, Klemens von, 79
Michelet, Jules (1798–1874), 118, 121
Mill, John Stuart (1806–73), 125
mir, 113, 120, 122
Miser Knight, The, 102
Misery, 204
Misfortune of Being Clever, The, 88, 89, 90
Mohammedanism, 2
Mokhila, Peter, 28
Molière (Jean-Baptiste Poquelin) (1622–73), 49, 51, 57, 63, 65, 66
Mongolian occupation, 14, 16–17, 21, 22, 23, 24, 32, 35, 38
Montesquieu, baron de (1689–1755), 46
Month in the Country, A, 154
Monument to Myself, A, 104
Moore, Thomas (1779–1852), 85
Moscow Art Repertory, 213
Moscow Art Theater, 211
Moscow Chronicle, 26
Moscow Journal, The, 69, 74
Moscow Telescope, 112, 115
Moskvityanin, 159
Moussorgsky, Modest (1839–81), 97
Mozart and Salieri, 102
Muravyov, Nikolay (1796–1866), 85
My Country, 107
My Past and Thoughts, 117

Namesday, The, 209
Napoleon, 76, 78, 80, 172
Narodniki (Populists), 123, 124, 125, 152, 157, 160, 169
Natalia, 70
Nechyev, S. G., 194
Nekrasov, Nikolay (1821–78), 115, 148, 157–59, 160, 161, 167, 169, 181
Nemirovich-Danchenko, Vladimir (1858–1943), 211
Netochka Nezhdanova, 182
Nevsky, Alexander (died 1263), 17, 18
Nevsky Prospect, 132, 133
New Time, 205
Nicholas I (1826–55), 81, 82, 83, 98, 111, 113, 120, 136, 157
Nightmare, 207
Nikitin, Afanasy, 26
No Way Out, 200
Nose, The, 133
Notes from the Fatherland, 108, 157, 161
Notes from the Underground, 184, 186, 191–92
Novice, The, 106, 107
Novikov, Nikolay (1744–1818), 58, 59, 61–62, 66, 67, 69, 70, 74, 92

Oblomov, 144–46, 152
Old-World Landowners, 132, 144
Oleg, 2
On Nebuchadnezzar, the Golden Calf, and the Three Children Who Were Unscathed in the Furnace, 50
On the Eve, 128, 149, 150
On the Road, 207
oprichina (recruited followers of Ivan IV), 20
oral literature, 36, 37–44
Ordinary Story, An, 144
Oriental Tales, 95
Orlov, Count, 76
Orlov, Mikhail, 85
Orthodox Christianity (also Russian Orthodoxy, Russian Orthodox Church), 4, 16, 18, 19, 113

Ostrovsky, Alexander (1823–86), 44, 127, 154–57, 212
Overcoat, The, 134, 141–42, 143, 181, 186
Ovid (Metamorphoses), 34
Ozerov, Vladislav (1770–1816), 88

Painter, The, 61
Palaeologa, Zoë, 19
Panayev, I. I. (1812–62), 115, 157, 181
Panayeva, Avdotya, 157, 158
Panin, Count, 63, 66
Parasha, 147
Parny, Evariste Désiré de (1753–1814), 87, 92
Pasternak, Boris (1890–1960), 165
Paterikon, 6
Paul I (1796–1801), 62, 76, 77
Paul, Grand Duke, 63
Peasants, 207
Persian Letters, 46
Pestel, Paul, 80, 81
Peter I (the Great) (1682–1725), 32–36, 39, 44–46, 52, 55, 72, 73, 91, 99
Peter II (1727–29), 46
Peter III (Jan–Jun 1762), 55, 56, 76
Peter of the Golden Keys, 30
Petrashevsky, M. V. (1821–66), 182
Philosophical Letter, 112, 115
Piron, Alexis (1689–1773), 92
Pisarev, Dmitri (1840–68), 127
Pobedonostsev, Constantine, 177
Polar Star, The, 119
Polo, Marco, 26
Polotsky, Simeon, 32, 50
Polovtsi (Kumans), 11
Poltava, 99
Polyxene, 88
Poor Liza, 70
Poor People, 142, 157, 166, 181
Populists (Narodniki), 123, 124, 125, 152, 157, 160, 169
Potemkin, Grigory, 55, 64
Portrait, The, 132, 133

Possessed, The, 185, 187, 188, 194, 195
Poverty is no Crime, 155
Power of Darkness, The, 178
Précieuses Ridicules, Les, 65
Primary Chronicle, The (The Tales of Bygone Years), 7–9
Prince Serebryany, 160
Privy Councillor, The, 207
Propertius, 92
Proposal, The, 211
Proudhon, Pierre Joseph (1809–65), 124
Proust, Marcel (1871–1922), 143
Pugachev, Yemelian, 56, 57, 59, 68, 103
Purse, The, 61
Pushkin, Alexander (1799–1837), 9, 44, 53, 54, 60, 68, 71, 74, 75, 83, 84, 87, 90–105, 106, 108–12, 116, 117, 118, 126, 127, 130, 133, 134, 137, 140, 143, 145, 150, 153, 156, 160, 173, 203, 208
Pushkin, Vasily (1767–1830), 84

Queen of Spades, The, 74, 102

Racine, Jean (1639–99), 49
Radcliffe, Ann (1764–1823), 187
Radishchev, Alexander (1749–1802), 59, 66–68, 70, 72
Radonezhsky, Sergey, 24
Raskolniki (schismatics, Old Believers), 29
Ravine, The, 144
Raynal, Guillaume (1713–96), 66
Razin, Stenka, 41
Resurrection, 178
Revelation of Paul the Apostle, The, 4
Revizor (The Inspector-General), 64, 134, 136, 139
Rhetoric and *Grammar,* 53, 54
Richardson, Samuel (1689–1761), 67, 68, 69, 109
Rimsky-Korsakov, Nikolay (1844–1908), 154

Riznich, Amelia, 96
Rodiovna, Arina, 98, 103
Romanov, Michael (1613–45), 21
Romanovs, The, 83, 98
Rousseau, Jean-Jacques (1712–78), 66, 69, 70, 170
Rublev, Andrey (c. 1370–1430), 24
Rudin, 149
Rurik, 2
Rus, 2, 4–7, 9, 11, 12, 15, 16, 21, 22, 23, 29, 30, 44
Ruslan and Lyudmila, 93, 94
Russian Messenger, The, 166, 185
Russian Sailor Vasily and the Beautiful Princess Irakliya of Florence, 34, 72
Ryleyev, K. F. (1795–1826), 105

Sail, A, 107
St. Cyril, 3
St. John Chrysostom, 4
St. Petersburg Gazette, 61
St. Petersburg Mercury, 65
St. Petersburg Stories, 132, 203
Saint-Simon, duc de (1675–1755), 182
St. Sophia, cathedral of, 9
St. Vladimir, 2, 6, 11
Saints' Calendar, 28
Saltykov-Shchedrin, Michael (1826–89), 160–63
Sand, George (1804–76), 143, 180, 187
Sarai, 15, 16, 18, 19, 22
Scandinavia, 1
Scandinavian sagas, 42
Scandinavians, 2
Schelling, Friedrich (1775–1854), 113, 114, 116, 123, 160
Schiller, Johann Christoph Friedrich von (1759–1805), 85, 113, 180
Schopenhauer, Arthur (1788–1860), 160
Scott, Sir Walter (1771–1832), 85, 131, 160
Seagull, The, 211, 212, 214
Seasons, 69
Sebastopol Stories, The, 169

Select Passages from a Correspondence With Friends, 140
Semenova, Catherine, 88
Sentimental Journey, 67
Shakespeare, William (1564–1616), 69, 97, 102, 127, 134, 164, 180
Shakhovskoy, Prince, 88
Shcherbatov, M. M. (1733–90), 72
Shelley, Percy Bysshe (1792–1822), 107
Shemyaka's Judgement, 31
Shishkov, A. S. (1753–1841), 75, 84, 88, 161
Sholokhov, Mikhail (1905–   ), 165
Singers, The, 148
skomorokhi (itinerant jesters), 43
49
Slavophilism, 113, 118, 132, 150, 156, 157, 159, 160, 161, 197
Slavs, 1
Slovo o Polku Igoreve (*Lay of the Host of Igor*), 11–14, 25, 37, 74, 132
Smoke, 149, 152
Snow Maiden, The, 154
Song of Lazarus, 38
Songs About Stenka Razin, 98
Southey, Robert (1774–1843), 85
Spectator, 61, 65
Speransky, Michael, 78
Spirit of Laws, The, 57
Sportsman's Sketches, 148, 203
Stanislavsky, Konstantin (1863–1938), 211, 214
Stankevich, Nicholas (1813–40), 118, 147
Stasov, V. V., 43
Steiner, George, 165
Stellovsky (publisher), 184, 185
Stendhal, (Henri Beyle) (1783–1842), 173
Stepmother, The, 154
Steppe, The, 205
Sterne, Lawrence (1713–68), 67, 68, 69
Stone Guest, The, 102
Story of the Merchant Karp Sutulov and His Wife, The, 31
Story of How Ivan Ivanovich Quarrelled with Ivan Nikiforovich, The, 132

Stowe, Harriet Beecher (1811–96), 148
Strakhov, Nikolay, (1828–95), 183, 184
Studies of the Age of Gogol, 125
Sue, Eugène (1804–57), 180, 187
Sumarokov, Alexander (1718–77), 46, 48–49, 51–52, 61, 69
Suslova, Apollinaria, 184, 185, 194
Suvorin, A. S. (1833–1911), 205
Suvorov, Alexander (1729–1800), 55
Svyatopolk, Prince, 6
Sylvester, 27
Symbala et Emblemata, 34

Tale of Frol Skobeyev, the Rogue, 31, 35
Tale of Savva Grudtsyn, The, 30, 35
Tale of the Squint-Eyed, Left-Handed Smith from Tula and the Steel Flea, 202
Talleyrand, Charles, 79
Taras Bulba, 131
Tartars, (see Mongolian occupation)
Télémaque, 48
Thomson, James (1700–48), 68, 69, 85
Three Sisters, 211, 213, 214
Thunderstorm, The, 156
Tieck, Johann Ludwig (1773–1853), 133
Time (Vremya), 128, 183, 184
Time of Troubles, 20
To My Mind, 46
Tolstoy, Alexey, 160
Tolstoy, Leo, 9, 44, 71, 83, 90, 127, 128, 143, 157, 159, 164–80, 190, 199, 200, 202, 203, 207, 208, 210
Tolstoy or Dostoyevsky?, 165
Torrents of Spring, 149, 152
Trediakovsky, Vasily (1703–69), 46, 47–48, 53, 75
Tristram Shandy, 139
Troitsa Sergeyeva Monastery, 24
Tsar Boris, 160
Tsar Theodore, 160
Turgenev, Alexander (1785–1846), 92, 94

Turgenev, Andrey (1781–1803), 84

Turgenev, Ivan (1818–83), 9, 44, 69, 71, 83, 101, 115, 116, 121, 125, 126, 127, 128, 143, 146–54, 57, 169, 181, 194, 195, 203, 208

Tyutchev, Feodor (1803–73), 159–160

Uhland, Ludwig (1787–1862), 85
Uncle Tom's Cabin, 67, 148
Uncle Vanya, 211, 212

Vanka, 206
Varangians, 1
veche (popular assembly of freemen), 22
Viardot, Louis, 147
Viardot, Mme. (Pauline Garcia), 147, 153
Virgin Soil, 149, 152
Visit of the Virgin to Hell, The, 4
Viy, 132
Vladimir Monomakh, *Testament* of, 9
Vogüé, Eugène-Melchior (1848–1910), 164
Voltaire (François-Marie Arouet) (1694–1778), 46, 57, 62, 69, 87, 92, 93
Voronstov, Count, 96
Vremya (Time), 128, 183, 184

Vyazemsky, P. A. (1792–1878), 84, 86, 102

Wagner, Richard (1813–83), 177
War and Peace, 153, 162, 166, 167, 171–74, 175, 179
Ward Number Six, 209
Waterfall, The, 60
Wedding, The, 211
What is Art?, 169, 177
What is Oblomovism?, 126
What is to be Done?, 125, 191
Whose Fault?, 118
Witch, The, 206
Woe, Misfortune, 31, 35

Yaroslav, Grand Prince, 6, 9
Yasnaya Polyana, 167, 170, 171, 176, 178, 180
Yazykov, N. M. (1803–46), 105
Yeruslam Lazarevich, 30
Young, Edward (1683–1765), 68
Your Drink—My Hangover, 155

Zidonshchina (Deeds Beyond the Don), 25, 37
Zhukovsky, Vasily (1783–1852), 85–87, 88, 92, 93, 94, 104, 108, 136
Zhidyata, Luka, 5
Zola, Emile (1840–1902), 153